THE
MESSENGER

"...there will be fearful sights and great signs from heaven.... And when these things begin to come to pass, then look up, and lift up your heads; for your redemption draweth nigh" (Lk. 21:11, 28) – JESUS CHRIST

THOMAS HORN

With Gary Stearman, Donna Howell, Allie Anderson-Hensen, Derek Gilbert, and Sharon Gilbert

THE
MESSENGER

IT'S HEADED TOWARD EARTH! IT CANNOT BE STOPPED! AND IT'S CARRYING
THE SECRET OF AMERICA'S, THE WORLD'S, AND YOUR TOMORROW!

DEFENDER

CRANE, MO

THE MESSENGER
IT'S HEADED TOWARD EARTH! IT CANNOT BE STOPPED! AND IT'S
CARRYING THE SECRET OF AMERICA'S, THE WORLD'S, AND YOUR
TOMORROW!
By Dr. Thomas Horn
With contributors: Gary Stearman, Donna Howell, Allie Anderson-Hensen,
Derek Gilbert, and Sharon Gilbert

Defender Crane, MO 65633 ©2020 by Thomas Horn.

ISBN: 9781948014380

A CIP catalog record of this book is available from the Library of Congress.

Cover illustration and design by Jeffrey Mardis.

All Scripture quotations from the King James Version unless otherwise noted.

Contents

1

I Was Dying to See the Messenger

Many years ago, I (Tom Horn) died and woke up in heaven. Contemplating my surroundings, I wondered where I was, where I had come from, and why I had no memories of getting here—wherever *here* was.

At that moment, before it was shortly confirmed, I knew this was no dream; it was too vivid to be anything less than real. In fact, it felt *realer* than any previous *reality* I had known.

Abruptly I found myself standing somewhere before a spectacular pillar of light (*or was it a throne?*). It was so bright, so intense, and penetrating—glistening with vibrant streams of silver, blue, and gold emanating with the most unexplainable, yet awe-inspiring presence—that I could hardly keep my eyes open or my face toward the radiance.

I was exclaiming something, and didn't know why I was saying it: "Please, Lord, don't let me forget! PLEASE DON'T LET ME FORGET!"

How long had I been here and what was I talking about? Why was I so desperate to recall something I had obviously been told I would not remember? And how did I know I was standing before the Lord?

Suspended there like a marionette on wires, I somehow was aware that "memories" from moments before stood just beyond my ability to reckon them back into my conscious mind.

But I *had* known something, something about the future. *I had seen it, and then I had been told I would not recollect the details.* But why? What would be the purpose of that?

Something else had happened, too. Somehow I knew that a scroll of some kind had unrolled before me…with scenes of a future, *my future*, playing out on what looked like a silvery parchment. It had been as clear and as believable as if I were watching a movie, with rich depictions of a destiny, or a possible future, where something extraordinary and miraculous was taking place—a cinematic conveyance of a personal fate, a "potential existence" that had been downloaded into my subconscious mind, or soul, and then…for some reason…had departed my intellect. Had a revelation of some type been sealed inside me? Something for a later time?

My thoughts raced, and I started to repeat, "Lord, please, don't let me forget," but I stopped short, as just then, a deep, still, small voice countered, *"You will not remember…and it is time for you to go back now."*

Then I heard a thunderclap…and found myself falling backward, drifting swiftly, as if I had been dropped out of an airplane window or let loose by some heavenly hands that had been holding me above, my arms and legs gliding up and down now against a cloudless sky.

As I fell, I gazed unblinkingly upward in amazement. The brilliance that had just been in front of me was moving rapidly away into the distance, yet I wasn't afraid. A high-pitched whistling sound began rushing in around my ears, and I thought it must be the air carrying me aloft as I plummeted toward the earth. A moment later, I watched as the oddest thing happened: The roof of my house literally enveloped me as I passed effortlessly through it, and then it felt as if I had landed on my bedroom mattress with a THUD!

I sat straight up, took a desperate, shuddering, deep inhalation, and slowly let it out, realizing that something extraordinary had occurred. Wherever I had been, whatever I had seen, I was back now to the so-called real world, and this material substance straightway felt far less authentic to me than the other place I had been.

It was the middle of the night, and I sat there for a few seconds, possibly in shock, trying to determine what had happened.

I could feel my chest burning...then I heard something.

Sobbing...right next to me...my beautiful young wife, Nita, with her head resting on her hands.

As my eyes adjusted to the darkness, I found her isolated stare. She looked as if she had been crying desperately, and she had an unfamiliar expression conveying what I somehow already understood: We both had experienced something far more irregular than we ever could have prepared for.

"Nita," I said softly, "what's going on? Why are you crying?"

It took a while for her to collect herself, but once she did, she tearfully described how she had awakened to find me dead. No pulse, no breath, no heartbeat. I had been cold to the touch—and not just for a few seconds, either. I had remained in that condition for approximately fifteen minutes while she had screamed for me to wake up, pounded on my chest, and attempted CPR.

We didn't have a phone in those days and no close neighbors, and since it was in the middle of the night, Nita had been unsure of what to do. She was about to try pulling me outside to the car to take me to the hospital when I jerked up, took in a deep breath, and looked at her.

For the reader, no matter how incredible the narrative above seems, this really did happen to me a long time ago. Later, and since then, I have understood why God allowed my wife to wake up to find me in that condition. Without her eyewitness account that night, uncertainties about the supernaturalism of the experience undoubtedly would have crept into my mind over the years. Also, the fact that I had been dead for a significant period of time, not breathing and therefore not taking in oxygen, yet experiencing no brain damage (though I'm sure some would argue otherwise), also attested to the preternatural quality of the event.

But why would God show me something and then not allow me to remember it? What would be the point of that? I can tell you that this was *the* question pressing me in the days immediately following the event, and in my youthful naïveté and impatience, I first went about trying to find answers to that mystery in the wrong way. I learned a valuable and biblical lesson as a result. In fact, that early mistake is why most haven't heard this story until now.

What happened next was this: A couple of days after my death and return from "over yonder," I told the pastor of our local church that I had an important question for him. In private, I recounted the events of earlier that week and probed what it could mean. "Why would God show me something, then tell me I wouldn't remember the vision?" I had inquired earnestly. The pastor's response was shocking to an honest and sincere young Christian man like myself. Basically, he offered that I had probably eaten too much spicy food, or had accidentally been poisoned, and was therefore delusional or simply had a vivid dream.

No kidding.

Of course, I wasn't yet familiar with such admonitions as, "Give not that which is holy unto the dogs, neither cast ye your pearls before swine, lest they trample them under their feet" (Matthew 7:6). I'm not saying that my pastor back then was a dog, you understand, but that this was a lesson I wouldn't soon forget about sharing sacred things with those who haven't had similar supernatural experiences and therefore can't appreciate or understand the otherworldly significance. In fact, besides my closest friends and family, from that day forward, I kept the event (and what I would soon understand about its measurable implications) a secret. Then, just a few years ago, well-known television personality Sid Roth asked me to repeat the story on his syndicated program, *It's Supernatural.* Because Sid, unlike some preachers, actually BELIEVES in the miraculous, I agreed that it was time to tell at least a part of that history—albeit, as legendary radio broadcaster Paul Harvey used to ponder, what was the rest of the story?

After the disappointing experience following my pastor's less-than-enthusiastic response to my question, I struggled to make sense of what had obviously been an extraordinary incident. I prayed daily, seeking understanding, and during this same period (undoubtedly God had all this timing in control from the very beginning), I happened to be reading the Bible from cover to cover for the first time in my life. I had made it to the oldest book of the Bible, Job, when, one day, my eyes suddenly fell upon Job 33:15–17. The Word of God dramatically came to life in what some charismatics might call a *rhema* moment, a time when the Scripture went from being ink on paper to becoming the living Word of God! The text that instantly conveyed the dynamic truth behind what had happened to me that fateful night read:

> In a dream, in a vision of the night, when deep sleep falleth upon men, in slumberings upon the bed; Then he openeth the ears of men, and sealeth their instruction [within them], That he may withdraw man from his purpose, and hide pride from man. (Job 33:15–17)

Though I was a very young and inexperienced believer, I clearly understood what this text was saying to me. Like the apostle Paul who couldn't tell whether he was "in the body…or out of the body" when he was "caught up to the third heaven" (2 Corinthians 12:2), or like Peter who experienced a "trance" (Greek *ekstasis* [see Acts 10:10; 11:5; 22:17], the thrusting of the mind out of its normal state where it is transported as it were out of self, so that in this rapt condition the individual "is wholly fixed on things divine" and "sees nothing but the forms and images" shown to them by God),[1] God, on that momentous night, had taken me to a heavenly place and sealed "instructions" within me. These directions would be there when I needed them during life, as they were like a roadmap that the Holy Spirit would "quicken" when, at different times, I needed guidance or information. Nevertheless, I was not to remember these details ahead of time; otherwise, I might be drawn away into my "own purpose" and lifted up in "pride," according to this passage in Job.

In other words, if, as a young believer, I had seen the ministries that God would later allow Nita and me to participate in—from pastoring large churches to owning a Christian publishing house and syndicated television ministry, to speaking at major conferences as a best-selling author, or any of the other opportunities He would give us permission to be associated with—I very likely would have made two huge mistakes. First, I would have immediately aimed at these later ministries and started working to try to make them happen—all without the benefit of the struggles, trials, setbacks, side roads, and experiences that are necessary for "seasoning" and (hopefully) qualifying one to eventually operate in them (thus God "withdrew me from my purpose"). Second, I would have been tempted by pride to think of myself as more than I should have as a young man, if I had seen myself ending up in high-profile ministries. So God, in His benevolence, also "hid pride" from me by keeping the revelations sealed until the appropriate times.

The Quickenings

In the Bible, it is clear that God does "seal" knowledge, wisdom, and revelations in the hearts of those who follow Him, and that these concealed truths can be "quickened" or made alive at the right moments as they are needed. This is depicted in such texts as Matthew chapter 10, where Jesus says to His disciples: "But when they deliver you up, take no thought how or what ye shall speak: *for it shall be given you in that same hour* what ye shall speak. For it is not ye that speak, but the Spirit of your Father which speaketh *in you*" (Matthew 10:19–20; emphasis added). That this reflects a deep partnership between our personal devotions and studies (2 Timothy 2:15, Psalm 119:11) and the indwelling Holy Spirit as part of the mystical union God has with all members of the true Church—the Body of Christ—can also be seen in Proverbs 3:6, which says, "In all thy ways acknowledge him [that's us doing our part], and he shall direct thy paths [His part]." Again, the book of John (6:63) refers to the Holy Spirit as the one "that quickens" (Greek: *zōopoieō*, "to cause to live, to make alive at that moment") the Word of God as well as those "sealed instructions" that Job talked about.

I'm not sure how this experience plays out for others, but several times in my life and at times completely unexpected (always at night when I am asleep), I have been jolted from bed with an extraordinary glimpse that I believe is taken from that original storyboard God gave me years ago, and about which I begged Him not to "let me forget." One time, for example, I was shaken from sleep by a very powerful and detailed list of things that would happen in the former religious institution in which I had been an executive. I jumped from bed, wrote down the vision as I had seen it—including names of people who would be involved, exactly what they would do, and how it would greatly damage the ministry if the district leaders did not intervene (they didn't, and it did)—then I sent that detailed letter to the state superintendent, plus gave copies to my son, Joe Ardis, and my wife, Nita. Within three years, everything played out exactly as I had seen it, down to the smallest details. In fact, my vision was so precise that it shook Joe up, causing him to come to me after the fact to express his amazement as to how it could have been possible for me to foresee such comprehensive events that accurately.

Another "quickening" that came to me in the middle of the night, and one that much of the world knows about now, involves how I was able to precisely predict the historic resignation of Pope Benedict XVI in the best-selling book *Petrus Romanus: The Final Pope Is Here,* as well as on television and radio more than a year in advance.

This began with a series of preternatural events too long to list in this book, during which time—in 2010—I was again rattled from sleep and instantly convinced that Benedict would step down in April 2012 using "health reasons" as a cover for his abdication. I went on television and radio (and out on a limb, quite frankly) in 2011, as the book *Petrus Romanus* was being written and rushed through editing, typesetting, and print so that it could be in stores before the anticipated resignation of the pope. We even wrote specifically on page 470 of that work that the pope would step down in April of 2012.

As the year 2012 came and went, and neither Pope Benedict nor the Vatican made any announcement that he was stepping down, I thought that perhaps for the first time since I had woken up in heaven years earlier, the "sealed," Job-like "instructions" mechanism either had not worked or I had been mistaken. Yet, as the months passed, I somehow remained convinced that I had seen the vision correctly! I would email friends and say, "It's not over till it's over," while at the same time saying to myself, *What are you talking about? Benedict is still the pope!*

Then something happened that the world knows about now: On February, 28, 2013, at 8 o'clock p.m., the resignation of Benedict was announced by the Vatican, which immediately gave the *New York Times* an interview in which it made the astonishing admission: Pope Benedict had SECRETLY AND OFFICIALLY resigned to select members of the Curia in April 2012, just as I had said he would. This was immediately confirmed by Giovanni Maria Vian, the editor of the official Vatican newspaper, *L'Osservatore Romano,* who wrote that the pope's decision had been "taken many months ago," after his trip to Mexico and Cuba ended in March 2012, and had been "kept with a reserve that no one could violate"[2] (meaning it was to remain top secret and was to be known only to a handful of trusted Vatican cardinals until preparations for Benedict's housing and the public announcement was ready).

Since no pope had resigned in nearly six hundred years and everybody had been saying I was crazy (because "popes do not resign; they die in office"), this revelation was astounding, and media everywhere went crazy! My office phone didn't stop ringing for weeks, with top media from around the world (including Rome) wanting to interview me to ask who my "insider at the Vatican" was. Even fake-news CNN begged me to come on their program, which I declined. The History Channel pleaded with me to participate in a special series, which I also declined.

But why am I talking about this now? Is it so I can pat myself on the back and brag about how accurate my prediction was?

Not at all.

I'm raising this issue because, early in 2019, the phenomenon happened again. And this "quickening" was the most vivid and terrifying of all such *ekstasis* yet.

So I would beg the reader: Given that, so far, these visions have been extraordinarily accurate and stated publicly beforehand against all odds, I pray that you will consider what was published in *The Wormwood Prophecy* (Charisma House, December 3, 2019) involving the newest spectacular revelation.

Like usual, I had gone to bed one evening in April of 2019, not anticipating anything unusual, when, at around 2 o'clock the next morning, I "awoke" in a hyperdimensional reality and saw in the heavens above me what looked like a horned, fiery serpent, hundreds of feet wide, plunging past the stars toward earth at an incomprehensible speed. This terrifying monster seemed to be swimming across the sky, past the planets, as it descended toward the earth.

Then, suddenly, my point of view shifted, and I was lifted above the massive object only to realize it was not a dragon after all, but rather a very large rock, and the way it was rolling through space it caused the light of the sun to glide over its contours, giving it the appearance of something undulating through space like a living thing.

The next thing I knew, I was on a tall hill or mountain somewhere, surrounded by thousands of people. We were running, terrified, and people were screaming for God to deliver us from the menace barreling through the sky toward this planet.

Moments later, I heard a deafening sound. It was as if the earth was splitting apart, the ground beneath our feet jerking violently, knocking us to the soil where we bounced viciously against the rocks, desperately reaching out for anything we could cling onto for stability.

Somehow, I knew an asteroid had plunged into the Pacific Ocean, its massive form sending a sequence of tsunamis hundreds of feet into the air.

As I glanced over my shoulder, I could see an overwhelming wall of water coming up over the hillside behind us. I perceived we wouldn't be able to escape.

But then, it was as if two very large hands slid under my arms, lifting me high into the sky, where, looking down, I watched in shock as people everywhere were swept away by astonishingly large waves slamming into coastal terrains as far as I could see. The atmosphere was simultaneously infused with scorched particles of aerosol and vapor as a blistering culmination of moisture and extreme heat subsequently combusted into a series of high-velocity hurricanes. Tornadoes, volcanoes, and earthquakes seemed to be going off like fireworks with what were likely some of the eleven deadliest volcanoes on earth—those of the Cascadia region of the United States—being triggered like dominos, releasing so much debris into the sky that, for about a week, darkness covered the heavens worldwide as the entire landscape was pounded by hurricanes and atmospheric annihilation circulating within the jet stream. By the time days later when the waters finally settled, storms subsided and the sky grew clear, much of life on earth was dead.

When I awoke, I nearly fell out of bed.

Grabbing for pen and paper to record what I had seen, I was unexpectedly interrupted by what seemed like an audible voice. It could have just been in my head, but it seemed spoken to me. The voice uttered a single word—*Apophis*.

Now, I knew there was an ancient Egyptian god of chaos and enemy of light known by that name.

I also knew that NASA (National Aeronautics and Space Administration) had named an asteroid Apophis, but didn't know any details about it.

When I got out of bed and headed for my computer to begin research on this particular space rock, I also didn't anticipate that a year-long investigation would ensue that ultimately would lead me to uncover evidence of a cover-up by NASA, ESA (European Space Agency), and other space organizations involving the likelihood of Apophis impacting the earth in less than nine years from now—Friday, April 13, 2029.

And, just so you know, my startling conclusions are shared by members of the government I spoke with, science experts of the first rank who have written peer-reviewed articles on this matter,[3] astronomers, and mathematicians (including one who has sent a warning letter to President Trump[4] seeking action on this case), and others, all cited and documented in the book, *The Wormwood Prophecy*.

But the mystery of that revelation has gotten deeper since I wrote *Wormwood*, and it wasn't until after that book was in print and I was doing media interviews on its claims that the biggest revelations involving Apophis came to light.

Those secrets are what this new book is about and involve why I am know calling Apophis "The Messenger." The "transmission" it is bringing with it will soon unveil one of the scariest—and strangest—wonders connected to Bible prophecy.

2

From Revelation to Revelation

It was 2 o'clock a.m. when suddenly I sat straight up in bed. A moment earlier, during what was perhaps REM sleep (that mysterious mechanism created by God called "rapid eye movement") when most dreams or "night visions" occur, glimpses of Wormwood impacting earth and the aftermath following it had startled my subconscious mind, shaking me from slumber.

I had been wrestling inside that spectacular vision moments before, trying to make sense of what was happening around me and what I was watching play out around the world. But not until I awoke did I hear the word "Apophis" whispered across the room, and something deeper—indistinguishable—troubled me. It was as if the ominous voice had only paused to follow later with more revelations from the beyond.

Of course, I was very familiar with transcendent subject matter. I had been involved with religious institutions for more than thirty years in official capacities, including as an executive in the largest evangelical organization in the world. During that same time, I had appeared on international television and radio programs with the opportunity to expand my presence to a regular audience, if desired.

Yet it wasn't until a brief stint working with exorcisms that I had come face to face with authentic supernaturalism, and had finally begun question-ing the differences between indoctrination and revelation, knowledge and wisdom, religion and relationship, or good and evil. It was here at last that my arrogant disposition, which had served my significant ego like a trium-phant battle horse for decades, fell weak. The sword of a superb memory that had allowed me to chop down others with proof texts and so-called writs of fact had at once become as empty as the tomb of Jesus Christ.

I wouldn't know until later how necessary that rebirth and change of heart and mind had been. Some of the very people I had mocked as "conspiratorial" had turned out to be closer to understanding enigmatic truths than I had ever been. Naiveté and blind acceptance—especially of specific, controlled versions of how the end of the world would play out—had kept me in the dark, blinded from the actual course that a frighten-ing network of hidden, Antichrist-seeking powers (what elsewhere I have called *Shadowland*) had set our nation and world upon years before.

Then came *The Wormwood Prophecy*, and pieces of the puzzle began rapidly falling into place. Things were making sense now—Jewish feasts; changes to US domestic and foreign policies (including Donald Trump's relationship with Israel); a renewed focus on the Middle East, Jerusalem, Iran, China, and Russia; and even the coronavirus pandemic—and I found it astonishing. The words, deeds, gestures, and coded language of the world's most powerful men clearly pointed to an ancient, prophetic, cryptic, and even terrifying reality.

As outlined in the forthcoming pages, the complete truths behind these facts and what soon followed the first version of the *Wormwood* book explode with heightened meaning as the reader learns how I became aware of mysterious hidden truths bursting with prophetic importance. What had been concealed in plain sight would suddenly and unexpectedly be exposed live in studio—and right as we were recording the first Sky-Watch TV broadcast programs (which aired November–December 2019) regarding my Wormwood *ekstasis* vision and supernatural encounter.

If you follow the link in the endnotes (here[5]) and watch the second program in that series, you'll see something interesting transpire between the 13–17 minute marks, when I was describing how evangelical dispensationalists (and some Catholic prophecy believers) might find the timing of the Apophis-Wormwood impact date (April 13, 2029) ominous regarding a possible "Rapture" of the Church as being soon to occur. (The Rapture is the eschatological, or end-times, event when all true Christians who are alive will be transformed into glorious bodies in an instant and joined by the resurrection of dead believers who ascend with them into heaven). During that program recording, as I was making the case that, depending on one's position, the asteroid's impact date as first set by NASA could place the last possible timing of a pre-Tribulation Rapture happening around October 13, 2025, you can see SkyWatch TV's host Derek Gilbert studying something on his MacBook. Unknown to me, while I was talking, he was searching a Hebrew calendar and checking whether anything interesting would be happening three and a half years before the date I was talking about involving when Apophis will strike earth. He was doing that because prophecy scholars say Wormwood will fall to earth in the *middle* of the seven-year Great Tribulation period, thus pre-Tribulation Rapture believers place the rapturous "catching away" of the saints three and a half years before then.

What Derek discovered raised the hair on our necks.

His eyes had fallen on a prominent timeline. Exactly three and a half years before the original date set by NASA for Apophis to come crashing down on this planet, the high holy days of the Feast of Tabernacles will be unfolding on earth. Just a few days before that will be the Feast of Trumpets. Both festivals are strongly tied by eschatologists to the Rapture of the Church.

When Derek pointed that out during the show, you could have knocked me over with a feather, as they say. How had I not known this before sending *The Wormwood Prophecy* to the printer?

Even then, things were about to get profusely more enlightening.

We had but scratched the surface of a much larger revelation tying Apophis-Wormwood with prophecy, Jewish feasts, and the ancient idea that asteroids and comets are "messengers" of the gods and omens of important coming events (for example when the magi in Matthew 2:2 see the "star" [Greek *aster*, from which the English word "asteroid" is derived]), they interpreted it as a "messenger" that the "King of the Jews" was born; they had seen "his star [*aster*] in the east, and are come to worship him" (Matthew 2:1–2). Similarly, the Apophis-Wormwood-feasts connection could imply that a countdown clock is ticking down at this very hour—a countdown that the world and the Church are unaware of.

In the following pages, based on these revelations, I will argue that mankind has likely entered the last decade of history as it has been known—what prophecy teachers call the Church Age—and how the several unusual things you will read herein set this book apart from all other works on prophecy.

We will discuss timelines, feast days connected to the Old Testament and the New Testament, and future prophecy, and why I strongly believe you need to prepare your family and friends as soon as possible for the end of the age.

Let's begin by discussing a countdown clock linked with the parable of the fig tree.

Israel and the Budding of the Fig Tree

The parable of the fig tree appears in three New Testament Gospel locations (Matthew 24:32–35; Mark 13:28–31; and Luke 21:29–33):

> Now learn a parable of the fig tree; When his branch is yet tender, and putteth forth leaves, ye know that summer is nigh: So likewise ye, when ye shall see all these things, know that it is near, even at the doors. **Verily I say unto you, This generation shall not pass, till all these things be fulfilled. Heaven and earth shall pass away, but my words shall not pass away.** (KJV; bold emphasis added)

The word "it" in Matthew 24:33 has been rendered also "he" or "the Kingdom of God." This passage, along with those that refer to the Holy

Land and God's chosen people together, make up the base Scriptures of what has become known as the fig tree prophecy.

On the Mount of Olives, the disciples asked Jesus Christ about the end of the world (or "end of the age"):

> And as he sat upon the mount of Olives, the disciples came unto him privately, saying, Tell us, when shall these things be? and what shall be the sign of thy coming, and of the end of the world? (Matthew 24:3)

After speaking for a moment about His Second Coming and the threat of the Antichrist, Christ tells His listeners that the first sign of the end of the age would be when the fig tree "putteth forth leaves" (or "buds"). Because the fig is the last of the trees to flourish in the springtime, when it buds, it is an indication that "summer is nigh" (or "imminent").

Note that in Hosea 9:10a, Israel is referred to as a fig tree: "I found Israel like grapes in the wilderness; I saw *your fathers as the firstripe in the fig tree* at her first time" (emphasis added). Joel 1:6–7a makes the same comparison: "For *a nation* is come up upon my land, strong, and without number, whose teeth are the teeth of a lion, and he hath the cheek teeth of a great lion. He hath laid my vine waste, and barked *my fig tree*" (emphasis added). In addition to these references, nations have historically been typified by symbols and/or emblems (America: eagle; Russia: bear; Canada: beaver and maple leaf; Britain: lion; and so on), and for Israel, the emblem is a fig tree.

Jesus also spoke the following:

> "I tell you, Nay: but, except ye repent, ye shall all likewise perish."
>
> He spake also this parable; "A certain man had a fig tree planted in his vineyard; and he came and sought fruit thereon, and found none.
>
> Then said he unto the dresser of his vineyard, Behold, these three years I come seeking fruit on this fig tree, and find none: cut it down; why cumbereth it the ground?

And he answering said unto him, Lord, let it alone this year
also, till I shall dig about it, and dung it:

And if it bear fruit, well: and if not, then after that thou shalt
cut it down." (Luke 13:5–9)

In Isaiah 5:7a, the "vineyard" is the property of God and the "house of
Israel" ("For the vineyard of the Lord of hosts *is* the house of Israel"; ital-
ics original). At the time Christ spoke the parable above in Luke 13:5–9,
He was three years into His public ministry. God's people (the vineyard)
needed to "repent" or they would "likewise perish." Also note that Christ
explicitly referred to the vineyard owner as "Lord" ("Lord, let it alone this
year also"). So, in the parable, the "certain man" who owned the vineyard
(God; "Lord") approached the "dresser" (Christ), and told him that for
"three years" (the length of Christ's public ministry up to that point), the
vineyard owner had tried to find fruit from this fig tree (Israel). Because
the tree would not produce fruit, the vineyard owner ordered the dresser
to cut it down. (Translation: God told Jesus to cut Israel down.) But the
dresser requested that the vineyard owner give the fig tree one more season of growth, during which the dresser would "dig about it" (make the
ground around it healthy) and "dung it" (fertilize it). (Translation: Jesus
requested more time to bring the nation of Israel to repentance.) If further
efforts to see the fig tree produce fruit did not deliver, then the vineyard
owner would cut it down.

Then, in AD 70, Israel was cut down by the Romans in the Siege of
Jerusalem. In Ezekiel, it is prophesied:

But ye, O mountains of Israel, ye shall shoot forth your branches
[bud], and yield your fruit to my people of Israel; for they are at
hand to come.

For, behold, I am for you, and I will turn unto you, and ye
shall be tilled and sown [made healthy again]: And I will multiply
men upon you, all the house of Israel, even all of it: and the cities
shall be inhabited, and the wastes shall be builded:

And I will multiply upon you man and beast; and they shall increase and bring fruit: and I will settle you after your old estates, and will do better unto you than at your beginnings: and ye shall know that I am the Lord.

Yea, I will cause men to walk upon you, even my people Israel; and they shall possess thee, and thou shalt be their inheritance, and thou shalt no more henceforth bereave them of men. (Ezekiel 36:8–12)

And in Amos, we are told of a replanting:

And I will bring again the captivity of my people of Israel, and they shall build the waste cities, and inhabit them; and they shall plant vineyards, and drink the wine thereof; they shall also make gardens, and eat the fruit of them.

And I will plant them upon their land, and they shall no more be pulled up out of their land which I have given them, saith the Lord thy God. (Amos 9:14–15; emphasis added)

Then, in 1948, Israel was replanted.

We now arrive at an important conclusion: If Christ said the "end of days" was "even at the doors" when the fig tree "putteth forth leaves," and that "this generation shall not pass, till all these things be fulfilled," then the establishment of Israel as a nation marks the last generation before the end of days.

This is the core of the fig tree prophecy.

Furthermore, because Jesus prophesied that "this generation shall not pass, till all these things be fulfilled," and a prophetic generation is at most eighty years, based on Psalm 90:10, some scholars believe a period of not more than that much time will elapse between the reformation of Israel as a nation and the return of Jesus Christ. When eighty years are added to May 14, 1948—the date Israel was formally recognized as an independent nation by the United Nations[6]—it brings us through April 13, 2029—at exactly eighty years, ten months, and thirty days later.

Of course, a Rapture or Second Coming could happen at any time, but these numbers intrigue when also compared to the prophecy-infused Jewish feasts connected with the Wormwood Prophecy and the date of the asteroid's arrival in 2029.

Now, we mentioned earlier that, exactly three and a half years before Apophis-Wormwood is set to smash into this planet, the Feast of Tabernacles will be unfolding on earth following the Feast of Trumpets a few days before.

However, exactly 120 days before the start of the Feast of Tabernacles in 2025 is Pentecost. And the number 120 in the Bible represents "the end of all flesh" (for example, Genesis 6:3 says, "And the LORD said, My spirit shall not always strive with man, for that he also is flesh: yet his days shall be an hundred and twenty years.") Moses is another example. He was 120 years old when he died (Deuteronomy 34:7).

And, while I do not know what to make of it, if anything, the mysterious "Tunguska" event where it is thought a meteor exploded near the Podkamennaya Tunguska River in Russia on the morning of June 30, 1908, was also 120 years before the much larger Apophis asteroid is scheduled to similarly impact earth.

But the number 120 is also tied to the Feast of Pentecost:

And in those days Peter stood up in the midst of the disciples, and said, (the number of names together were about an hundred and twenty),

Men and brethren, this scripture must needs have been fulfilled. (Acts 1:15–16)

All this in mind, and without "setting dates," consider the timeline graphic below and ask yourself if this is all just a coincidence? It certainly could be and time will tell, but I find it curious and worth consideration.

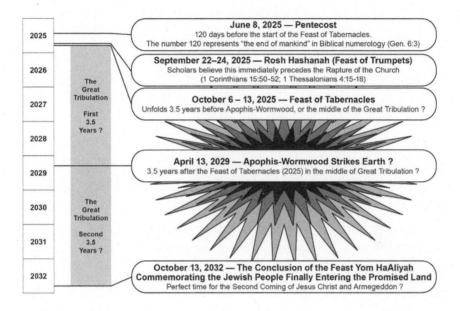

In the following chapter, before we analyze the feasts that will be fulfilled at the Second Coming of Christ, let's examine the amazing ways Jesus fulfilled the first three of the seven major feasts—Passover, Unleavened Bread, and Firstfruits, so we may appreciate the astonishing acts that are soon to be fulfilled, as heralded by *The Messenger*.

3

The Seven Feasts: Part I

Spring

The first three of the seven major feasts—Passover, Unleavened Bread, and Firstfruits—occur in spring. To the question of how Jesus fulfilled the feasts, the answer is they relate to His First Coming, the work He did on the cross.

Passover

Scripture References

- Commanded to do in: Leviticus 23:4–5 and Exodus 12:1–4; 13:8
- Talked about in the Old Testament: Numbers 9; 28:16–25; 2 Chronicles 35:1–19; Ezra 6:19; Ezekiel 45:21
- Talked about in the New Testament: Matthew 26; Mark 14; Luke 22; John 6:4; 11; 13; 19; 1 Corinthians 5:7

Observance Date
Passover begins on 14 Nisan on the Hebrew calendar, which occurs sometime during March or April on our calendar (we use the Gregorian calendar today).

The Hebrews began and ended their day with different timing than we do, as 6 o'clock in the evening, around sundown, is considered the start of a new day. This concept of daytime was wrapped around the phases of the moon and light, and is so alien to us now that it's hard to wrap our brains around, but this is why Nisan days cannot be solidly linked to specific dates in March or April. (This is true for the next feast dates as well.)

The lamb of the tenth-plague narrative was slaughtered and the blood was sprinkled around the door at 3 o'clock in the afternoon on 14 Nisan. The subsequent feast then took place *only three hours later*, at 6 o'clock in the evening, which, to the Hebrew calendar, was precisely at the beginning of a new day, 15 Nisan. (However, see the explanation later under "Astoundingly Prophetic Links" for why there appears to be another dating/timing system in place for at least some of the Jews at the time of Christ.)

Practice

Passover commemorates the Jews' deliverance from slavery in Egypt. The Passover meal, called the Seder (pronounced "say-der"; Hebrew for "order"), is consumed by families or communities, involving the gathering of multiple generations.

The *Haggadah*, an ancient writing that acts as a kind of script read intermittently during the entire feast, is a collection of readings composed by writers of the Mishnah and Talmud before the fifth century, though there are modern translations that include contemporary (and sometimes quite progressive) circumstances. The *Haggadah* includes the whole narrative from the Exodus story, and parents or mentors often stop in the middle of a reading to expound upon the ritual to their children and youth, so the feast can sometimes be lengthy. Family members take turns with the reading, and often they speak with flare and emphasis to dramatize and "act out" the event.

Jewish oral laws (the *Halakhah*) orders that the language spoken during the *Haggadah* be one that those present can understand, but a more traditional Passover meal will involve certain family members (usually the head of the household) reciting portions of it in the original Hebrew or Aramaic, in addition to the language of their nearby peers.

The food items served are specific and symbolic to the unfolding story. The lamb, which has to be flawless and without blemish, according to Exodus 12:5, is chosen on the tenth of the month and is closely observed for four days before the ritual killing for Seder. During this time, the animal is loved and treated like a member of the family—being hugged, petted on, and adored, etc. For many families, especially for the children, this makes the killing of the lamb harder, yet this difficulty is intended. It is only by learning to care about the lamb and seeing its precious innocence that its sacrifice to cover sin can be felt with the corresponding guilt over the fact that it had to die for us in the first place. (That prophetic element would certainly come into play on a deeper level on the day of Jesus' sacrifice.) In the Exodus narrative, it was the blood of the first sacrificial lamb that was spread on the doorpost.

Greatly Misunderstood Origins and Meanings

Passover, the Hebrew *Pesach* (pronounced "pay-sahk")—*as a feast*—was named after the evening when the homes of the Israelites were spared from the fate of the tenth plague of Egypt, which involved the angel of death taking the lives of the first-born males in any home that wasn't covered with the blood of a perfect lamb.

Even this early on in our reflection, most readers are probably wondering why we haven't already said that Passover is named for the night that the angel of death "passed over [or around]" the homes with the doorposts that were sprinkled in blood. This is by far the most popularly referenced explanation for the name of the feast. But the word *pesach* existed prior to both the feast and the tenth plague, and going farther back in history unveils a layer to the subject of the Passover that many Christians today have never heard of. A deep dig into the etymological roots of the word in ancient Hebrew blatantly exposes that the angel-passed-over definition is not only incorrect, but that the true meaning is *far* more significant!

Etymological Origins of Pesach and Sap

The term "folk etymology" (sometimes "pseudo etymology") refers to when an errant word origin is assigned to a word, and most times this is because it phonetically (though coincidentally) sounds like what it's describing. For centuries and beyond, the "angel passed over" definition of what was originally a Hebrew word of much greater antiquity has been widely accepted because the phrase "pass over" literally describes a person or thing skipping or avoiding something along the path to a destination (like the angel of death would have done with the marked Israelite houses).

To clarify, there was quite a bit of a mess in the meaning of the word "wormwood" in *The Wormwood Prophecy* released earlier this year due to folk etymology, and part of that discussion helps us here:

> In the case of "worm-wood," many have assumed, understandably, that this is a compound description of the woody texture of the [*Artemisia*] plant family's outer skin, and the herb's historical connection to being used as a remedy for intestinal worms. Although this makes perfect sense, as far back as we can trace it, our English "wormwood" actually stems from the German *wermōd*, meaning vermouth (an herb-infused wine).

Just prior to this statement in that book, it was also illustrated that "'licorice' (a variant of the French word for 'sweet root') was respelled 'liquorice' in Britain and Ireland because of the mistaken assumption that the 'licor' sound at the front had something to do with making 'liquor' from the root." Ironically, because some alcohols *are* made from the licorice root, the "sounds like it" false explanation behind the origin of the word having anything to do with alcohol is still popularly accepted and reported as truth from many sources. Nevertheless, it is pure coincidence that the sound for "sweet root" in French sounded to the British like a reference to alcohol, despite the fact that, by quirky happenstance, distilleries make hard liquor from it.

And let's don't even get started on the whole "o-bel-isk" breakdown that was tackled in *Unearthing the Lost World of the Cloudeaters*. The way we arrive at "obelisk," meaning literally "the shaft of Baal," and the role that plays in association with the Washington Monument is a story too long for us to get into here, and we don't need any distractions from the Passover trail we're on. It should only be reiterated that people, during the earliest formations of languages, assigned sounds to what they saw in their own place, time, religion, culture, and political climate. Only after those sounds have been picked up by other languages and assumptions have been made do we lose the history behind those sounds' names, and therefore their *story.*

This is why etymology is so important, because many times we can't see the full picture without going back to the beginning, and that has never been truer than with the naming of the Passover! Missing the deeper meaning of *pesach* is like trying to appreciate a blurry-mouthed Mona Lisa, or like turning to Psalm 23:4 and reading, "Yea, though I walk through the valley of the shadow of marginal discomfort." There's just a glaring missing element to a thing that was designed to pack a serious punch.

So the idea that the compound "pass-over" describes the act of the angel of death passing over (or around) the houses marked with blood on the doorpost and suggests that the feast of the same name commemorates that event is poetic for sure, but much of that ultimately is *folk* etymology. It works by coincidence. (Actually, it might not be coincidence. It *could* be that God, in His infinite, transcendent design, planned it all along to denote both its true, original meaning as well as describe what occurred that night in Egypt. It wouldn't be surprising if He so thoughtfully maneuvered how those terms would trickle down through history.)

But hold on. Doesn't Exodus 12:13 specifically say "I [God] will pass over you"?

Well, yes, in *English* that's what it says. In Hebrew, it simply says *ra'ah dam pesach negeph*, which translates in its most basic form to "see blood *pesach* plague," or, "when I see the blood, I [God] will *pesach* you [from or during] the plague." So first, we must understand what *pesach* means before we can know what He is doing to us or for us in this moment.

What many don't know today is that the threshold of one's home served as the altar in many ancient religions in the days before worship structures were available, so it was there, on these doorway altars, where sacrifices were often carried out. The ritual, called a "threshold covenant," marked a family's doorway for a dual purpose. First, the practice served as the residents' invitation for God or the gods to enter the dwelling and live with them there. In fact, mankind's earliest civilizations—including those of the Sumerians and Assyrians—involved elaborate entryway and archway ceremonies that sought to attain "good omens" through important imitative magic. Colossal stone creatures stood guard at the gates and palace entries to keep undesirable forces from coming through the portals while these same sentinels were often accompanied by carved winged spirits holding magic devices and/or other enchanted statuettes concealed beneath the thresholds. Second, this covenant provided a way for a deity to stand guard and protect those inside. An animal—such as a lamb, goat, dove, pigeon, ox, or calf—would be slain and the blood spilt right there over the threshold of the home as an offering to the deity. As such, it would be necessary to jump, step, or leap over the blood and into the home, because walking on the sacred, covenantal sacrifice blood showed disrespect and dissolved the covenant made with that deity.

Let's spend a minute looking at another element of support for this thread. Remember the "basin" (sometimes alternatively "bason" in the KJV) mentioned in Exodus 12:21–22, into which the Israelites were instructed to dip their hyssop branches for spreading blood over the doorpost (lintel)? As it turns out, the Hebrew word translated as "basin" here is *sap*, and although it can describe a bowl-like object, that's not what it's talking about in this instance, according to some scholars who have studied the earliest etymological origins. The translators of the KJV were likely to assume, especially if they were unfamiliar with the threshold covenant ritual of the East, that God and Moses intended the Israelites to kill a lamb and catch the blood in a bowl, then spread it upon the doorposts. Because of the Hebrew word's association with various precious-metal carrying vessels elsewhere in the Old Testament (for example, in 1 Kings 7:50 and 2 Kings 12:13), this assumption is not outrageous.

However, before younger books like the Kings, the Hebrew *sap* in Judges (c.f. 19:27) directly translates to "threshold." Since Exodus is one of the oldest books written, the "threshold" translation of *sap* would be more accurate (and would certainly fit the description of the threshold covenants of the East, which we will visit at greater depth in a moment). From *The Anchor Yale Bible Dictionary*, we read that the noun "*sap*... belong[s] to the architectural vocabulary of ancient Israel and denote[s] an essential component of an entrance, whether gate or doorway. In the Hebrew Bible, that component is always the threshold, with the one exception of Ezek[iel] 40:6–7, where a gate chamber may be indicated."[7] So, rather than collecting blood in a bowl and spreading it with a branch, what is most likely being talked about in Exodus 12:21–22 is the animal being slain right on the doorstep and the blood flowing freely about the walkway. From there, the Israelite would dip the hyssop branch in the spilled blood and spread it up and over the two side posts and lintel.

Certainly, over time, *sap* came to mean "basin" or "bowl" in the context of the Passover, and that has been the assumed interpretation since, which is why Jews for thousands of years have been collecting the blood in the bowl. However, remember that thirty-nine years passed between the first and second Paschal offering. Many folks miss that detail. The first lamb was, as we're about to show in more detail, sacrificed directly on the threshold of Hebrew houses. According to Logos Bible Software's biblical timelines, as well as Tyndale's masterful *Complete Book of When & Where in the Bible and Throughout History*, this was in the year 1446 BC.[8] The next forty years were spent in the wilderness with manna. Then, according to the same sources, the Jews celebrated their first Passover in Canaan in 1405 BC (cf. Joshua 5:10–12).[9] By then, the Jews had the *Shema Yisrael* ("Hear, O Israel") prayer straight from the Mosaic Law, as documented in Deuteronomy (6:4–9; 11:13–21), which reminded the Jews that: 1) God is One, and 2) He will not tolerate idolatry. Twice in this prayer—once at the beginning and again at the end—God instructs the Jews to write these important reminders "upon the posts of thy house, and on thy gates [6:9].... And thou shalt write them upon the door posts of thine house, and upon thy gates [11:20]." (A quick aside for those who are curious: This string of passages also commands that His words be kept like a binding upon the hand and a frontlet [ornamental jewelry that hangs on the forehead] between the eyes, which is where the Jewish "phylactery" or "tefillin" comes from, which are those long black straps of leather with a tiny box on the hand or forehead that Jewish adult males wear during prayer times. The little boxes contain the *Shema Yisrael.*)

Thus, the covenant between God and the Israelites no longer needed to involve the blood of the lamb on the threshold for two reasons: 1) The threshold covenant was already established, God was already within their homes to protect them, and there would be no more angel of death; 2) The markings upon the door would now be permanent, year-round reminders of the covenant through the prayer of *Shema Yisrael.* The threshold covenant was rendered obsolete when two generations of Israelites later resumed the Passover. Now, with a different kind of altar and a different mark on the doorpost, *sap* would evolve from defining "where the lamb was slaughtered" to describing "an instrument used in the slaughtering." It's just our own etymological theory for how "threshold" became "basin," but it all fits (including the location of both the threshold and the bowl being under the lamb's neck), and we authors find it more probable in the natural evolution of a word than to assume that any ancient people groups would coincidentally make these otherwise completely unrelated words homonymous.

Back to *pesach.*

Dr. Richard Booker, founder of the Institute for Hebraic-Christian Studies and author of *Celebrating Jesus in the Biblical Feasts,* acknowledges this historical threshold connection, explaining that *pesach,* before the Exodus, meant "to come under the protection of a deity by crossing over, jumping over, stepping over, or leaping over...the threshold" and into the protection of a home sprinkled with the animal's blood.[10] World-famous Sunday School Movement trailblazer and Yale Divinity School academic, Henry Clay Trumbull, published an entire volume in 1896 on the threshold covenant in ancient religions. His preface explains that the purpose of his book was to teach about "the beginning of religious rites, by which man evidenced a belief, however obtained, in the possibility of covenant relations between God and man; and the gradual development of those rites, with the progress of the race toward a higher degree of civilization and enlightenment."[11] His research into these religious practices—involving the consistent and corresponding contributions of thirty-six well-known and respected professors, scholars, and theologians alive in his day (including John Henry Wright)—shows that the original family altar was the "threshold, or door-sill, or entrance-way, of the home dwelling-place."[12] He goes on to explain:

> This is indicated by surviving customs, in the East and elsewhere among primitive peoples, and by the earliest historic records of the human race. It is obvious that houses preceded temples, and that the house-father was the earliest priest. Sacrifices for the family were, therefore, within or at the entrance of the family domicile.
>
> In Syria and in Egypt…when a guest who is worthy of special honor is to be welcomed to a home, the blood of a slaughtered, or a "sacrificed," animal is shed on the threshold of that home, as a means of adopting the new-comer into the family, or of making a covenant union with him. And every such primitive covenant in blood includes an appeal to the protecting Deity to ratify it as between the two parties and himself. While the guest is still outside, the host takes a lamb, or a goat, and, tying its feet together, lays it upon the threshold of his door…. [A few sentences of potentially disturbing content is omitted here. Trumball explains specific details about how the animal is sacrificed. Then he goes on to say that the host:] retains his position until all the blood has flowed from the body upon the threshold. Then the [lamb] is removed, and the guest steps over the blood, across the threshold;

and in this act he becomes, as it were, a member of the family by the Threshold Covenant.[13]

So, far before it was a "Hebrew thing," a "Jewish thing," or an "Israelite thing," *pesach*—in many ancient languages that are *not* phonetically similar to the sound the mouth makes when we say "passover," by the way—was a custom that would have been carried out in many religions of our old world, including paganism. Technically, the compound "passover" is better translated today as "cross over," as in the act of crossing over a threshold. It never meant "to avoid" or "float by," as we imagine when we think of the angel of death. It's actually quite the opposite! *Pesach*, in the context of the intended purpose of a threshold covenant ritual, meant "to invite in" (the humans' appeal to the deity) or "to enter in" (the deity's acceptance of the humans' appeal). As Trumbull explained, this rite was even observed between two people with the invisible deity in the middle of them as a witness to a covenant.

Some scholars and theologians even acknowledge that, in the ancient East, kings would travel throughout their land with their armies and advisors, interacting with the people from door to door. Kings would do this for several purposes, such as to gain further support from nobility, to ensure that their laws were being carried out, or to personally deliver important changes to the law. However, if that had been all these kings were attempting to do, most of that could have been tended to in the kings' courts and via the town criers and messengers. One central reason the kings would directly lead a march from castle grounds was to weed out their enemies. When people in these territories heard that the king was coming, they would complete a sacrifice upon their threshold, using their most prized animals as a covenant sign to the king and his men that he was welcome to "pass over" their threshold, enter their homes, and receive homage. If the royal troop happened upon a threshold that wasn't marked with blood, that family would be seen as enemies of the king, and the home would be invaded and everyone killed.

Although variations of this custom are still practiced in some parts of the Middle East, over the years, the veracity of the threshold covenant's history would be greatly blurred into oblivion in the West, even though there are quite a few traditions we still perform despite not knowing why.

For instance, the custom of a groom carrying his bride over the threshold actually began in the earliest records of human history as a woman stepping over the animal-sacrifice blood, right foot first, into her new husband's home during or immediately after a matrimonial ceremony. No part of the threshold could be touched during the crossover, lest the covenant be then and there voided. However, because of the long veils involved in much of the wedding attire of the day, getting the bride from one side of the door to the other without disturbing the blood was a challenge. Thus, as a practical matter, the groom would lift his bride while she clasped on to any flowing fabrics; in this way, the couple completed the crossover as a joint effort, once again with their deity present (in their belief). As readers may have already imagined, because not every man is the buff jock he needs to be to carry out this tradition without clumsily bumbling and ruining the whole *pesach* ritual for both of them, some cultures switched to seating the bride in a chair that was then carried over by the groom and several others (a custom still practiced in some tribes of West Africa). Because of its association with the altar, some countries traded the blood for fire (which, in accordance with not burning one's house down, actually meant a red-hot blade or a few coals from the fire were placed at the door for a brief time, though the Romans somehow used a torch); this is how we arrive at some of the earlier Eastern ceremonies in which brides are carried over smoke.

Of course, over time, eventually the brides, grooms, adopted family members, contractual agreements, and so on would extend the rite to involving blood above the door, and not just where a foot can tread, as a way of coming *under* covenant (as in "under" the obligations of the promissory pact). Ironic, then, that "pass-over" now becomes its own opposite, "pass-under."

Are you starting to see how the angel of death has nothing to do with this word?

Anyway, you get the idea. The *pesach* exchange floods into nearly countless other rites and customs of almost all world cultures, always (as far as we can tell) related to a sworn covenant—and we could have mentioned another thirty examples…but a bride being carried over the threshold is a tradition still practiced in the US today, so we chose that illustration because we knew it would be most familiar. (We can't help but chuckle a little, however. Most young men today have no idea that it's not just about carrying his bride through the door, but that it's also about not allowing his feet to tread on the threshold. These authors can imagine many well-meaning gentlemen in their struggle unknowingly stomping all over the "sacred" place in their eagerness to show chivalry, symbolically canceling or insulting their union.)

The Pesach Covenant Changes Common Tenth-Plague Imagery

Speaking of what's familiar, Trumbull explains that God, Himself, reestablished the *pesach* for His own purposes on the night of the tenth plague not out of the blue, but because of the intense, covenantal overtones the Israelites would have easily recognized from common culture. He puts it this way:

> How the significance of the Hebrew passover rite stands out in the light of this primitive custom! It is not that this rite had its origin in the days of the Hebrew exodus from Egypt, but that Jehovah then and there emphasized the meaning and sacredness of a rite already familiar to Orientals. In dealing with his chosen people, God did not invent a new rite or ceremonial at every stage of his progressive revelation to them; but he took a rite with which they were already familiar, and gave to it a new and deeper significance in its new use and relations.
>
> Long before that day, a covenant welcome was given to a guest who was to become as one of the family, or to a bride or bridegroom in marriage, by the outpouring of blood on the threshold of the door, and by staining the doorway itself with the blood of

the covenant. And now Jehovah announced that he was to visit Egypt on a designated night, and that those who would welcome him should prepare a threshold covenant, or a pass-over sacrifice, as a proof of that welcome; for where no such welcome was made ready for him by a family, he must count the household as his enemy.

In announcing this desire for a welcoming sacrifice by the Hebrews, God spoke of it as "Jehovah's passover," as if the pass-over rite was a familiar one, which was now to be observed as a welcome to Jehovah. Moses, in reporting the Lord's message to the Hebrews, did not speak of the proposed sacrifice as something of which they knew nothing until now, but he first said to them, "Draw out, and take you lambs according to your families, and kill the passover"—or the threshold cross-over; and then he added details of special instruction for this new use of the old rite.[14]

Understanding the threshold covenant brings new life to the story of the tenth plague. The *pesach* act of the Exodus narrative was the direct and intentional cross-over step of God, Himself, into the doorway of a faithful family, where He would now actively guard His people against the danger of the angel of death.

Pesach means to jump over something, as we have certainly discussed, but in proper context of the threshold, the term means "protect"! And whereas the translators of the KJV and other early translations rendered Exodus 12:13 to read "I [God] will pass over you," the English translation of the Septuagint (LXX) actually has it: "I [God] will protect you"!

It gets even more beautiful and theologically profound when we consider that God was *protecting* those families from the vehicle of His own wrath, since He is the One who sent the judgment plague in the first place.

The tenth plague in movies, books, and plays, and generally in the minds of Westerners, is a moment when the Israelites cowered in fear and smeared blood above their doorposts as a way of warding away an angry God. In this view, God is not even *with* His people! This is a stark contrast to the historically true story behind the tenth plague, which tells of when the Israelites carried out a threshold covenant as a way of welcoming the King who would identify the other doors as the enemy of His kingdom and people.

Let's turn to how this all connects to Christ.

Jesus' Role in and Fulfillment of the Passover

The New Covenant was prophesied in more than one place in the Word, but in Jeremiah 31, we see some of its specific accomplishments:

> Behold, the days come, saith the Lord, that I will make a new covenant with the house of Israel, and with the house of Judah: Not according to the covenant that I made with their fathers in the day that I took them by the hand to bring them out of the land of Egypt....
>
> But this shall be the covenant that I will make with the house of Israel; After those days, saith the Lord, I will put my law in their inward parts, and write it in their hearts; and will be their God, and they shall be my people.
>
> And they shall teach no more every man his neighbour, and every man his brother, saying, Know the Lord: for they shall all know me, from the least of them unto the greatest of them, saith the Lord: for *I will forgive their iniquity, and I will remember their sin no more*. (Jeremiah 31:31–34; emphasis added)

The death of "a" lamb *covered* sins. The death of "the" Lamb *removed* them entirely from God's memory. The sins are forgiven and remembered no more, because of the New Covenant made with the perfect sacrificial Lamb—which, as confirmed by forerunner John the Baptist, is Jesus (John 1:29). This sacrifice, accomplished on the cross where He suffered, bled, and died, was described by the prophet Isaiah about seven centuries before Christ's birth (Isaiah 50–53).

By now, a few Passover/Christ parallels should be clear:

- A) The Israelites spread a perfect lamb's blood on the door to establish a threshold covenant between God and them; B) Jesus is the Perfect Lamb, whose sacrifice of blood established the New Covenant between God and all people.
- A) The threshold covenant involved all Hebrews inviting God into their homes through belief in the lamb's blood on the doorpost; B) The New Covenant involves all believers inviting Christ into their lives through belief in the saving power of the Perfect Lamb's blood on the cross.
- A) The threshold covenant saved the Israelites from the plague God sent upon the land; B) The New Covenant saves all believers from the judgment of God upon sin.
- A) The threshold covenant ultimately led to the Israelites' deliverance from bondage in the hands of the Egyptians and onward to the Promised Land; B) The New Covenant immediately made possible our deliverance from the bondage of sin and onward to the Kingdom of God.
- A) The lamb's blood marked the doorway of a common house, where the Israelites invited God the Father; B) Jesus' blood marks the doorway of His Father's house, where God the Father invites His children.

Already, the message conveyed by these parallels is beautiful. In the West, when we hear about blood, we tend to cringe and think of death. In the East, and embedded in the foundations of Christian doctrine, blood represents *life*, as many verses from the Bible directly declare (Genesis 9:4, Leviticus 17:11, Deuteronomy 12:23, and many others). All this talk of blood should inspire imagery of the celebration and transferal of life, not death.

Fresh Light on Old Words
Comprehension of the threshold covenant brings the Passover parallels and prophetic fulfillments through Christ into view, but it also casts new

light on Jesus' words, "This is my blood of the new covenant" (Matthew 26:28, Mark 14:24, Luke 22:20).

But the big picture is even more astounding when we see Christ literally referring to Himself as the threshold covenant for all people before His own death, irrefutably positioning Himself as the fulfillment of the promise that was begun that night in Egypt (brackets below for clarification):

> "Verily, verily, I say unto you, He that entereth not by the door into the sheepfold, but climbeth up some other way [some way other than the threshold], the same is a thief and a robber. But he that entereth in by the door is the shepherd of the sheep [Himself].
>
> To him the porter openeth; and the sheep hear his voice: and he calleth his own sheep by name, and leadeth them out. And when he putteth forth his own sheep, he goeth before them, and the sheep follow him: for they know his voice.
>
> And a stranger will they not follow, but will flee from him: for they know not the voice of strangers."
>
> This parable spake Jesus unto them: but they understood not what things they were which he spake unto them.
>
> Then said Jesus unto them again, "Verily, verily, I say unto you, I am the door [threshold] of the sheep [believers].
>
> All that ever came before me are thieves and robbers [because they didn't establish a threshold covenant]: but the sheep did not hear them.
>
> I am the door: by me if any man enter in, he shall be saved, and shall go in and out, and find pasture.
>
> The thief cometh not, but for to steal, and to kill, and to destroy: I am come that they might have life [through a blood sacrifice on the cross], and that they might have it more abundantly.
>
> I am the good shepherd: the good shepherd giveth his life for the sheep." (John 10:1–10)

Jesus not only fulfilled the *pesach* for us to enter His Father's house; He *was* the Threshold, the Doorway upon which the *pesach* occurred. It doesn't get any more poetic and sweet than that. A couple of chapters later in John, Jesus makes sure His parallel has been received, saying for ultimate clarification, "I am the way, the truth, and the life: no man cometh unto the Father [or into His eternal dwelling], but by me [as threshold covenant]" (John 14:6).

The writer of Hebrews also apparently sees the link between Christ as the Threshold and location of the blood covenant, as well as the cancellation of a covenant if the blood is stepped upon:

> For if we sin willfully after that we have received the knowledge of the truth, there remaineth no more sacrifice for sins....
>
> He that despised Moses' law died without mercy under two or three witnesses:
>
> Of how much sorer punishment, suppose ye, shall he be thought worthy, who hath *trodden under foot the Son of God, and hath counted the blood of the covenant, wherewith he was sanctified, an unholy thing*, and hath done despite unto the Spirit of grace? (Hebrews 10:26–29, emphasis added)

Further, Jesus told His disciples on the night he was betrayed:

> With desire I desired to eat this Passover with you before I suffer:
>
> For I say unto you, I will not any more eat thereof, until it [the *pesach*/Passover] be fulfilled in the kingdom of God [which was later accomplished through His sacrifice]. (Luke 22:15–16)

Because of the New Covenant that was established through Him (Luke 22:20, Ephesians 2:11–13), He became the Passover Lamb, "our passover [who was] sacrificed for us" (1 Corinthians 5:7) on the threshold of His Father's Kingdom, fulfilling the purposes of the Passover feast. The

Jews were commanded to observe the Passover (Leviticus 23:4–5; Exodus 12:1–4, 13:8). Christians are commanded to observe the replacement of the Passover in the form of Communion (Mark 14:22–25, Luke 22:18–20, 1 Corinthians 11:23–25).

But, when we say He became the Lamb, some readers may not know just how deep that parallel goes…

The most obvious example would be the way Christ conducted the Last Supper. It confuses a lot of people at first. Without a theological understanding of the symbolism, Christ's references to His own body and blood as the bread and wine sound cannibalistic (and of course, that's what most people think at first, though they rarely dare to say it aloud). But once believers understand the parallel between the sin-*covering* Passover lamb that is sacrificed for the Seder feast and the sin-*removing* Jesus as the Lamb that replaced all others, it sheds fresh light on why Jesus presented Himself as such. As uncomfortable as it may be for some to imagine Jesus breaking bread and saying, "Take, eat; this is my body," followed by the passing of the wine cup, over which He said, "Drink…this is my blood" (Matthew 26:26–28), it was necessary to establish that imagery and practice precisely in that way, since Jesus was establishing Himself as the replacement of the Seder lamb.

As for the unsettling and cryptic phrasing about "partaking" of Jesus' body and blood, believers are required to be mature enough to see the Last Supper as it really played out: *purely* symbolically. The whole scene would be much harder to take if Christ had maimed Himself in any way and required His disciples to literally "partake." (Goodness, just the thought. And though we wouldn't launch into a diatribe about transubstantiation at this moment, these authors think the fact that the Last Supper was only symbolic says something about whether Jesus intended the communion/ Eucharist sacrament to be also.) It would likewise be uncomfortable if Jesus had raised an arm outward and instructed His disciples to mimic a "partaking." But that is certainly not what happened, and it behooves the reader to, for a moment, set aside how this representative act lands on *us*, and consider how it would have landed on *them*.

The disciples were very well accustomed to the Passover feast, and it was no small thing. By their time, the lamb was no longer slaughtered over a threshold, since the temple in Jerusalem had now been built. (By then, the sprinkling of the lamb's blood by the priests at the base of the temple's altar was symbolic of the past sprinkling of the blood on the doorposts.) Historians acknowledge that hundreds of thousands of Jewish pilgrims from near and far traveled in enormous caravans to the same place at the same time each year, selecting lambs, checking them for perfection, preparing them for sacrifice, setting up extra ovens all over Jerusalem, and making accommodations. If you were a Jew in those days, you were either a part of the procession toward Jerusalem for Passover, or you were in Jerusalem getting your city ready for the endless barrage of pilgrims, which required months of planning: selectively breeding lambs for their sole purpose of sacrifice, cleaning ritual baths, ensuring that all roads and bridges leading in and out of the city were ready for mass travel, and so on. The population of Jerusalem during the Passover jumped from twenty thousand to about one hundred and seventy thousand.[15]

This annual event was so grand that it was, to borrow one of President Donald Trump's favorite expressions, "YUUUGE!" We can hardly imagine it today, but to the people of Jesus' time and in His area, the tremendous focus on the sacrificing, bloodletting, and eating of a lamb for one's sins was on everyone's mind—not just one day a year, but throughout the year in preparation.

So, at the Last Supper, Jesus wasn't trying to be dark or cryptic; the disciples would never have taken His words that way. He was giving them a revelation by saying (if we might suggest a modern rewording), "Remember that Passover lamb who only covers your sins? You won't need it anymore. *I* am the Lamb that completely removes your sins. It is not an animal every year, but the Son of God only once and for the benefit of all that will be sacrificed. I am the door, the way, the threshold upon which the New Covenant will be established between My Father and men. My blood will be spilled once for all, and My body will be broken once for all, in replacement of your lambs. So, when you see wine or bread, like these here at this table, when you think of the Passover feast, think of My blood that is shed, My body that is broken for your sin and in replacement of the Passover. Now take this bread and eat it, take this wine and drink it, with that in mind."

What a powerful image!

But that was only to point out the most obvious comparison. The lamb/Lamb parallel continues.

Astounding Prophetic Links

Recall that, in Exodus 12:46 (see also Numbers 9:12), the Israelites were commanded to prepare the Passover lamb in a way that wouldn't break a single bone.

You're probably already trekking with us on this one. This is a "what comes first, chicken or egg?" conundrum, as we wonder whether God didn't want the Israelites to break the lambs' bones because not one of Jesus' bones would be broken (Psalm 34:20, John 19:30–37), *or* if none of Jesus' bones would end up broken because that's how the Passover lamb was to die. Either way, God orchestrated this additional layer. Neither the lambs' bones nor the Lamb's bones would be broken in the carrying out of the sacrifice.

We all saw that one coming, we authors can believe we hear the readers thinking.

Ah, yes, but do we all know *how* the Israelites had to prepare the Passover lamb in order for no bones to break? Do we know how they carefully roasted the animals in such a way that the entire flesh could be accessed and devoured (Exodus 12:10) without breaking any bones?

The process isn't one we will go into in great detail, because those with weak stomachs may not appreciate it. Put simply: Once the lamb's organs were removed, a pole (or branch from a sturdy source such as a pomegranate tree) was inserted horizontally to splay open the chest and upper arms of the animal, guaranteeing even and thorough roasting. Then another pole was inserted vertically and driven into the ground in order to hang the animal upright near the fire. The removed entrails were coiled atop the lamb's head, an ancient tradition called the "Crown Sacrifice" or the "Crown of the Passover Lamb." The result was literally a blood-crowned lamb hanging on a cross…a visual foreshadowing of Christ's death. No regular human imagination could have planned that element centuries before He was crucified.

We could explore countless other parallels on this trail to understanding how Christ fulfilled the Passover. Here are just a few more that we can mention quickly:

- Jesus was thoroughly examined by the Pharisees, Sadducees, and scribes for four days and found to be spotless (1 Peter 2:22), just as the Passover lamb for Seder was continuously examined for four days to ensure perfection before the sacrifice.
- After the building of the temple, when the Jews would gather en masse, preparations took more time to complete, and all the Passover lambs would have to be gathered and tied to their altars at 9 o'clock in the morning in order for the families to assemble to sing the Psalms. Nine in the morning was the same time Jesus would be nailed to the cross.
- In order for the lamb to be prepared in time for the feast, however, it needed to be slain at 3 o'clock in the afternoon—the same time of day Jesus died.
- At 6 o'clock in the evening, the Passover meal is complete and a new day begins. This is the same time Jesus was laid to rest in the tomb.
- When the temple's high priest had completed the ritual killing of the lamb on the altar, he lifted his hands apart in the air and said, "It is finished." This was the position of Jesus' body on the cross when He spoke those same words and then gave up the Spirit.

The list goes on and on, detailing hundreds of intricate links and connections between the manner in which Jesus died and the feast that had been established or ages before He was born, many of which (like the timing of His crucifixion and death) couldn't have been planned to symbolically align so perfectly.

Note that not every scholar agrees on the *dates* of these events. Some state that the Last Supper Jesus shared with His disciples was a true Passover Seder (i.e., happening on the official Jewish Passover day at the same time the rest of the Jews were sitting to supper), while others claim it was conducted ahead of the rest of the Jews so Jesus could have one last Passover experience before He was arrested (as He knew He would be). Theories abound as to what day of the week on which Jesus was crucified, and there are arguments for a number of different possibilities. This is all in addition to the fact that the Gospel of John mentions the urgency of taking the bodies down from the cross because it was a Sabbath day (John 19:31), which leads to numerous interpretations as to whether it was a literal or symbolic Sabbath day. (This discrepancy is no doubt related to the heated discussions between the Pharisees and the Sadducees regarding whether the "holy" day of Unleavened Bread would be considered the real Sabbath Day of Passover week...a quarrel we will visit at more length later on.) Likewise, the year is in question, though most sources are willing to agree that Jesus went to the cross in either AD 30 or 33. And then, of course, the "what day did which event happen" puzzle gets even more complicated when we compare Gregorian "days" (that begin at precisely midnight) with Hebrew calendar "days" (beginning at 6 o'clock p.m., or sundown).

You may be wondering why the timing of any of this matters.

Bear with us; we want to show you something astonishing. It will take some explaining, since the subject is a little complicated, but it's well worth the effort.

The Double-Calendar Issue: Was the Last Supper a True Seder?

For centuries, scholars, historians, researchers, and even Hebrew and Greek linguists have visited all the considerable details available in Scripture, in culture, and in various extrabiblical texts. In the research for this book, we consulted many sources, including the following two New Testament scholars and seminary professors who subscribe to the AD 33 theory: Dr. Harold W. Hoehner, holder of multiple doctorates in Bible and theology from several respected universities (including Cambridge), and author of *Chronological Aspects of the Life of Christ*; and Dr. Darrell L. Bock, senior research professor over all New Testament studies at Dallas Theological Seminary, editor of *Christianity Today*, and author of *Studying the Historical Jesus: A Guide to Sources and Methods* (although most readers will remember Bock for his book, *Breaking the Da Vinci Code*, in which he exposed Dan Brown's best-selling "Jesus married Mary Magdalene" fiction, *The Da Vinci Code*, as the historical and theological train wreck that it was). These men have spent a significant portion of their professional lives looking into what dates, times, and customs are mentioned in the Scriptures surrounding the Passion Week, and then comparing them to the writings of early Church historians and several contributing calendars of that time (Gregorian, Judean, Galilean, etc.; more on this in a moment). The conclusion, once these and other "AD 33" timelines are compared, is that Jesus was killed on 14 Nisan, Passover's "preparation day." Remember that technically the Seder lamb was killed on 14 Nisan and then consumed at sundown, the beginning of the Hebrew calendar's 15 Nisan.

We also checked sources that land at the AD 30 theory. On this end of the spectrum, in addition to some convincing scholarly discussions, a few expert astronomers with cutting-edge computer calculation technology have taken all the data that can be collected about feast days, rules of crucifixion, calendar dates, and astronomical movements within the universe since the New Testament, and they have concluded that Jesus was crucified in AD 30, yet still on 14 Nisan.[16] Once again, Passover "preparation day" is *14 Nisan*; the Seder meal began at sundown hours later, on *15 Nisan*.

In either case, AD 30 or AD 33, a massive number of scholars and historians agree that the order of weekdays, as they line up with the Passover week observations of the Jews, still place Jesus' death on "preparation day," *not* on or after the Passover Seder.

So, was Jesus' last meal—the meal He *called* a Passover meal (Luke 22:15)—a real Seder or not? If He was killed on "preparation day," then He couldn't have been sitting down to the Last Supper hours later, right?

Before we go any farther, let's stop for a moment and address why this is such a hotly debated issue.

If you're familiar enough with the four Gospels, you will have already likely stumbled onto what we're about to dissect, and perhaps you've even wondered about the apparent "discrepancy" between what the Synoptic Gospels say and what the Gospel of John says. The Bible seems to give two different days of Christ's death.

Mark 14:12 appears to force the interpretation that Jesus' Last Supper was an official Seder: "And the first day of unleavened bread, when they killed the passover, his disciples said unto him, 'Where wilt thou that we go and prepare that thou mayest eat the passover?'" At first glance, that looks like a clear description of 14 Nisan, during the hours when the lambs were slaughtered, which presses the idea that the Lord would have sat to His meal with the disciples at dinnertime, sundown, the moment 15 Nisan began. (Also see Luke 22:7 and Matthew 26:17. They refer to the same time stamp, but for the sake of simplicity, we will use Mark as a representative text for the other two.)

But as we turn to John 19:14, we read about a moment in what can only refer to early 14 Nisan—"preparation day"—when Jesus has already been arrested and is now standing before Pilate, soon to be crucified: "And it was the *preparation* of the passover [14 Nisan], and about the sixth hour [noon or midday in Hebrew time]: and he [Pilate] saith unto the Jews, 'Behold your King!'" (emphasis added).

Both Mark and John look as if they're talking about events occurring on early 14 Nisan. However, Mark shows Jesus prior to His arrest preparing for a peaceful meal just after having been anointed with expensive perfumes in Bethany. John places Him in Pilate's presence, well *after* His arrest: flogged, beaten, slapped, taunted, crowned with thorns, dressed in a mock-royalty robe of purple, and bleeding from head to toe, all while a crowd stands nearby demanding "Crucify him!" (John 19:15). Jesus, because He is God, certainly *could have* been in two places at once, but that obviously isn't the case here.

A few verses later in John, another reference to "preparation day" (14 Nisan) is quite clearly noted; this time, it's after Jesus has died:

> When Jesus therefore had received the vinegar, he said, "It is finished": and he bowed his head, and gave up the ghost.
>
> The Jews therefore, because *it was the preparation*, that the bodies should not remain upon the cross on the sabbath day, (for that sabbath day was an high day,) besought Pilate that their legs might be broken, and that they might be taken away. (John 19:30–31, emphasis added).

Yet, just when we might start to think we've discovered a biblical discrepancy or contradiction—just when we're getting the impression that Jesus died "on 14 Nisan in John" but "on 15 Nisan in Mark"—Mark suddenly delivers this gem over in 15:39–43:

> And when the centurion, which stood over against him, saw that he so cried out, and gave up the ghost [note: Jesus just died in this passage], he said, "Truly this man was the Son of God."
>
> There were also women looking on afar off: among whom was Mary Magdalene, and Mary the mother of James the less and of Joses, and Salome; (Who also, when he was in Galilee, followed him, and ministered unto him;) and many other women which came up with him unto Jerusalem.
>
> And now when the even was come, because *it was the preparation* [14 Nisan], that is, the day before the sabbath, Joseph of Arimathaea, an honourable counsellor, which also waited for the kingdom of God, came, and went in boldly unto Pilate, and craved the body of Jesus. (Emphasis added)

Hold on a second… Mark describes Jesus as both preparing for the Last Supper on "preparation day" (Mark 14:12) *as well as* already being dead on "preparation day" (Mark 15:42), when the Word is clear that there was a whole night and day filled with trials, sentencing, beatings, mockeries, bleeding, and hanging on the cross between the Last Supper and Christ's death?

Further, if John and the Synoptics don't agree with each other…and Mark doesn't even agree with itself…then why do all *four* Gospels agree that Jesus died on Friday, the day before the Sabbath (Matthew 27:62; 28:1; Mark 15:42; Luke 23:54, 56; John 19:31, 42)?

If you're confused, it's okay. You're only finding yourself in the same pickle that has caused many a brilliant Bible scholar to blink a few times. This is merely one of several areas of Scripture nonbelievers love to refer to as "proof" that the Bible is fallible and untrustworthy. However, the explanation is simpler than a lot of folks make it, and the answer can be found with a little diligent digging.

Today, many who study this subject initially believe the Hebrew calendar is a singular dating system for all the Jews. However, after the Diaspora separated the Israelites into many different sects for generations, which eventually saw to the establishment of slight variations in custom and tradition, not all sects within Judaism agreed on how to interpret the passage of a day. Eventually, the Galileans (including Christ) considered a day to be "from sunrise to sunrise." The Judeans, along with the Sadducees (and therefore the high priest), considered a day to be "from sunset to sunset." Though both of these considerations are "Hebrew," once the instructions from God regarding the Passover are interpreted through these contrasting lenses, they effectively produce *two* Passover Seder meals the Jews would have been celebrating at the time of Christ.

Using AD 33 as an example:

- For the Galileans, 14 Nisan started *at 6:00 in the morning* on Thursday, April 2, and ended *at 6:00 in the morning* on Friday, April 3. However, because the Galileans' "evening at the end of 14

Nisan" was on April 2, they would have celebrated their Passover Seder on Thursday night. In this, their "preparation" and their "Seder meal" were *both* on the Galilean 14 Nisan.

- For the Judeans, 14 Nisan started *at 6:00 in the evening* on Thursday, April 2, and ended *at 6:00 in the evening* on Friday, April 3. However, because the Judeans' "evening at the end of 14 Nisan" was on April 3, they would have celebrated their Passover Seder on Friday night, just as the low sun whisked them into 15 Nisan. In this, their "preparation" was on 14 Nisan and their "Seder meal" was in the first moments of 15 Nisan.

Bottom line for us Gregorian calendar folks: One of these Seders would have been on Thursday and one would have been on Friday, while *both days* would have been "preparation day" for one or the other of the Galileans or Judeans. And whereas it might be seen as a point of contention between Galileans and Judeans as to whom was correct in their traditional interpretations, many scholars have noted that this discrepancy of celebration days actually brought some relief to the Jews in Jerusalem, since there were thousands upon thousands of lambs for the priests to slaughter. Exodus 12:10 required the lamb to be eaten the evening after it was slain, and if there was any leftover, it was to be burned in the morning. The differentiating interpretations of 14 Nisan allowed the slaughter, the preparation, the roasting, and every other massive arrangement to be broken essentially into two national Seder observations—one on Thursday and one on Friday—the latter of which would be the more public display of the two in the temple, since the high priest was among this group.

Semitic language master, Bible scholar, former president of Hebrew Union College, former honorary president of the Central Conference of American Rabbis, and a founder of the World Union for Progressive Judaism, Dr. Julian Morgenstern, acknowledged this in his 1955 article, "The Calendar of the Book of Jubilees, Its Origin and Its Character." Prior to that article, scholars were at times aware of this double-Hebrew-calendar problem due to the grace of God and/or their own passionate analysis of

Gregorian Calendar

	Thursday, April 2, 33 AD	Friday, April 3, 33 AD
Hour	12 1 2 3 4 5 6 7 8 9 10 11 12 1 2 3 4 5 6 7 8 9 10 11	12 1 2 3 4 5 6 7 8 9 10 11 12 1 2 3 4 5 6 7 8 9 10 11

Galilean Calendar — Sunrise to Sunrise

14 Nisan - Day of Preparation | 15 Nisan

Jesus' Seder / Communion; Washing of Feet; Upper Room Discourse; Departure to Gethsemane

Gethsemane to the Cross; Arrest; Trials; Torture

Crucifixion of Jesus — Jesus Nailed to Cross; Work on Cross in Progress — Jesus Dies; Prepped for Tomb — Jesus Laid to Rest

Judean Calendar — Sunset to Sunset

14 Nisan - Day of Preparation | 15 Nisan

Lamb Sacrifice

Passover Seder and Ceremonies

Lambs Bound for Slaughter — Jews Gather for Hallel — Lamb Sacrifice; Prepped for Seder — Lamb Sacrifice; Passover Seder and Ceremonies

Night | Day | Night | Day | Night

14 Nisan, AD 33. © James Howell; used by permission."

biblical cultures. However, since the academic quarterly *Vetus Testamentum*, which is sponsored by the International Organisation for the Study of the Old Testament, ran Morgenstern's study,[17] it has paved the way for many more modern scholars to delve even further into what this would have meant for the "Passover Day discrepancy" we just reflected upon.

One scholar who personally benefitted from the Morgenstern piece was Dr. Harold W. Hoehner, who, as we mentioned before, believes the crucifixion year to be AD 33. He wrote in his book, *Chronological Aspects of the Life of Christ*:

> Thus, according to the Synoptics, the Last Supper was a Passover meal. Since the day was to be reckoned from sunrise, the Galileans, and with them Jesus and His disciples, had the Paschal lamb slaughtered in the late afternoon [3:00 p.m.] of Thursday, Nisan 14, and later that evening [6:00 p.m., but the same Hebrew day for the *Galileans*] they ate the Passover with the unleavened bread. On the other hand, the Judean Jews who reckoned from sunset to sunset would slay the lamb on Friday afternoon which marked the end of Nisan 14 and would eat the Passover lamb with the unleavened bread that night which had become Nisan 15. Thus, Jesus had eaten the Passover meal [the Last Supper with His disciples] when His enemies, who had not as yet had the Passover, arrested Him.[18]

So, the reference to the preparation slaughter in Mark 14:12 relates to the Galilean Hebrew calendar, and the reference to the preparation day in Mark 15:42 relates to the Judean Hebrew calendar. *All* talk of "preparation" was on 14 Nisan, but with different interpretations of when 14 Nisan begins and ends; this means "preparation day" at the time of Christ would have been on *both* Thursday and Friday.

Okay, but why wouldn't the writers of the Gospels mention the two different Passover meal days?

Why would they feel the need to?

The audience of their time would have been very familiar with the ongoing incongruity between Jewish sects and their post-Diaspora variations of tradition. And don't forget that the first rule of biblical interpretation is that readers need to interpret the Word *as it was written to the original audience*, lest we find our contemporary lens warping what was originally said.

The conclusion, in these authors' opinions, and as is shared in the judgment of many scholars: Jesus' Last Supper *was* a legitimate Seder, celebrated with the Galilean sect of the Jews, on Thursday evening. Then, later that same night, He was arrested, Peter denied Him three times before dawn (the crowing of the rooster) on Friday, and by 9 o'clock a.m. Friday morning, He was being nailed to the cross. He died and was removed from the cross just before the Judeans had their Seder meal.

What This All Means: Astonishing!

This is where we get to the rewarding part of all this calendar reflection.

Add the fact that Jesus died on 14 Nisan, "preparation day," to the previously discussed times of day that Jesus was nailed to a cross, died, and then was taken down.

Do you see it yet?

The parallel, and Christ's fulfillment of the feast, reaches an ultimate apex. Every single step taken throughout His last days was a moment-by-moment, exact playout of what the feast lambs over in the temple grounds faced in their own last days.

The massive Jewish crowds escorting lambs into the gates of the city and onward to the temple would have been aligned with Jesus' triumphal entry into the city amidst shouts of "Hosanna!" and the waving of palm leaves.

The lambs were being loved, praised, doted on, and eventually inspected by the Temple priests to be proven worthy as the sacrifice, just as Jesus was being loved, praised, doted on, and eventually tried before the secular and religious authorities, upon which He proved Himself worthy as the only sacrifice for all mankind.

At 9 o'clock a.m. Friday, as the sacrificial lambs were led to the holding pens where they would be bound for slaughter, Jesus was led to the hill at Golgotha, where His hands were bound to the cross by nails.

Before, during, and after midday, between the binding of all the lambs and their mass slaughter, the Jews gathered for the singing of the Hallel, an event dedicated to thanking Jehovah for His love, grace, and provision. Simultaneously, Jesus was on the cross, *completing* Jehovah's love, grace, and provision in the ultimate act of redemption.

The very second that Jesus died was at 3 o'clock on Passover day, after moving His lips one last time to say, "It is finished," precisely in accordance with the high priest in the nearby temple proclaiming, "It is finished," as he ended the life of the sacrificial lamb. A spiritual transferal occurred in that instant, from the kosher knife of the Old Covenant Passover lamb to the forever accessible grace of the New Testament Covenant Lamb.

Once the no-bones-broken lambs of the Jews had been roasted with their bloody crown while hanging, arms outward, on their cross-shaped spit, they were prepared for the Seder.

Then, at precisely sundown—when the Judeans were sitting down to the Seder to consume the now-deceased, no-bones-broken lamb that had been hung, arms outward, on their cross-shaped spit with the bloody "crown of the sacrifice" atop their heads—Jesus was taken to the tomb to be washed and laid to rest.

One final thought on how all this might be additionally connected to *The Messenger* Apophis.

- According to NASA's original dating, the asteroid Apophis could strike earth Friday, April 13, 2029, six days after Passover, and six is the number of man, sin, and judgment.
- Passover is also connected to the Rapture and Second Coming, as Jesus was the firstfruits of our resurrection (1 Corinthians 15:20–23).
- Lastly, the Apophis-Wormwood strike is one morning after HaShoah, Holocaust Remembrance Day, and the number "one" in biblical numerology represents God and His power displayed.

The best writers in Hollywood can't produce a more poetic drama…
and now we're going to see how this masterpiece is still, unbelievably, only
the beginning.

Unleavened Bread

Scripture References

- Commanded to do in: Leviticus 23:6–8; Exodus 12:15–20

Observance Dates

The Lord commanded that all the people of Israel eat unleavened bread for
seven days (Leviticus 23:6–8). The *Hag HaMatzot* (pronounced "Hawg
Hah-Maht-zot") Feast, or the "Feast of Unleavened Bread," is a continual observance from 14–21 Nisan. In Scripture, the Feast of Unleavened
Bread is often treated like a separate feast than *Pesach* (though not always;
cf. Matthew 26:17, Mark 14:12, and Luke 22:1, 7), but because the dates
overlap, today's tradition involves the observance of all three together over
a week: Passover, Unleavened Bread, and Firstfruits (which will be discussed shortly). This is why, today, when we hear "Passover," it's in reference to a week-long celebration instead of a single meal.

Practice

As Passover commemorated the Jews' deliverance from slavery in Egypt,
the Feast of the Unleavened Bread observes the "going out" of Egypt.

Leaven (an ingredient used to make bread dough rise) was a symbol
of sin (cf. 1 Corinthians 5:7–8 and Luke 12:1), so the unleavened bread
of the Passover week, known as *matzah* (or *matzoh*), became a symbol
of either sinlessness or the removal of sin from one's life. In fact, though
the etymology of *matzah* only partially connects to this concept, as it
first meant "sucked out" or "drained out" (note this original meaning for
later!), after the establishment of the Passover, the use of *matzah* more
heavily implied "without sin." This flatbread, which looks quite a bit like

a cracker, must be prepared and baked in less than eighteen minutes to prevent it from rising by fermentation, and during the preparation process, the dough cannot touch anything (cooking utensils, etc.) that has ever been in contact with leaven.

Before Passover, the Jews had to take serious measures to remove all traces of leaven from their houses, including an aggressive scrubdown of all walls, floors, ceilings, tables, chairs, cupboards, and any other surface that might have ever touched leaven at any point. Any leaven or leavening agents stocked in the home had to be destroyed or sold to a non-Jew.

The "Search for Leaven" Ceremony

Then, the *Bedikas Chametz* ("Search for Leaven") ceremony takes place, conducted by the homeowner and/or head of the household: After sundown, the following blessing is recited:

> Blessed are You, our God, Ruler of the world, who sanctifies us with mitzvot [commandments] and calls upon us to remove chametz.

Once this blessing has been spoken, all others present say "amen," then it becomes forbidden to speak about anything other than the search.

Carrying a lit beeswax candle and shining its flame high and low into every crevice, the homeowner thoroughly inspects the house on a mission to find any trace of leaven left behind or overlooked during the prior cleansing. The homeowner or his assistants bring along a small bag, a wooden spoon, a feather, and often a bell. When leaven is found, the bell is rung to herald the discovery. The feather is then used like a tiny broom to carefully sweep the substance onto the wooden spoon, and then the leaven is collected in the bag. When the search is over, the wooden spoon, feather, and candle are placed in the bag with the leaven, and a safety-measure "nullification statement" is spoken to cover any crumb that might not have been found throughout all these previous endeavors:

All leaven and anything leavened that is in my possession, which
I have neither seen nor removed, and about which I am unaware,
shall be considered nullified and ownerless as the dust of the earth.

The next morning, the bag, now more flammable, as it contains the
wooden spoon and feather (thus the reason behind why these otherwise
odd utensils would be used), is burned. During this somber moment of
watching flames engulf the bag and its contents, ceremony participants
are to think of their own lives and their own sin and pride, and they are to
reflect on the God-given gift of sanctification.

The ceremony is celebrated at night because, in ancient times, the
Jews didn't have the kind of lighting needed to see in every nook and
cranny of their home, and the candlelight tended to cast hyper-focused
illumination in areas where daylight wouldn't suffice. It's common today
for the custom to be carried out with a candle and supplemented with
a flashlight (and even regular electric lights) for areas in a home where a
flame would present potential danger.

Early on, it was decided that the blessing spoken at the beginning
of the search was less meaningful (some even believed it was in vain) if
there was no leaven anywhere in the house at the time to substantiate the
recitation. On the other hand, the house cleansing is such a tedious and
involved process that it wouldn't be logical to leave it until the *Bedikas
Chametz* to justify the blessing of removal, because it's likely there would
never be enough time to have it all done between the start of the "search"
ceremony and the time the Jews must be leaven-free.

Just like their calendar, the precise time of day in reference here is difficult to calculate because it depends on what area of the world a Jewish
family might live in and that geographical location's relationship to the
sun, known as the "*halachic* [seasonal] hour." Suffice it to say that, for
their purposes, it was midmorning, or one *halachic* hour before midday.
Also, they weren't allowed to start the *Bedikas Chametz* early (unless they
had good reason, such as traveling far from home to join another family or a medical emergency, etc., in which case there were provisions in

place to help families schedule the search around that event). This meant that they would have between sundown one evening and midmorning the next to start the search with all the candles, feathers, bell-ringing, etc., *and* complete all the washing down of the house to ensure that it was leaven-free. It could be that this was more possible in the beginning, when Israelite houses were much smaller than today, but before long, it became impractical to squeeze all this activity into such a narrow time frame when there were so many other Passover-related preparations to be done simultaneously.

So, the Jews essentially had no choice but to complete a pre-cleaning in the days leading up to the Passover, in which all the leaven would be removed. Then, to ensure that the "Blessed are You...who sanctifies us with [commandments] and calls upon us to remove [leaven]" words still had spiritual significance during the ceremonial search, a compromise was reached: Ten small pieces of leavened bread (a nod to the ten plagues) were separately secured in wrapping that wouldn't allow them to leave crumbs behind, and they were hidden by a member of the family throughout the house. Notes were made as to where the pieces were placed, just in case the homeowner didn't find all ten, to make sure that locating them later would not depend entirely on anyone's memory. (For modern Jewish families, this hunt is often a favorite part of Passover week for young children who get to stay up late and wander the dark with flashlights looking for anything out of place. It's like an Easter egg hunt with an Indiana-Jones twist. A similar hunt is the "search for the *afikomen*," which takes place at the beginning and the end of the Seder, but it's related to unleavened bread, so we'll address that at the end of this section as well.)

With the *Bedikas Chametz* finalized and the bag burned (along with any leftover leaven stored up that the household wasn't able to sell to non-Jews), the family is now set up to remain chametz-free for Passover week.

Now, comparing the leaven to sin and the symbolism enacted in this custom, we arrive at the early, pre-Christ representation: They had set out to acknowledge the presence of sin in their lives (planning the search and hiding the pieces of leavened bread), thanked the Lord for His command to remove it (the blessing), systematically searched all nooks and crannies for any sin that may have been either hidden or overlooked (the ceremonial search), claimed nullification of any sin they weren't aware of (the nullification statement), and destroyed any remnant of sin (the burning of the bag).

As to why, of all things, flat, cracker-like bread would be so important as to be assigned the central symbol of sinlessness, there are several excellent reasons, but discussing those at length crisscrosses our reflection of Jesus' personal fulfillment of the feast, so we will deal with both subjects simultaneously in the following pages.

Note going forward: As to what leaven, *matzah*, the *Bedikas Chametz*, and ultimately the entire Feast of Unleavened Bread would eventually all have to do with Jesus—those details, like the Passover links, couldn't have been planned beforehand by any brilliant mind save for the Creator's. Keep your eyes peeled to see the glory and wonder of all God designed, those elements that the best of human imaginations couldn't have contrived just to make religion look pretty. For those with eyes to see and ears to hear, the next bit is as profound as all we've discussed regarding the Passover.

Origins, Meanings, and Jesus' Role and Fulfillment

Leaven, and Christ's relation to it, naturally relates to a historical as well as a spiritual explanation. Since the former of these two is easier to address than the latter, we'll tackle that first.

Historical Reasoning for Leaven-Link

The historical and circumstantial origin of the unleavened bread is simple to clarify looking back on just a few relevant verses (pay attention to italics/emphasis):

[The tenth plague:] And it came to pass, that at midnight the Lord smote all the firstborn in the land of Egypt, from the firstborn of Pharaoh that sat on his throne unto the firstborn of the captive that was in the dungeon; and all the firstborn of cattle. And Pharaoh rose up in the night, he, and all his servants, and all the Egyptians; and there was a great cry in Egypt; for there was not a house where there was not one dead.

[Pharaoh's sudden, middle-of-the-night release of God's people:] And he called for Moses and Aaron by night, and said, "Rise up, and get you forth from among my people, both ye and the children of Israel; and go, serve the Lord, as ye have said. Also take your flocks and your herds, as ye have said, and be gone; and bless me also."

[Israelites leave in a hurry:] And the Egyptians were urgent upon the [Jews], that they might send them out of the land *in haste*; for [the Egyptians] said, "We be all dead men."

And the [Israelites] took their [bread] dough *before it was leavened*, their kneadingtroughs [a rectangular bowl about the size of today's average kitchen sink in which the ancients would knead their bread together with yeast] being bound up in their clothes upon their shoulders…. And they baked unleavened cakes of the dough [the first *matzah*] which they brought forth out of Egypt, for it was not leavened; *because they were thrust out of Egypt, and could not tarry.* (Exodus 12:29–39, emphasis added)

Before the feast of the same name was instituted, having unleavened bread was a result of being in a huge rush to get out of Egypt. Normally, the Jewish families' bread would have been leavened, and until this point, nothing was inherently sinful about fluffy bread.

However, because of this speedy deliverance from Pharaoh's totalitarian and tyrannical oppression—the leader's polytheistic religions opposed and greatly offended God—the lack of yeast in the bread took on a spiritual importance. It was a separation of God's people from the old life—when they weren't allowed to worship God freely, when they grew accustomed to not worshiping God the way He longed for them to—and into the new life, where they were liberated to worship God without the sin of the Egyptians' prohibitions preventing them. The *matzah* marked the moment when, for the first time in hundreds of years, God's people ran toward Him and His provisions. A couple of other passages drive home the importance of this unleavened bread as a symbol of the transition from the old life to the new:

> Remember this day, in which ye came out from Egypt, out of the house of bondage; for by strength of hand the Lord brought you out from this place: there shall no leavened bread be eaten....
>
> Unleavened bread shall be eaten seven days; and there shall no leavened bread be seen with thee, neither shall there be leaven seen with thee in all thy quarters.
>
> And thou shalt shew thy son in that day, saying, "This is done because of that which the Lord did unto me when I came forth out of Egypt." (Exodus 13:3–8)

> Thou shalt eat no leavened bread with it; seven days shalt thou eat unleavened bread therewith, even the *bread of affliction; for thou camest forth out of the land of Egypt in haste*: that thou mayest remember the day when thou camest forth out of the land of Egypt all the days of thy life. (Deuteronomy 16:3; emphasis added)

God wanted more than just the path away from Egypt to be remembered. His deliverance from slavery, oppression, and discomfort would have been enough, but that wasn't the whole picture. God wanted His people to be able to worship Him (translation: have the fullest relationship with Him), and Pharaoh repeatedly stood in the way of that (Exodus 8–10), which was the greatest of sins against the God of the Hebrews. So, the item that marked their quick, middle-of-the-night abandonment of Egypt (unleavened bread) came to represent of leaving behind all else and hurrying toward a spiritually free relationship (righteousness) with God.

With the seemingly coincidental, historical association of leaven/yeast addressed, let's look at the layers behind why leaven/yeast ended up being the prophetically perfect icon for sin.

Spiritual Reasoning for Leaven-Link

First, leaven and/or yeast, because of its effect on bread dough, is an excellent metaphor for something that spreads uncontrollably and swells larger than it started out to be, as well as something that can't be removed from the mix, as it is, by nature, inherently there from the beginning. Sin, too, spreads uncontrollably and swells beyond the first offense (we will look at one example of this shortly), and the sin nature cannot be removed from mankind, as it has been there since the Fall.

The difference between "leaven" and "yeast," just to proceed with clear terminology, is that "leaven" can be *any* ingredient added to a bread recipe that makes the bread rise, expand, or puff up, as well as a common way of referring to the leavened bread, itself; "yeast" is a *specific* ingredient, a popular, yellowish fungus that creates a leavening (lifting) effect in baking goods through a fermentation process. Whereas there can be several different leavening agents in baking (such as baking soda, baking powder, cream of tartar, etc.), the most well-known and referenced ingredient in baking since ancient times in Israel is and always has been yeast, which is why so many sources discussing the Hebrew feasts use "leaven" and "yeast" interchangeably.

Jesus Fulfills Both Pre- and Post-Passover Matzah Definitions

Remember that we've already discussed the etymological transition of the word *matzah* from "to suck out," "to drain out," and "to remove," to "without sin" after the first Passover (glance back to the "Practice" subhead for reference if needed). One fact that will pop up several times in this section is that Jesus *is* the ultimate *Matzah*. He was, is, and always will be "without sin" (1 Peter 1:19, 2:22; Hebrews 4:15, 9:14; 2 Corinthians 5:21; 1 John 3:5; Isaiah 53:9). Therefore, His nature is identical to the very *post*-Passover definition of the word *matzah*. It describes Him, and

He describes it; the two are inseparable as early as the Israelites' rushed exit from Egypt. However, because our Redeemer and Savior allowed His own blood to be spilled and His own body to be broken for our sins to be taken away, He also fulfills the "removing" angle of what the Hebrew *matzah* or *matzoh* meant *eons before* the plague or the feasts. He is absent of sin; He removes sin: It's a literal fulfillment of the word from before and after *matzah* adapted a new meaning...yet this was foretold far in advance of His birth.

This can be a lot to take in for those reading these facts for the first time, so let's reiterate that the word *matzah*, itself: 1) originally described the removal of something, which was unrelated to any Messiah; 2) came to represent both the absence and removal of sin *hundreds* of years before the Messiah; and then 3) eventually became a precise descriptor of both who the Messiah would be to us (the "sinless One") and what He would accomplish for us (the "Remover of our sins"). This is similar to how *pesach* originally had nothing to do with any feasts or angel of death, then became the "sounds-like" descriptor of the angel's actions, as well as the precise definition of the threshold covenant with Yahweh and later the New Covenant through Christ as the ultimate Threshold and Door.

Another tier of beauty is added to the Communion sacrament: Jesus instructed us to "take, eat," as His body *was* the bread. Remember that He said this as He was handing the disciples literal chunks of *matzah*? (Whether He was celebrating Passover on the correct day or not—discussed in the last section—is not a concern here. He called together His disciples for a meal, referring personally to it as a "Passover," and therefore, unleavened *matzah* would have been the *only* kind of bread the sinless, Jewish Son of God would have passed to them at this time, regardless of that fluffy, soft bread depicted in many faith films and stage plays about Jesus at the Last Supper.) Here again, just like with the threshold covenant, Jesus is calling *Himself* the very central element of the feast. He is our Unleavened Bread. That much is clear, and that much, by itself, would be enough to call Christ a "fulfillment" of this feast.

But the Last Supper wasn't the first time a parallel between Jesus and bread had been brought up. In the Gospel of John, chapter 6, we see that Jesus was making a name for Himself far before the crucifixion. In this portion of Scripture, He has quite the crowd of eyewitnesses to the miracles He was performing for the sick. These were men, women, and children pilgrims who were near Jerusalem for the Passover, and their curiosity about the Healer was so strong that they were willing to wander as a great multitude away from any readily available food source. One small boy had immense faith, which led to what appeared to be a tremendously insufficient donation of food for the gathering: five loaves of barley bread and two fish. Jesus took these petite offerings and multiplied them, feeding thousands of people (the five thousand men recorded, plus the unnumbered women and children present) as much as they wanted until they were completely full, and then watched as His disciples gathered up twelve full baskets of the excess. This miracle, according to verse 14, proved to the crowd that Jesus was the Messiah—the Prophet they had been told would come in Deuteronomy 18:15–18.

The next day, when the enormous assembly continued to trail after Jesus, He challenged them not to set their appetites for perishable foods, but upon that which lasts forever. They couldn't comprehend what Jesus was telling them, and proved as much by asking for further signs, citing the "manna from heaven" events in Exodus 16:4–36 as justification. If the Israelites had manna in the wilderness, surely Jesus, if He were sent and sealed by God (as Jesus just claimed to be in verse 27), was capable of cranking out more miraculous food for His followers. Jesus, seeing the truly superficial motive behind those in the crowd who requested a repeat of the events of the day before, offered a gentle correction, leading to the moment He explicitly and unequivocally refers to Himself as the "Bread of Life":

> "Verily, verily, I say unto you, Moses gave you not that bread from heaven; but my Father giveth you the true bread from heaven.
>
> For the bread of God is he which cometh down from heaven, and giveth life unto the world [Christ]."

Then said they unto him, "Lord, evermore give us this bread."

And Jesus said unto them, "*I am the bread of life*: he that cometh to me shall never hunger; and he that believeth on me shall never thirst....

All that the Father giveth me shall come to me; and him that cometh to me I will in no wise cast out. For I came down from heaven, not to do mine own will, but the will of him that sent me.

And this is the Father's will which hath sent me...that every one which seeth the Son, and believeth on him, may have everlasting life: and I will raise him up at the last day....

I am that bread of life. Your fathers did eat manna in the wilderness, and are dead.

This [referring to Himself] is the bread which cometh down from heaven, that a man may eat thereof, and not die [but inherit eternal life]....

The bread that I will give is my flesh, which I will give for the life of the world....

[Once again, in words that would have been familiar to *them* but sound odd to us today, Jesus summarizes His own sacrifice in that Communion language:] "Verily, verily, I say unto you, Except ye eat the flesh of the Son of man, and drink his blood, ye have no life in you.

Whoso eateth my flesh, and drinketh my blood, hath eternal life; and I will raise him up at the last day.

For my flesh is meat indeed, and my blood is drink indeed.

He that eateth my flesh, and drinketh my blood, dwelleth in me, and I in him." (John 6:32–56; emphasis added)

Follow this rundown: a) Leavened bread is a symbol for sin; b) the New Testament clearly teaches that sin equals death (Romans 6:23); and c) symbolically and spiritually partaking of the leavened bread (engaging in or tolerating sin) leads to death. As a symbol, unleavened bread could be called the "bread of death." The Feast of Unleavened Bread was established to remove this deathly bread (sin) from the lives and homes of God's people. Now, Jesus *is* the Unleavened Bread, or, *the Bread of Life*. In this teaching, it is clear that Jesus positioned Himself as a direct replacement of the *matzah*—a fulfillment of the Feast of Unleavened Bread. Believing in and following Christ and making an effort to be forgiven, sanctified Christians in our homes and lives is the replacement/fulfillment of the "Search for *Chametz*" ceremony.

But there is another physical-resemblance angle on the bread. We glanced before at the extraordinary resemblance between the Seder lamb's spilled blood and "crucifixion"-style roasting spit, as well as the Eastern understanding of blood as the essence of life, and that explained a lot where "blood" was concerned. Here, we can comprehend not only the symbolism of Jesus referring to His body as the "bread" that the Hebrews' sin-free *matzah* foreshadowed…but we can literally *see* the symbolism.

The *matzah*, when the baking rules are strictly followed, is striped and pierced, just like Jesus' flesh on the cross. This regulation was decreed by the Jewish leaders as the mandatory preparation method during the intertestamental age, well before the birth of the Messiah, prophetically pointing to His sacrifice.

Why stripes and holes?

Yeast feeds on sugar, creating carbon dioxide gases and, through fermentation, ethyl alcohol. In *sugar water*, these excretions release bubbles outward into a foamy, carbonation-like froth that rises to the top of the water in a yellowy-brown slurry. (It's quite unappealing to look at in liquid.) In dough, however, the flour and yeast enzymes immediately begin to interact to make the existing starch molecules break down into sugars, which the yeast metabolizes and converts to gas and alcohol. The bubble gum-like elasticity of the "viscoelastic matrix" (basically, that's the early protein combinations leading eventually and collectively to "gluten"), especially after sufficient hand-kneading, traps the bubbles within the bread dough like tiny balloons. These balloons, or air bubbles, when exposed to the heat from the oven, maintain their shape and harden, producing a bread that is soft, fluffy, airy, and delicious.

When unleavened bread is made for the feast, the baker has eighteen minutes from the moment the ingredients are mixed to the time the bread is extracted from the oven. If the baker tarries at all beyond that timing, there is risk of fermentation and, therefore, some rising of the bread. So, the entire process is done in a hurry. To allow the air to escape from the *matzah* dough in the oven, and therefore avoid any yeast-rising, the Jews would (and still do) line their *matzah* with stripes and pierce it with holes.

But Jews don't put any yeast in their bread, anyway… These authors can hear our non-Jewish readers thinking that. So if unleavened bread doesn't have yeast, why would it ferment and rise? Wouldn't unleavened bread be as simple as not putting in the expanding agent?

Not entirely, and that's yet another beautiful puzzle piece involving God's intricately connected design about the Feast of the Unleavened Bread and its fulfillment through Christ.

Obviously, the unleavened bread made by the Hebrews wouldn't contain "added" yeast or other leavening agents. Symbolically, this would mean that the Jews accomplished not "adding extemporaneous sin" between themselves and Yahweh that they would later nonchalantly expect unending grace for. It essentially means that, through the covenant with God, they have chosen to conscientiously avoid sin (a precursor to Paul's "die to sin" reflections of Romans 6:1–2) as they conscientiously avoid yeast during Passover.

However, if it stopped here, this "added" yeast/leaven symbolism wouldn't account for unintentional sin or the inherent sin of human nature after the Fall; the no-added-leaven bread dough picture by itself might suggest that people can be, by their own efforts, sinless, merely by choosing to avoid "added" sin to the recipe of their faith.

Relating to actual yeast and bread, God's creation and design deepened the parallel when He made sure that *spores of wild yeast are already naturally found on grain*! (This is also true for many other food-related sources, like milk) This is because yeast develops in and travels through the air, naturally.

Like human nature that is marred by the reality of inherent sin from before we're born, flour is "marred" by the reality of inherent yeast from before it's ground. Fermentation is already a factor for all bread-baking processes, which is why Jewish customs and rules require that the *matzah* goes from start to finish in eighteen minutes.

And if yeast is to the nature of grain as sin is to the nature of man, then, from a technical perspective, there would be no way to completely remove the yeast from bread, regardless of how masterful the baker is. The fermentation of dough *will* happen, which means, in our symbolism trail, that festering temptation of sin *will also* happen, and it can never be removed.

It can never be removed, that is, unless you had a yeast remover powerful enough to grant a clean slate. Remember that the Seder lamb could only represent the *covering* of sin, not the complete *removal* of it. Now, the *matzah* can only represent the *avoidance* of sin, but not the complete removal of it. The striped, pierced *matzah*, then, like the Seder lamb, would be replaced by the striped, pierced body of Christ. We now "take" and "eat" the bread of Communion as a commemoration of Christ, the Unleavened Bread of Life, the only *wholly* "without sin," yeast-free *Matzah* that, paradoxically, also achieves the *first* meaning of *matzah*, which is "to remove [sin]."

Now, as with the "Astounding Prophetic Links" section in the Passover earlier, things are about to get even more amazing as we set our sights on the *afikomen*. And you may have heard about the Passover *afikomen matzah* being associated with Jesus before, but, after checking the market at length, these authors cannot find a single book anywhere that digs as deeply into this as we're about to. So grab yourself a cup of coffee and put Professor Grampy's thinking cap on. If you're anything like we were when we first learned about this, that lightbulb above your head might just blow up.

Links of the *Afikomen*

The Passover Seder meal, itself, involves a custom that is a little too striking and obvious a parallel for most scholars to write off as coincidence. It relates to the final piece of *matzah* that is eaten the night of Passover. This is, according to Jewish history (and modern scholarly reports), a "search for the future Messiah" symbolism. (But note that it's more complicated than that, as you will see shortly.)

Three pieces of *matzah* are brought to the father of the family at or near the beginning of the feast. The middle *matzah* (now called the *afikomen*) is broken, hidden until the end of the meal, searched for by the children, found, and traded to the father for a prize. Without a formal title, the hunt is simply referred to in modern Jewish literature as "the hiding of [and later the "search for"] the *afikomen*." The Seder cannot be concluded until this ritual is over. Upon its completion, the Seder is officially ended; no food or drink can be taken beyond that point (with obvious exceptions, such as water to wash down medication, etc.).

So rich is the subject of the *afikomen* that it requires breaking down and organizing subcategories of thought in order to fully address it, lest we end up with a messy, enormous chapter that trips over itself and delivers incomprehensible and seemingly unrelated facts. As such, we have decided to address the origins of the tradition first, followed by some additional layers of mind-blowing symbolism that couldn't have been planned by anyone other than God to point to a Christ-fulfillment. Finally, as to what the word *afikomen* really means, there are plentiful reasons why we can't explain that quickly in any simple terms. For now, suffice to say that it describes "that which comes later." After readers have gained a fundamental understanding of the tradition, we'll then tackle the evolution of this rare and bizarre word in a section appropriately called "Etymological Nightmares."

The Origin of the Search

Although not every source agrees, the most popularly referenced idea is that an innocent misinterpretation from an ancient teaching launched a new tradition that would be observed by the Jews (evidently without their knowing that they were reenacting Jesus' redemptive story). In the case of this theory, the *afikomen* wasn't even supposed to be what it came to be, making the strong prophetic link to Christ even more authentic and fascinating if this theory is true, because it can't be manufactured, contrived, or staged when it comes about by accident.

Based on the Talmud, Pesachim 108b–109a, children are to participate in the drinking from the four cups of wine (to remember the four promises of Exodus 6:6–7: "I will bring out," "I will deliver," "I will redeem," and "I will take"). The wine, late evening hours, festivities, stimulation, excitement, etc., can make children tired, so families must do whatever they can to keep the young kiddos from falling asleep before the end of the ceremonies, including the Talmud's suggestion here of handing out roasted grains and nuts. From this, the Talmud goes on to say: "It was taught in a *baraita* that Rabbi Eliezer says: One grabs the *matzot* [plural for *matzah*] on the nights of Passover…on account of the children, so that… they will not sleep and they will inquire into the meaning of this unusual practice."[19] Another common translation states: "We snatch matzahs on the night of Passover in order that the children should not fall asleep."

What's being described here, based on the context of the original Hebrew *chotfin* ("grab," "snatch," or "steal"), was originally only meant to describe a swift consumption; in other words, the *matzah* should be eaten before the kids fall asleep. It was that simple. However, some scholars explain that Rabbi Eliezer's teaching was (quite harmlessly) interpreted to mean that another tradition be implemented—one that keeps young ones alert and excited to the end of the night and involved the act of "grabbing" or "snatching."

This explanation is the one offered almost everywhere you look. However, the problem with this idea is that it relies on the fact that the hunt for the *afikomen* tradition began at the circulation of Eliezer's rabbinical teaching. As we will discuss in the coming pages, there is evidence that, though the tradition's execution was slightly different, the *afikomen's* role in the Passover is far older than that. And of course, that would cancel out any theories suggesting that the hunt started as a result of Rabbi Eliezer wanting children to remain awake. Another fairly major issue that surfaces a lot with the Eliezer-origin trail is how many times Jews associate the word *chotfin* with "steal" instead of just "grab" or "snatch," and this has been offered as an explanation for why some modern Jewish families disregard the *afikomen*, because they are under the impression they would be teaching their children that there are justifiable occasions to commit theft (or mimic the act). If that is a problem today, it would have been back in his day as well, suggesting that a "stealing game" may not have launched into a widely accepted rite at any point in the history of a people whose very Ten Commandments forbid it.

Another *afikomen* tradition origin theory involves some scholarly mud-flinging between a few passionate men in the 1920s: Robert Eisler, Hans Lietzmann, and Arthur Marmorstein. The lengthier story is quite dramatic and the telling of it honestly only serves to make them all look less intelligent than they all truly were (and all three of them were incredibly well known and respected theologians/scholars). Suffice it to say that Eisler had connected a few dots linking the *afikomen*-search tradition to ancient Jews prior to the time of Christ and possibly, as far as anyone knows, could have begun in Canaan. After Eisler published his findings and his interpretations in a German scholarly journal,[20] Lietzmann and Marmorstein wrote their own opposing arguments, which Eisler refuted in another article, and Lietzmann and Marmorstein responded again, and so on. Eventually, lawyers were pulled into the triangle, and Lietzmann, who held certain authority over what the German journal would publish, cut Eisler's writings from the magazine completely, allowing himself and Marmorstein to have the official last word. Eisler, whose voice had effectively been silenced, composed a list of final responses and arguments for his ideas, but they went unpublished. By presenting evidence his scholarly colleagues didn't agree with, his name and some of his work fell into obscurity.

Forty years later, in 1966, Eisler's work would be revisited and greatly compounded upon by renowned legal analyst and Oxford professor of Jewish law, David Daube. The conclusions of Daube's research alongside those of his predecessor were so convincing and reputable that the London Diocesan Council for Christian-Jewish Understanding endorsed

Daube giving a lecture called "He That Cometh" at St. Paul's Cathedral.

Daube is correct in pointing out that, at many points in Jewish history (notably that delicate era just before the destruction of the second temple in Jerusalem), the Passover Seder looked to the past (Egypt) as well as the future (the coming Messiah and ultimate redemption). Indeed, this is easily found in variously recorded Seder recitations and in the directives of respected rabbis from the beginning. Even contemporary authorities have no problem linking the *afikomen* to a forward glance toward a Messiah that has not yet come. In an online article called "Why Do We Hide the *Afikoman*," Jewish scholar Yehuda Shurpin explains that the *afikomen's* (or, *afikoman's*, as spelled in the article) symbolism is linked to the deliverance, and therefore redemption, from Egypt. He goes on to say: "That redemption, however, was not a complete one, as we are still awaiting…the coming of Moshiach [Messiah]…. Hiding the larger half of the matzah reminds us that the best, the real redemption, is yet to come, still hidden in the future."[21]

It is clear that in some of the oldest Seder traditions, there would have been elements of the meal mentioning, and symbolically reflecting upon, the coming Messiah. *What* that element was would be, without the *afikomen*, hard to identify. On the other hand, because of the association between Jews and "poor afflicted bread" from their days in Egypt (in other words, unleavened; cf. Deuteronomy 16:3), the Jews considered poor bread to be a symbol for them as a people. The breaking, hiding, and rediscovery of the "poor bread" *afikomen*, these scholars explain, were therefore symbolic of Israel as incomplete until that future day when the Messiah is revealed and joined back to her.

The fact that we don't have reliable literature that specifically identifies the first *afikomen* ritual, for some, casts doubt on whether the rite existed before the Rabbi Eliezer-origin theory. For others, like Eisler and Daube, the idea that almost all Jewish households would eventually implement the same ritual with the same symbolism because of an obscure passage by a rabbi who ambiguously instructed them to "steal," "grab," or "snatch" something to keep kids awake is its own high-speed, one-way street toward doubt. It's far more logical to admit the likelihood that the ritual immensely predates the Eliezer line from the Talmud. That doesn't have to mean that every Jewish household practiced it early on, as it could have been a less conventional observation for a time until it was written into the *Haggadah* later on.

With origin theories behind us, the question of Christ's involvement comes to the forefront.

To someone who is willing to have an impartial, open mind, the three pieces of *matzah* given to the father of the household, the search and recovery of the hidden *afikomen*, the prize—*all of it*, moment by moment, points to the Messiah and His work on the cross. It's considerably harder to look at all the layers of the ritual and cut Christ out of the picture than it is to admit it's all about Him. For many Jewish families today, keeping the kids awake for the prize competition is all the *afikomen* needs to represent. For some Jewish apologists, the similarities between the *afikomen* and Jesus is pure coincidence, and they go on to show conflicts in the comparison between Him and the feast custom. However, *if* these men are wrong—and these authors posit that they are, for many reasons too astonishing to ignore—then it could mean…

Well, it could be an unleavened bread game-changer.

It *could* even change everything we modern Westerners thought we knew about Communion…

Let's move on to the moment when the *afikomen* is first brought into the feast observances and take a look at how, from the very moment it enters the room, it takes on a Jesus quality.

The Three Matzahs

As stated earlier, three pieces of *matzah* are brought to the feast table and handed to the father of the household. They are wrapped in perfect, snow-white linen. Some claim that these are for the patriarchs (Abraham, Isaac, Jacob), but the most popular explanation is that they were named after the three tribes of Israel as it was divided after the Babylonian exile: Kohen, Levi, and Yisrael. The comparison between these tribes to God the Father,

God the Son, and God the Holy Spirit is remarkable. We will explain briefly how that is, so readers can understand how intense the relationship is between Christ and the *afikomen* custom.

Moses' brother Aaron was chosen to be the high priest, so his descendants were the Kohenim (priests), and it was from this bloodline the Kohen tribe continued to serve at the highest level in the temple. The *Kohen Gadol* ("high priest") was the most holy and pious man in all of Israel subject to the strictest laws of purity. He wore the eight temple garments, one of which was the *hoshen* (priestly breastplate). On the outside of the *hoshen* was twelve stones, each inscribed with the name of one of the original tribes of Israel. On the inside, behind the stones, was the *Urim VeTumim*, meaning "light and truth," a piece of parchment paper with the ineffable Holy Name of God (the Tetragrammaton—"YHWH") written upon it.

If one were to consider the three *matzahs* with the Trinity in mind, the *Kohen* has a "Father" feel to it—like One who is the spiritual leader over all His people whose names are written on His heart, who embodies and upholds the essence of all that the holy temple stands for like the ultimate *Kohen Gadol*, who literally bears the ineffable Holy Name Yahweh upon His chest. Tuck that in the back of your mind for a minute as we move on to the second *matzah*, the Levi.

When Moses wasn't as quick as the Israelites wanted him to be in coming down from Mt. Sinai, the golden calf debacle occurred, and the Levites refused to be any part of it. For this, they were "set apart to the Lord" and "blessed" in an exclusive position of intimacy with the Father (Exodus 32:26–29). The Levites were priests of the temple, journeyed as teachers (rabbis) of the Torah (their unique travel harmonizes with the fact that they were never given land to cultivate like the other tribes), and they were known for being the greatest servants to the rest of their people. Literature compiled by scholars, historians, and Jewish sages acknowledge the Levites to have been supremely devoted to God, collectively representing "a universal ideal for people of pure faith, ready to abandon the world and cultivate a life of inner tranquility and supreme wisdom."[22]

Aaron was a Levite, and therefore all Kohenim are Levites, but not all Levites are Kohenim: "Leviim are believed to be the direct patrilineal descendants of Levi, while Kohanim are Leviim who descend directly, through their fathers, from Aaron."[23] This is why, though the two are "one" in a way, Levites are considered a separate category of tribe than the Kohenim. Compare: Jesus is God, just as the Father is God, but the Father is not Jesus and Jesus is not the Father. Jesus is a "descendant" of the Father, though the two are "one."

The comparison of Jesus, the Son of God and second-listed member of the Trinity, to the Levi *matzah* is fairly obvious: Just like the Levites and the golden calf, when tempted, Jesus refused to worship anyone or anything besides the Father (Matthew 4:10). He was more devoted to and intimate with the Father than any entity in the history of the eternal cosmos (John 17), as He and the Father are "one" (John 10:30). Scripture repeatedly outlines Him as a priest and High Priest (references are rife throughout the entire book of Hebrews). Nobody would question whether He was the absolute Rabbi (or Rabboni), as He was commonly called as He traveled about and journeyed to minister and teach; John 3:2, one of many examples, candidly refers to Jesus as "a teacher come from God." Like the Levites, He both taught and demonstrated servanthood to those around Him as one of the highest priorities (John 13:4–17, Mark 10:45). And of course, He stands as *the* "universal ideal for people of pure faith."

This leaves the third *matzah*, the Yisrael. Anyone of Israel who was not a Levi or Kohen, and who therefore did not work in the temple, was considered Yisrael—the "congregation" as it is sometimes called. In other words, Yisrael represented all the tribes together, undivided, without favoritism: 100 percent equal in importance to and "one with" Kohenim and Leviim, but highly versatile and flexible in service to and for God.

Similarly, the Body of Christ operates with many "parts": different people from different "tribes" all over the world working together for the universal Church, impartial to backgrounds, racial divides, social statuses, and so on. Versatility and flexibility in service to God is vital. How is this accomplished? Through the third member of the Trinity, the Holy Spirit, the giver of gifts (1 Corinthians 12:8–10, Romans 12:6–8). He inspires personal service to God in many ways and to any believer. With the Holy Spirit, the "division of tribes" (to speak in equivalent terms) is irrelevant, as we are all one congregation called the Body of Christ. By itself, this would be enough to satisfy a reasonable comparison of the Holy Spirit as the One whom the Yisrael *matzah* represents, but there is more to it than merely this. The timing surrounding the Resurrection, Ascension, and Day of Pentecost also plays an unusual role in the *afikomen* custom. The Holy Spirit's role as the Yisrael *matzah* continues on through that.

The next few details are really unbelievable.

The "Promise of the Father" Prize

So, once the Kohen, Levi, and Yisrael *matzah* pieces are brought to the table in white linen, the father of the household takes hold of only the *middle* (Jesus/Levi) piece, blesses it, and then breaks it in half. The smaller half is placed back in the middle of the two other *matzah* pieces, while the larger half, now called the *afikomen*, is placed in a separate white linen wrapping and hidden somewhere dark in the house.

Remember: Jesus' body was broken, placed in its own white burial linen (Mark 15:46, John 20:5), and hidden away in a dark tomb.

After the meal, the children go in search of the *afikomen*. Once it is found, it is customary that the child only gives the *matzah* piece back to his or her father in exchange for a prize. The refusal to surrender the *afikomen* until a prize has been agreed upon is called a "ransom"; the prize is called—and we quote—"The Promise of the Father."

Remember: Through the sacrifice of the sinless, "unleavened" Savior's broken body (and the "precious blood"; 1 Peter 1:18–19), He paid a "ransom for many" (Matthew 20:28, Mark 10:45). Actually, He paid a "ransom for *all*" (1 Timothy 2:6). *Actually*, He paid a ransom for people from "every tribe" (Revelation 5:9). The entire Bible points toward, and shows fulfillment of, Jesus Christ as the Promised Messiah, sent from the Father. Jesus literally *is* "The Promise of the Father" whose *afikomen* body "ransomed" us all.

Now, the father of the household takes the *afikomen* and breaks it into as many pieces as there are people gathered, and each partakes of the piece in remembrance of the paschal lamb whose blood was shed to cover their sins.

Remember: Jesus instructed us to break bread together and partake in remembrance of Him, the Lamb whose blood was shed to remove our sins.

Some orthodox Jewish scholars have tried throughout the years to explain how all this correlation is mere coincidence. They attempt, from every angle, to point out ways that the *afikomen* does *not* resemble the Messiah, but despite their greatest efforts, people continue to, *understandably*, think the similarities are too great to ignore. One of the most frequent arguments is that the paschal lamb and unleavened bread are literally to be eaten, and the Messiah was/is obviously not. But, the fact that Jesus personally symbolized Himself as the unleavened bread and wine, using the very words "eat" and "drink" in reference to His body, cancels that case and even argues for *greater* attention toward the *afikomen* as a representative of the Messiah. Nevertheless, what comes next takes it to yet another level…

Exactly forty days from the child's *afikomen* ransom-exchange, the father of the child gives the gift agreed upon. An additional ten days later (fifty days total from Passover), the Feast of Pentecost (or "Weeks"; Hebrew *Shavuot*) is observed. The Feast of Pentecost/Weeks is, in part, a celebration of the day the Israelites were given the all-guiding Torah from the Father, "when God made Israel one people in the Law."[24] (More on this later.)

Remember: Exactly forty days from the Resurrection, Jesus gives the apostles another gift, telling them, *word-for-word*, to "wait for the promise of the Father" (Acts 1:4). An additional ten days later (fifty days total from the Resurrection), the Day of Pentecost (Greek word for "fiftieth") occurred. The Day of Pentecost was the day the early Church was given the all-guiding Holy Spirit from the Father, when God made the Church one people in equal efficiency toward the Gospel's Great Commission (Acts 2). (And thus, the third *Matzah*, Yisrael, the Holy Spirit, comes round about through the delivery of the promise of the Father!)

Once the Communion-style partaking of the final *matzah* is over, nobody eats or drinks anything else; the Passover meal is finished. As Jesus hung His head on the cross, He acknowledged specifically that the redemptive work of His sinless, broken, "unleavened," *afikomen* body was "finished" (John 19:30). Yet "finished" here doesn't just mean something is over; it is from the Greek *tetelestai*, which translates "paid in full."

The Jews awaited and looked for their Messiah, just like their children today await and search for the *afikomen*. Jesus was, is, and always will be the Promised Messiah, whose body was broken for us and hidden away, but whose Resurrection revealed Him once again. Jesus is therefore the sovereign *Afikomen*: broken, hidden, and revealed.

It's absolutely beautiful.

Through Jesus, the blood redemption transaction is paid for. The *afikomen*, for those who believe in Christ, can no longer mean "that which comes later," for the Messiah has already come, paid the price for our sin, risen from the dead, and ascended to heaven, where He sits at the right hand of the Father. Jesus Christ is our "rediscovered *Afikomen*." Now you can see why we felt we had no choice but to address the meaning of this rare word *after* we showed the symbolism between it and Jesus.

Nevertheless, that doesn't mean the etymology of this term was as easy as seeing Jesus assign it new meaning. As is usually the case with etymological pursuits, a good dig for origins will reveal unexpected gems.

Let's now turn to, shall we say, "the rest of the story."

Etymological Nightmares

The word *afikomen* (alternatively *afikoman*, as spelled in the Shurpin article) has a most difficult origin to trace. We spent days rummaging around the gnarling thorns of misinformation and folk etymology on this particular word before we were able to piece it all together. But without forcing readers to go on that tedious journey as well, we'll simplify: Nobody knows for sure where it came from.

Jewish tradition expert Dr. Ronald L Eisenberg acknowledges as much in his book, *The JPS* [Jewish Publication Society of America] *Guide to Jewish Traditions*, when he says that the "precise meaning is unclear,"[25] and it was refreshing to read that rare and transparent report. We (especially Donna Howell) found it to be problematic that many writers on the subject made unsubstantiated claims that *afikomen* meant any number of the following: "dessert," "food eaten for pleasure," "revelry," "evening entertainment," "festival song," "after-meal tradition," and so on, most concepts contextually relating to a food or activity that consummates a ceremony. In sources written by authors wanting to lift up the Name of Christ, it appeared over and over that the meaning was something like "One Who Came" or "I Have Come," even flatly "Messiah," and it was stated as a fact, glorified like a miracle. But as much as we might be tempted to pick our favorite definition and take off with it in a study like this, going from "dessert" to "Messiah" without proof or background is journalistically irresponsible (and makes the same mistake as these other sources).

There's also the issue that many don't agree on whether the word was Greek first, and then Hebrew, or Hebrew first, and then Greek…and others even claim it was originally Aramaic. (Scholars generally attribute it to a Greek-first origin.) Because the word is so rare in antiquity—leaving hardly a trace of itself prior to the Mishnah—*honest* scholars will admit that we cannot be sure what culture or people uttered the sound first and what it meant to them. What we *can* do is look at the closest traceable word derivatives, compare those to contextual uses in literature as far back as we can, and watch as the picture clears a bit.

It appears most likely that *afikomen* is an early transliteration of the Greek *epikomen or epikomion* (later transliterated into *afikomenos*), which generically means "that which comes after." This is why, when translated from an ancient sentence, it can mean things like "dessert" or "evening entertainment," etc., because these festive, special-occasion activities come after something else, like a meal or a long day of work. Obviously, "that which comes after" could also easily relate to a Messianic translation of "the One who comes later" or something equivalent.

Breaking this word down further, we arrive at: the Greek *epi*, meaning "after," "over," or "later"; *komos*, which is a pre-Greek verb (Sanskrit or Proto-Indo-European, some believe), likely meaning "announce," "proclaim," or "declare"; and finally, *ios*, which is the Greek suffix simply meaning "pertaining to." It's not a stretch to see how *afikomen* could be interpreted to mean a special "after-dinner dessert" indulgence, so long as it could also "pertain to" an "announcement" or "proclamation" (such as the news that the hidden *afikomen* had been found). And considering that the *afikomen* is the last thing eaten at the Passover meal, the stretch between "dessert" and "unleavened bread" may be allowable in the interest of "after-the-meal" symbolism.

For the Jews, "dessert" eventually became the only definition of *afikomen*. This would explain why their own "waiting for the Messiah" tradition became harder to trace back to a point of origin predating that of Rabbi Eliezer's "keep the kids awake" Talmud instruction. Among common households, what could have been an ancient ceremony looking forward to the Messiah could have been lost and replaced with just another thing to eat. Several scholarly sources have considered this as well. Hermann Strack and Paul Billerbeck's heavily sought-after German work, *Kommentar zum Neuen Testament aus Talmud und Midrasch* ("Commentary on the New Testament from the Talmud and Midrash"), agrees with this conclusion, stating that the eventual "dessert" definition was "erroneous," yet unwavering: "The meaning of the word *afikoman* was forgotten early on. Already the Tosephta [earlier Jewish Law compilation than the Mishnah or Talmud] understands the word as 'the dessert.' This erroneous explanation then held its sway throughout the entire period of Jewish antiquity."[26]

We can prove that the rare word stretches back to before the time of Christ, and its meaning gets fuzzier the farther back we travel. We likewise know that it was misinterpreted for a long time to mean an after-dinner treat, when the first word meant something much closer to "a proclamation that occurs sometime in the future [or "after"; "later"; etc.]." But for our purposes of showing Christ's fulfillment of the whole unleavened bread picture, we need to look at two things: 1) whether "the search for the *afikomen*" was a Passover observance established well before the time of Christ; and, therefore, 2) whether at, or at least around, the time of Christ, there had been a cultural shift in its interpretation: an explanation behind why, today, Jewish sources say "dessert" and Christian sources say "One Who Came"—both claiming it as fact and neither alluding to the other.

Thanks to a written work by David Daube, we have a lead. The Greek *afikomenos* appears in the *second-century* writing *Peri Pascha* by Bishop Melito of Sardis! And, as this ancient text attests, by the second century, the context of the term most certainly did refer to Jesus Christ as "The Coming One," "He that has come," or more directly, "the messiah who has come."[27] Daube's collective work on this subject clarifies that this reference by Bishop Melito refers to "an awaited redeemer who, symbolically united with his people, makes them whole as they contemplate their past, and future, redemption."[28]

This fact raises the common-sense question: If the Jews had *not* been practicing a Messianic element at the Passover feast related to *afikomen* this whole time—in other words, if, at the time of Christ, the term *only meant dessert* to the Jews and there was no prior "Messiah" meaning behind the name of their feast custom—then why would Christians like Bishop Melito use that word to describe their Messiah? Why would they name their Savior after the Jewish word for "dessert"?

More blatant than that, however: If the Jews merely set out to instruct parents how to keep little ones awake, why would their ritual look *so much like* Jesus, both in His redemptive acts *as well as* the Communion He instructed His disciples to do often in remembrance of Him?

None of this makes sense...*unless* the Jews held the custom first, and then the Christians continued it while simultaneously establishing Christ as the fulfillment of their antiquated ritual. The Jews' reaction to that, however, may not have been too agreeable. The Talmud writing by Rabbi Eliezer that came hundreds of years *after* the Sardis document *might* have actually been attempting to dumb it down or revive the casual treatment of this word.

Scholars behind the Sheffield Academics' "Biblical Seminar" series involving one title, *New Testament Backgrounds*, also subscribe to a similar theory, stating that:

> It seems that a ritual involving the *afikoman* was preserved but over time its meaning was, perhaps even deliberately, distorted....
>
> How could such an important idea have been lost? It seems likely that as Christianity emerged from Judaism, Jewish ideas which had been taken up and developed by the followers of Jesus were played down or even suppressed by Jewish authorities.[29]

If these scholars are correct, then: The Jews *suppressed a custom from their own feast* because Messianic Jews of their day—aka the first "Christians"—believed it to have been fulfilled in Jesus Christ. The true picture of an early, now all-but-lost Messianic *afikomen* ceremony was buried under religious bureaucracy and repainted as a "keep kids awake dessert." All the components that held on past this potential alteration—the breaking, hiding, hunting, revealing, dividing, and eating of the unleavened bread—would become confusing, inconsequential to Jewish descendants who would later understand the symbolism of every *other* step in the Passover. This one element, which acts as the beginning and the end of the feast (a position of great importance, clearly), is reduced to a teaching by a beloved rabbi who could think of no other tool for parents to keep kids awake than to come up with a new ritual that "coincidentally" parallels Christ's death.

Thus, *afikomen* went from "Messiah" to "dessert." (See why we had to leave etymology until the end on this one?)

Please don't miss what just happened...and what else it implies. It's not *just* that a long-standing Messianic custom would have been fulfilled in Christ. That satisfies why a book like this would show Jesus' fulfillment of a feast, certainly, but if all of this evidence is properly understood by the theologians who have made it their lives' work, then there's something else here that almost *everyone* misses...

The *afikomen* ritual was the very first Communion.

Afikomen Communion Ceremony Established by Christ, Himself

The Jews tried to suppress it as best they could, and certainly their efforts were marked with some success as Christians have largely no idea what Christ was pointing to when He took and broke the Passover *afikomen* and likened it to His body. But, one might say that none of the Jewish rulers of that age understood it; if they had, they may not have attempted to suppress the feast of the Lord of Glory.

Follow this trail:

1. *If afikomenos* was being used, by *Christians*, to refer to the Messiah shortly after the Ascension in the area of the world Jesus walked, this tells us that Jesus *became* the *Afikomen* to those Jews who believed in Him, since Christianity stemmed from Judaism. It means that the now-Messianic Jews had to rebrand the word (and the custom) that was familiar to them already. It always meant "Messiah," but this shift was from future tense ("that which comes after") to past tense ("He that has come").
2. And *if* the Jews had a longstanding Messianic custom within their feasts, as we have shown herein to be the most likely scenario, then *Jesus would have known about it as well.*
3. And *if* Jesus knew about it, then, when He, *a Jew of the orthodox kind*, conducted His own Passover with His disciples, He would have participated in this important, Messianic, bread-breaking custom as well.

But wait. You might be thinking the similarities aren't exact. Jesus never hid anything, or released children to go hunting, or…

We're aware. It's another layer that blows the mind, actually. Jesus, Himself *the* Promised Messiah, was telling them He was no longer hidden. No one needed to ever again go on a search for this Man, this *Afikomen*.

He had come.

At this Passover meal, when Jesus took and ceremoniously broke the *afikomen*, the *matzah* representing Himself, He went straight to the end, passing by the search. Why would He do anything but that?

He was revealed.

He then explained in no uncertain terms that the *afikomen* He broke *was* His body, that which would be broken and traded as ransom, as the Messianic fulfillment of the "Promise of the Father." He instructed His followers to partake of it in remembrance of Him, the Paschal Lamb, just as the Jews instruct their youth to partake of it in remembrance of the paschal lamb.

And then, just like the Jewish child who would pass the *afikomen* to the "father of the household" in exchange for a prize, Jesus became that Child, willingly submitting His *Afikomen*, His body, to be the ransom to the Father: a symbol of the completion of a promise. The Father acknowledged the handing over of the Great *Afikomen* and gave redemption to all.

A few days after Christ's Resurrection, two followers entertained His company unaware. These men were not in attendance at the Last Supper. They also didn't recognize Jesus by His robe, His scars, or anything supernatural as they walked alongside Him on the road to Emmaus. Ironically, they continued lamenting the loss of their Savior—who joined them on the walk. And then, the Word says, they recognized Him only by how He broke bread.

Observe:

And it came to pass, that, while [the two men] communed together and reasoned, Jesus himself drew near, and went with them. But their eyes were holden that they should not know him. And he said unto them, "What manner of communications are these that ye have one to another, as ye walk, and are sad?"

And the one of them, whose name was Cleopas, answering said unto him, "Art thou only a stranger in Jerusalem, and hast not known the things which are come to pass there in these days?"

And he said unto them, "What things?"

And they said unto him, "Concerning Jesus of Nazareth, which was a prophet mighty in deed and word before God and all the people: And how the chief priests and our rulers delivered him to be condemned to death, and have crucified him....."

And beginning at Moses [Genesis] and all the prophets, he [Jesus] expounded unto them in all the scriptures the things concerning himself....

And it came to pass, as he sat at meat with them, *he took bread, and blessed it, and brake, and gave to them. And their eyes were opened, and they knew him*; and he vanished out of their sight.

And they said one to another, Did not our heart burn within us, while he talked with us by the way, and while he opened to us the scriptures?

And they rose up the same hour, and returned to Jerusalem, and found the eleven gathered together, and them that were with them, Saying, "The Lord is risen indeed, and hath appeared to Simon."

And they told what things were done in the way, and how *he was known of them in breaking of bread*. (Luke 24:13–35; emphasis added)

Jesus walked and talked with these two men personally, long enough to tell them "all" of what the Scriptures said regarding Himself, and in all that time, they didn't know they were in the presence of their Risen Messiah. They became comfortable enough to invite this Man into their house for a meal during Passover week (when unleavened bread would still be the rule), yet they did not know His true identity. That revelation *only* came as a result of His breaking bread.

But how could a simple act of breaking bread divulge identity so immediately? It's not that hard to believe that His disciples might have spread the word that Jesus had established Himself as the *Afikomen* at their Passover meal. It's actually more likely than not that those in the intimate circle of followers would have heard all about how much emphasis the Messiah placed on the breaking of the *afikomen* and the subsequent announcement that it was His body. Later on, in the home of those He shared a roadside with, Jesus blessed the unleavened bread, and then didn't say another word as He broke it and handed it straight to them. He never hid it or proceeded to talk about a search for the Messiah. He bypassed the search and hunt. That act alone made the statement: The *Afikomen* is no longer hidden. Therefore, He made Himself known "by the breaking of bread."

Then, forty days after Christ's death, on the day the children of Jewish homes redeem their prize for discovering the hidden *matzah*, Jesus ascended to be with His Father, whom He was one with, which was an immense gift for Christ, indeed. The promise of the Father was fulfilled for all.

It all fits.

The puzzle is put together, all pieces in their rightful place, and the picture is clear. At this point in our reflection, it's harder *not* to believe that the search for the *afikomen* was the first Communion. When we pass those pretty, artificial-gold communion plates around the sanctuary every few Sundays with those already-broken crackers in a stack, many of us don't know how deep and how beautiful the final image of our Savior really is. The days leading up to His death feel, to us today, so lonely, tragic, and sad. And there are moments that capture that for certain, such as His prayers in the garden just before His arrest. But there are other moments we miss, like the one when He broke bread, and in so doing broke the old custom with a triumphal roar in the unseen realm. We authors can only imagine that the angels sang a praise so loud as to deafen human ears the second that unleavened cracker's surface first sounded its prophetic, splintering snap.

It was a small noise. But, like many scholars who have fine-tooth-combed this subject, these authors believe that the tiny cracking vibrations, by the power of Jesus as the Supreme *Afikomen*, signaled a sacrament that, no matter who tries to suppress what, will stand until He comes again. That small ripple echoed irreversibly that *Afikomen now* means "the One who came...and who will come again":

For as often as ye eat this bread, and drink this cup, ye do shew the Lord's death till he come. (1 Corinthians 11:26)

Final Thoughts: Our Unleavened Attorney
Let's take a look at a few mentioned yeast/sin parallels:

- A) Yeast is part of the nature of bread dough, since it has been on the grain from the beginning. B) Sin is part of the nature of man, since it has been within man since the Fall of mankind in Genesis.
- A) Leavening bread dough makes it "puff up." B) Sin is "puffed up" (Proverbs 28:25; Habakkuk 2:4; Romans 11:21; 1 Corinthians 4:6, 18–19, 5:2, 13:4; 1 Timothy 6:4; 2 Timothy 3:4).
- A) Bread that has become too puffed up (over-proofed) will fall (collapse). B) An overly puffed-up believer will fall to the enemy (1 Timothy 3:6).
- A) Yeast might be hidden within the dough, but the effect it has inside the bread can never be hidden from the baker. B) Sin might be hidden within mankind (John 3:20), but its effect inside of people can never be hidden from God (Romans 1:18, Jeremiah 16:17, Isaiah 29:15).
- A) Leaven presents the bread to be more than what it is, when truthfully, there's nothing but hot air under the surface. B) Some, like the Pharisees and Sadducees, present themselves to be more spiritual or holy than they are, when truthfully, the Lord knows there's nothing but hot air under the surface ("Watch out and beware of the *leaven* of the Pharisees and the Sadducees" [Matthew 16:6, emphasis added]).

More than anything else in that bullet list is the obvious parallel that yeast, whether natural or added, once activated, spreads uncontrollably throughout the dough. Looking to the New Testament and the New Covenant through Christ, Paul also used the ingredient as a metaphor to explain that sin can expand and spread, leading to more sin in one's life, or even causing us to influence others to participate in sin, just like one lump of leaven or yeast can affect a whole lump of dough (1 Corinthians 5:6–8).

If you think about how far that could go, the reach is actually limitless. Just as one example: Here at SkyWatch Television, Defender Publishing, and Whispering Ponies Ranch, one of our highest priorities is to underwrite the rescue of and directly minister to sex-trafficked children, youth, and women. We have learned since the beginning of this venture that traffickers are supported by countless avenues that most people don't consider, like Internet pornography (and many others). Websites that produce content with these victims are accessed all the time by browsers belonging to folks who had no idea who or what they were supporting when they clicked. Follow just this *one* cycle with us for a moment. In the case of a criminal site like those developed in the human-trafficking rings:

1. Certainly, accessing a pornographic website is a sin in the first place, whether or not the viewer knows what kind of abuse may be occurring on the other end of the site.

2. The criminal behind the website continues in this profitable arena, supported by those who browse where they shouldn't. As his pockets increase in jingle, more children, women, and teens are kidnapped to expand his pornography business. Without a doubt, kidnapping and sex slavery are sin.

3. Drugs play an enormous role in sex trafficking. It is administered to the victims for pain after abuse, to keep them numb and emotionless during the abuse, and for those who are addicted, it keeps them reliant upon the drug and therefore willing to do whatever it takes to get their "next fix." (Drugs are also the reason many of these sites look like they involve willing participants; they have been instructed to act like the event is consensual, and the appearance of willingness—or even instigation—is an easier feat when a person is numb.) Obviously, making addicts out of these victims is a terrible sin.

4. The criminal abusers in the ring are frequently (some would say "always") addicted to drugs as well, which makes the sin of illegal drug use a bigger part of this chain.

5. Drug cartels and all the unimaginable crimes they are linked to (including murder, rape, violence, money laundering, etc.) are now also supported, which makes the spread of sin even wider.

6. Repeated defilement and illegal drug administration to and upon children, teens, and women—even upon an unlikely rescue and release—contributes to psychological damage that makes these victims far more likely to struggle in their faith and commit further sin against God in their hurt and pain. In some tragic cases, the victims may feel that further abuse of their body is all they know how to do to make a living. In the *worst* of cases, a victim may believe he or she is outside of God's grace, or even outside of the realm of His concern. Now that the effects of psychologically numbing drugs has been experienced, there is a high possibility that a victim would turn back to that "friend" as comfort later in life. Relationships these victims make down the line will be further hurt by these complications, possibly leading to more abuse even outside the trafficking ring. All of these "future" factors feed a cycle of sin all its own that is heartbreaking to God!

7. And finally, it all circles back to that first person browsing the Internet: He or she has put images in his or her mind that are hard to forget. Haunted by such deviant imagery, this person slips back into the computer chair when nobody is looking and returns to the site that funds all the above-listed twisted evils all over again. The power of porn sticks with the person, taunting, drawing in, weakening his or her resolve to refrain until addiction to that world takes over. What was a titillating enough picture or video yesterday is not enough today, and something even more deviant or disturbing is clicked on in order to satisfy the curiosity of the mischievous mind, making the trap worse. Eventually, the addiction can lead to a destroyed marriage, a broken home, and

even a person's abandonment of faith. The sin seemingly never ends...

Of course, we don't intend to suggest that every pornographic site is related to human trafficking. This example is close to our heart after hearing our ministerial associates (like "Eight Days Ministries" founder Jaco Booyens) explain how oblivious most people in our society are about just how much of the porn industry traffickers have taken over. This is even more clearly illustrated in the astonishing details uncovered in the groundbreaking new documentary, *Silent Cry: The Darker Side of Trafficking*. But we also know that people who click around the World Wide Web in private, thinking they are only affecting themselves, quite often unknowingly support these criminal rings. (But even if they *don't* support this kind of heartbreaking victimization, they contribute help to those who are willingly in the pornography industry, who make their money by selling bodies, which is, biblically speaking, prostitution of the worst and obscenest kind. We wonder how many people who have visited porn websites liken themselves to one who hires a prostitute...)

Using only one illustration, we can more appropriately appreciate how sin (leaven), once activated and allowed to take hold (like yeast), can spread to the entire person's heart and life (to the whole lump of dough), and its effects can't be stopped or removed by the sinner's own efforts. Paul understood the use of leaven as a representation of sin very well.

The fulfillment of the Passover was a once-and-done act by Christ, remembered through a sacrament (Communion), which is a physical acknowledgment of a spiritual work. Communion, *especially* when taken with unleavened bread (though we wouldn't judge those who take it with regular bread, as Christ replaced the *matzah*), also fulfills the Feast of the Unleavened Bread in acknowledgment of Jesus' redemptive work. However, the Feast of Unleavened Bread with its corresponding *Bedikas Chametz* ("Search for Leaven") ceremony represents a search for *all* sin in our lives, including that which is hidden in tiny nooks and crannies, followed by the quick removal of it, the cleansing from it, and the casting of it away. The

Feast of Unleavened Bread is a time to acknowledge a *continual, conscious* abstinence from sin. The fulfillment of the feast through Christ requires more than just a casual "thanks" for what He's done. We celebrate Christ's work/fulfillment with a daily choice—a faith-through-works relationship. What He did for us should never be smeared by our taking it for granted, and we can never miss what that means in the light of eternity.

Consider it like this: Passover looked forward to the Crucifixion, which was the event in which we were forgiven of all our sins and became new through acceptance; The Feast of the Unleavened Bread, as fulfilled through Christ, marks what *our responsibilities* are in continuing to accept His sacrifice and *separating ourselves from sin* as the Jews separated themselves from leaven.

God loves us, but He cannot love sin, so our sin, prior to Christ, separated us from Him. Jesus came so we might reach the Father, and that He accomplished in spades without a doubt, but not so that we might continue to sin to spite His grace!

Paul refuted this detestable concept: "What shall we say then? Shall we continue in sin, that grace may abound? God forbid. How shall we, that are dead to sin, live any longer therein?" (Romans 6:1–2). The NLT phrases this passage: "Well then, should we keep on sinning so that God can show us more and more of his wonderful grace? Of course not! Since we have died to sin, how can we continue to live in it?"

What Christ did for us by becoming the Lamb was a legal move in the spiritual judicial system.

We must have at least a basic comprehension of the following information in order to appreciate the separation between God and sin, and how that requires *our* involvement: For us, for you, and for all the world, in the courtroom of the unseen realm, Jesus became an Attorney...one that a good friend to us SkyWatch folks, John McTernan, calls "the best Jewish Attorney that you could ever imagine."[30]

McTernan is a Christian evangelist, teacher, and author of multiple books, as well as one of the founders of International Cops for Christ. As a profoundly successful criminal investigator in practice since 1972, he has spent countless hours in court, observing our justice system at work firsthand; therefore he has a unique insight as to how the justice system of God works. When Tom invited him to come on SkyWatch Television to share about his book, *When Jesus Sets You Free, You Are Free Indeed*, a book that uses the United States court methods as a way of explaining the legal action Jesus took on our behalf, McTernan shared:

> In our society, we have a penal code. And doesn't that penal code direct what we can do and what we can't do? And there's all these penalties for the penal code. Well, *God* has a penal code.... If you break [the *human* law], you have, you know, felonies, there's misdemeanors and violations, some are "A to B to C" type felonies. But God has sort of like *one* felony, and that is separation from Him for eternity because He is holy.
>
> In our system, if you commit a crime, we do an investigation, and there is evidence presented in court. In God's government, you could say there's an investigation, there's evidence presented: The Bible says, "For by your words you shall be justified, for by your words you shall be condemned," [and,] "Every action, whatever we do in darkness, in the Day of Judgment it will be brought out to the light." In God's system, He has evidence procurement. In fact, if you look at Revelation chapter 20 and the Great White Throne Judgment, there are books that are open that contain the deeds that people did. All of it will be brought out.
>
> In our system, there's a court.... And *we* provide an attorney. "If you can't afford one, one will be provided for you." You know, we have the rights, the Miranda rights we read to people. Well God provides an Attorney: Jesus Christ the Righteous. If any man sin, we have an advocate with the Father: Jesus Christ the Righteous. The difference is, in God's system, the Attorney is willing to pay the price.... Let's say you owe fifty thousand dollars in penalties for some crime you've committed, and I say, "Well, you're honor, [the convicted person] can't afford it, but I'm going

to write the check on [his] behalf." That's what the Lord did, in a physical sense to pay the penalty for *our* sin.

See, the key to all of this is: God is holy. He's *holy*. And sin is a great offense to Him, so He has to separate Himself from sin, but He also has love. He has a tremendous amount of love. So that's why He sent Jesus Christ to bridge His holiness and His love, so that whoever will receive the Lord as that person's Savior, no matter what they have committed, He will forgive.[31]

The fulfillment of the Passover in Jesus Christ removes the separation between us and God. It obliterates the eternal sentence we earn in being found guilty of sin. We are, though we committed the crime, found "not guilty." This spiritually legal act carried out on our behalf is called "justification." Remember what Paul said about justification in Romans and Galatians, and note how he, too, uses a parallel of legal terminology between Christ's redemptive act and the Mosaic Law of his day:

> For all have sinned, and come short of the glory of God;
>
> Being justified freely by his grace through the redemption that is in Christ Jesus:
>
> Whom God hath set forth to be a propitiation through faith in his blood, to declare his righteousness for the remission of sins that are past, through the forbearance of God;
>
> To declare, "I say, at this time his righteousness: that he might be just, and the justifier of him which believeth in Jesus."
>
> Where is boasting then? It is excluded. By what law? of works? Nay: but by the law of faith.
>
> Therefore we conclude that a man is justified by faith without the deeds of the law. (Romans 3:23–28)

Knowing that a man is not justified by the works of the law, but by the faith of Jesus Christ, even we have believed in Jesus Christ, that we might be justified by the faith of Christ, and not by the works of the law: for by the works of the law shall no flesh be justi-fied. (Galatians 2:16)

Redemption isn't just about doing something wrong and being for-given (although that is certainly part of it). More than anything else, it's about God, in His holiness, being naturally and characteristically incapa-ble of joining Himself with us in our sin, even while He loved His creation and yearned for our company. Therefore, we needed a Passover Lamb Interceder-Attorney to present our criminal case to the Father, then to take our sin, remove it from us "as far as the east is from the west" (Psalm 103:12), and cast it "into the depths of the sea" (Micah 7:19).

The only cost *we* are responsible for is placing our faith in Jesus and accepting His redemptive work on the cross as our Savior. We are "justi-fied" before God by *faith alone*, as Martin Luther so correctly insisted upon in his *Sole fide* doctrine of the Reformation.

However, James, the half-brother of Jesus Christ, also had a thing or ten to say about faith. He made it clear that his outwardly observable life decisions revealed his faith without him having to pitch it to others, and that just believing in God was a feat even the demons could accomplish, yet they tremble (James 2:18–19). He drove home the point that *continu-ally* resisting temptation and removing any potential sin in a believer's life is necessary for *living out* the faith that a Christian claims to have.

The fulfillment of Passover celebrates the work of the Lamb in the past, which freed us from the bondage of sin and granted us access to a new life in Him. The fulfillment of the *Bedikas Chametz* ("Search for Leaven") ceremony during the Feast of the Unleavened Bread observes the *going forward* of believers into that new life with accountability to Christ, just as the Israelites left Egypt to enter a new life with accountability to God. Our spiritual *matzah* requires effort on our behalf. We must repeti-tiously carry our *chametz* tools through the rooms of our lives, discovering the leaven of our choices, acknowledging/confessing the ugly yeast we have scattered, and, through the sin-removing blood of the Lamb and body of the Supreme *Matzah*, be considered completely cleansed.

Responsibility now goes beyond what happened on our behalf in court and follows us home to where we live. In a contextually relevant, modern rewording of Paul's berating in Romans 6:1–2: "Well then, should we keep on ending up in the courtroom of God's justice system so that our Attorney can show us more and more of His wonderful defense skills? Of course not! Since we have died to that old life of crime, how can we continue to be criminals?"

Firstfruits

Scripture References

- Commanded to do in: Leviticus 23:9–14 and Deuteronomy 16:9–12

Observance Date

The date of this feast is a bit tricky to cover, as there is some interpretational discrepancy (again) between Jewish sects. Leviticus 23:11 specifies that this annual feast should be observed "on the morrow after the sabbath."

Which Sabbath is in mind, though? Was this original command referring to a literal, weekly Sabbath, or does this "Sabbath" refer to a day of no work? Is it 15 or 16 Nisan like the Pharisees believed, holding the day as a "holy convocation" (Leviticus 23:7) alongside the Feast of the Unleavened Bread because it, too, required that no work be done on that day? Or, should we be inclined to follow the practice of the Sadducees, who said that it's simply whatever day in Nisan that lands on the Sabbath during Passover week?

This discrepancy has led to an enormous debate among Jewish authorities, and we have no intention of specifying a date in Nisan that would be most appropriate *today* for observance (though, without the temple, Jews have largely stopped observing this feast).

However, using the year AD 33 for example, the Feast of Firstfruits would have landed on the Sunday (literal day after Sabbath) halfway through 16 Nisan for the Judeans, or, for the Galileans, when 16 Nisan slipped into sunrise on 17 Nisan. Amazingly, upon analyzing the biblical narrative, that happens to be the very calculated moment when Jesus rose from the dead.

Quick note: Some people ask how Jesus died on a Friday and rose on a Sunday, yet the Word says He rose "on the third day" (Matthew 16:21, 17:23; Mark 9:31; Luke 9:22, 18:33). But just as we can't consider Hebrew "days" in the same way as we would for the Gregorian calendar, we would be wrong to think that the Jews counted a "day" as "twenty-four hours" like we would. If Jesus was crucified on Friday, or "day one" of His death; remained in the tomb all day Saturday, or "day two" of His death; and then completed His work by returning to life on Sunday, or "day three," then He was raised to life "on the third day," just as Scripture says.

Practice

In thanks to God for His providence, and as a sign of their dependence upon Him, Jews reserved the first portion of barley grain to be cut from their fields and waved before the Lord as an offering in the temple of Jerusalem. The non-local Jews who were gathered in that city for Passover "were delegated to go after sunset into different barley fields with sickles and obtain samples from each field…[which was] lain together in a sheaf."[32] Additionally, the nearby Kidron Valley held a reserved property specifically for the Jews to harvest at this annual event.[33] These handfuls would be brought together to create only *one* barley bundle that represented all of the Jews together. God's acceptance of this single barley offering meant the rest of the harvest was also satisfactory to Him.

This sheaf offering of grain had to be an *omer*, a unit of dry measurement equal to one-tenth of an *ephah* (Exodus 16:36). Once brought to the temple, the sheaf was treated with oil and incense, then the priest would wave it in the four cardinal directions, consecrating the harvest. *Barnes' Notes on the Bible* commentary elaborates:

Until this was done, it was not lawful to partake of the harvest. The offering of this was regarded as rendering the mass holy, that is, it was lawful then to partake of it. The first-fruits were regarded as among the best portions of the harvest; and it was their duty to devote to God that which would be the best expression of their thanksgiving. This was the general practice in relation to all that the land produced.[34]

(Note: As the readers will soon see, this feast is bridged into the next one, so much of the symbolism of fulfillment connected to the Feast of Firstfruits will continue into the next feast, Pentecost.)

Jesus' Role and Fulfillment

The following are scriptural time stamps related to the Resurrection event: "In the end of the Sabbath, as it began to dawn toward the first day of the week" (Matthew 28:1); "The first day of the week cometh Mary Magdalene early, when it was yet dark" (John 20:1); "Now when Jesus was risen early the first day of the week" (Mark 16:9).

So far, Matthew says it was beginning to dawn, which is about 6 o'clock a.m. Gregorian time. John states that Mary came just before dawn, while it was still dark out, placing the time just prior to the moments when the sun lightened the day. Mark just says "early" on Sunday. The Greek word for "early," *proi*, allows for slightly more precision to the timing of Mary's arrival, as this was a technical word used to describe a Roman official's watch post from three to six in the morning.

Earlier, in the reflection on the Passover sacrifice, we noted that a spiritual transferal took place from the kosher knife of the Old Covenant Passover lamb to the forever-accessible grace of the New Testament Covenant Lamb. Here, we note another spiritual transferal. The Resurrection of the Messiah at the dawn of the Feast of Firstfruits profoundly changed the meaning from a merely agricultural holiday to a day when Jesus became the "firstfruits from the dead." On this fateful day in spring, just as the very first light of day bled over the hills, Jesus sprang to life in His tomb, the stone rolled away, and He emerged both victorious over death and in fulfillment of the Feast of Firstfruits.

The apostle Paul said this was the case, literally, stating in 1 Corinthians 15:20–23:

> But now is Christ risen from the dead, and become the firstfruits of them that slept.
>
> For since by man came death, by man came also the resurrection of the dead.
>
> For as in Adam all die, even so in Christ shall all be made alive. But every man in his own order:
>
> Christ the firstfruits; afterward they that are Christ's at his coming.

The high priest was in the temple, raising the sheaf in a wave-offering to God so that He might consecrate and accept all the new-life harvest of the fields. This sheaf was a single bundle representing all Jews, together, as one. Over in the tomb, Jesus, our High Priest, was raised from the dead; in this act, He conquered the grave, which *completed* the work He began as the Passover Lamb. He was now the New Life, through which the soul harvest could be equally consecrated and accepted from the fields of sinful mankind. He, as the Great Sheaf, would be found acceptable, this single bundle representing all believers who would then also be found acceptable to God, as Romans 11:16 states: "For if the firstfruit be holy, the lump is also holy."

In Jesus' becoming the "firstfruits from the dead," there was most certainly a spiritual and eternal fulfillment of the feast. However, His authority over life and death established a literal, *physical* fulfillment as well, involving more than just His own body. Note this bizarre turn of events found in Matthew 27:51–53:

> And, behold, the veil of the temple was rent in twain from the top to the bottom; and the earth did quake, and the rocks rent;

And the graves were opened; and many bodies of the saints which slept arose,

And came out of the graves after his resurrection, and went into the holy city, and appeared unto many. (Emphasis added)

The Church Fathers also wrote about this event:

Ignatius to the Trallians (AD 70–115): "For says the Scripture, 'Many bodies of the saints that slept arose,' (Mat[thew] 27:52) their graves being opened. He descended, indeed, into Hades alone, but He arose accompanied by a multitude."[35]

Irenaeus (AD 120–200): "He [Christ] suffered who can lead those souls aloft that follow His ascension. This event was also an indication of the fact, that when the holy soul of Christ descended, many souls ascended and were seen in their bodies."[36]

Clement of Alexandria (AD 155–200) "'But those who had fallen asleep descended dead, but ascended alive.' Further, the Gospel says, 'that many bodies of those that slept arose,'—plainly as having been translated to a better state."[37]

So, as the Jews were celebrating the turnover of new grain on their lands, the graves were turned over as saints with new life flooded Jerusalem to be witnesses of Jesus' power and authority over death.

What a picture! What a moment in time!

...And it's a moment in time that we believers will also witness:

But if the Spirit of him that raised up Jesus from the dead dwell in you, he that raised up Christ from the dead shall also *quicken your mortal bodies* by his Spirit that dwelleth in you. (Romans 8:11; emphasis added)

For the hour is coming, in the which *all that are in the graves* shall hear his voice,

And shall come forth; they that have done good, *unto the resurrection of life.* (John 5:28–29; emphasis added)

Until that day, we can remember the Supreme Sheaf who presented Himself as representative of all believers bundled with Him, to be accepted, made holy, and consecrated to God. We Christians observe this every year on Resurrection Sunday, even though most of us are unaware of the feast connection.

4

The Seven Feasts: Part II

Summer

The fourth of the seven major feasts—Pentecost—occurs in summer. In regard to the question, "How did Jesus fulfill the feasts?" this one relates to the current Church Age that He ushered in when He ascended and sent the Holy Spirit to guide and be with His people until His Second Coming.

Pentecost

Scripture References
- Commanded to do in: Leviticus 23:15–22
- Talked about in the Old Testament: Exodus 34:22; Deuteronomy 16:9–10; 2 Chronicles 8:13; Ezekiel 1
- Talked about in the New Testament: Acts 2:1–41, 20:16; 1 Corinthians 16:8; James 1:18

Observance Date
Beginning with the wave offering of the barley firstfruits, each day for seven weeks, the Israelites observed the "Counting of the Omer." This involved the blessing—"Blessed are You, Lord our God, King of the Universe, Who has sanctified us with His commandments and commanded us to count the Omer"—followed by the number of the day: "Today is

the first day of Omer," "Today is the second day of Omer," and so on. The end of this seven-week counting lands at precisely forty-nine days. The following day, then, makes fifty, which is what the Greek word *pentecost* means; the Feast of Pentecost takes place on the fiftieth day. This is why there is no official observance date. Nevertheless, it falls in the early days of the Hebrew month Sivan, which, on our Gregorian calendar, overlaps the second half of May and the first half of June.

This counting ritual bridges the Feast of Firstfruits to the Feast of Pentecost (or Feast of Weeks). When the temple was destroyed in AD 70, the wave offering of the firstfruits was largely discontinued. The Counting of the Omer, however, remained. (Note, also, that the section in the coming pages under the heading "Greatly Misunderstood Origins and Meanings" will further address relevant dates and times as we unravel an incredible mystery about this feast!)

Practice

There are many names for the Feast of Pentecost, the alternative "Feast of Weeks" being the most referenced. However, the nature and practice of this feast has gained it several other titles worth mentioning as well: "Feast of Harvest," "Day of Firstfruits," and "Latter Firstfruits." The first wheat crops (not to be confused with the barley of the last feast) would be harvested, and the first two loaves of bread baked from that yield would then be presented to the Lord in a wave offering. The offering of these "firstfruit" loaves is the reason behind the numerous names of this feast or festival.

Unlike the bread prepared during the week of Passover, these two loaves of bread are to be baked with leaven. And, unlike any other ordinary bread, the flour for these two loaves must be the finest—not just in quality, but also in that it is sifted over and over until completely free of any course material. As an odd detail to note for later: The Feast of Pentecost is the only occurrence in the Word of a two-loaf offering.

Prior to the Diaspora (the scattering of the Jews), this feast was an acknowledgment of dependence on God's providence in the abundance of wheat for their daily bread, a thanksgiving to Him for the harvest, and a day to remember when the Torah had been given to the people. After the Diaspora, when Jews were no longer united to celebrate the same land harvests as they were all over the known world at that time, the agricultural roots of the feast faded, and the focus turned heavily on the delivery of the Law on Mt. Sinai.

Greatly Misunderstood Origins and Meanings

By now, you're probably no longer wondering why we believe dates, times, and symbols are so important to our reflection on the feasts. We've observed that, hour by hour, Jesus walked the same steps the paschal lambs did during Passover week, and that He was killed in a manner that the cross-shaped roasting spit and blood-crowned lambs had foreshadowed. We reflected on how the unleavened bread is a perfect image—both physically and symbolically—of the sinless Jesus Christ. And we've looked at how He arose on the Day of Firstfruits, positioning Himself as the Great Sheaf. You're likely expecting the exact parallel-fulfillment comparisons to unveil something as mind-blowing as those we have already visited.

You wouldn't be wrong…

Let's start with the timing.

Establishing 6 Sivan

A mathematical equation most Christians miss involves: 1) the days between the Exodus from Egypt and the time the Israelites arrived at Mt. Sinai, and 2) the few calculated days between that day and the establishment of the Law.

According to the most devout Jewish sages, Christian scholars, and experts in Hebrew, there were exactly fifty days between the Israelites' departure from Egypt and the giving of the Torah. This interpretation begins with an irrefutable reference to Sivan, the third month on the Hebrew calendar: "In the *third month*, when the children of Israel were gone forth out of the land of Egypt" (Exodus 19:1a; emphasis added). As to what *day* of the third month, the Word only goes on to say, "the same day came they into the wilderness of Sinai."

They came to the wilderness the same day as *what*, though?

Some have suggested that the following verse's reference to their departure from Rephidim is all the clarification needed, essentially arranging the facts in contemporary English, like this: "The same day that the Israelites left Rephidim, they arrived at the foot of Mt. Sinai, which was sometime in the third month, Sivan." Others interpret that the day's "same as" description is grammatically joined to the word "month," rendering: "The Israelites arrived at Sinai in the third [3rd] month, and on the day that is numerically the same as the month, the third [3rd] day." (In other words, the third day of the third month.)

However, the most straightforward and literal explanation reveals itself when we take a quick peek at the original Hebrew. The word translated "month" is *chodesh*. Hebrew language uber-master, dictionary writer, and man of widespread influence in the academic world, Heinrich Friedrich Wilhelm Gesenius, paid close attention to this word. His classic work was the foundation upon which the groundbreaking 1906 *Brown-Driver-Briggs Hebrew and English Lexicon* was based; the scholars behind this lexicon referred to Gesenius as "the father of modern Hebrew Lexicography."[38]

In Gesenius' *Hebrew-Chaldee Lexicon*, the word *chodesh* was shown to refer to "the new moon" or "the day of the new moon"—i.e., "the first day of the month."[39]

This brings us to *yowm*—here translated "the same day." Gesenius, in a lengthy explanation, shows that *yowm* stems from another root word meaning "to be hot," and therefore etymologically evolves to refer to "the heat of the day."[40] (Some of this is related to a moment when new Hebrew-language root words and accents were formed by the softening of throaty or "guttural" sounds by the Hebrews in the attempted pronunciation of an Arabic word meaning "to glow with anger."[41])

Lastly, the location of Rephidim is unknown today. Sources reporting the distance between Rephidim and the foot of Mt. Sinai rely on knowing the precise location of that mountain, and even that is still up for debate. However, we can calculate at least an elementary idea from our Logos Bible Software's "Biblical World Atlas" tool, more specifically from its "Route of the Exodus" map.[42] The most likely Mt. Sinai site, according to this source, is the mountain modernly referred to as Jebel Musa. From there, the land that most accurately matches what is being described in the Old Testament as Rephidim (the place where Moses struck the rock for water and the last location of the Israelites prior to Sinai) is between ten to fourteen miles away, depending on the foot path traveled. These latitudinal and longitudinal coordinates can link directly from Logos to Google World maps today, where the calculations are similar.

Now, putting modern language together with what Gesenius (and countless language scholars after him) believes were the true origins behind *chodesh* and *yowm*, these two verses (Exodus 19:1–2) communicate:

> On the first day of the third month (Sivan), during the heat of the day, after traveling [somewhere from ten to fourteen] miles from Rephidim, as the children of Israel were still travelling from out of the land of Egypt, they came into the wilderness of Sinai.

Or, as an even more concise and modern potential translation:

> On 1 Sivan, the same day that the Israelites left Rephidim on their journey away from Egypt, around noon when the sun was at its hottest, the Israelites arrived at the foot of Mt. Sinai.

Amidst the ocean of Hebrew linguists that have adopted this same conclusion are a number of classic biblical literature commentators who have assisted in working out the timeline of events between 1 Sivan (their arrival) and the day the Law was given to Moses:

- The Israelites arrived at the foot of Mt. Sinai on 1 Sivan.
- On 2 Sivan, Moses went up the mountain to hear from the Lord and take His Word to the Israelites (Exodus 19:3).
- On 3 Sivan, Moses took the agreeable response of the Hebrew elders back up Sinai to God (19:7–8).

- On 4, 5, and 6 Sivan, the three-day period God gave His people to sanctify themselves and wash their clothes, they prepared for the promised appearance of God, "for the third day the Lord will come down in the sight of all the people upon mount Sinai" (Exodus 19:11).

Altogether, this is a total of exactly fifty days from the first *Pesach* threshold covenant with God Almighty to the day when He, Himself, descended upon Sinai. Thus, we have the event that instigated the annual Feast of Pentecost, or, the Feast of "the Fiftieth Day."

The *Jamieson-Fausset-Brown Bible Commentary* reflects this order, documenting that the first day of the month, 1 Sivan, was:

...forty-five days after Egypt—one day spent on the mount (Ex[odus] 19:3), one returning the people's answer [to God] (Ex[odus] 19:7, 8), three days of preparation [sanctification], making the whole time fifty days from the first passover to the promulgation of the law. Hence the feast of pentecost, that is, the fiftieth day, was the inauguration of the Old Testament church. [43]

Let those last few words ring in your thoughts as you proceed. This day at Sinai was "the inauguration of the Old Testament Church."

Understanding the Sinai Manifestation

Interestingly, however, God didn't *just* show up when and where He said he would. He appeared in a most bizarre manifestation. It was a highly supernatural event that had the Israelites trembling in reverent fear of God. Read the full account, and pay special attention to what is said about thunder and lightning:

And it came to pass on the third day [of their preparing themselves for God's appearance; i.e., 6 Sivan] in the morning, that there were thunderings and lightnings, and a thick cloud upon the mount, and the voice of the trumpet exceeding loud; so that all the people that was in the camp trembled.

And Moses brought forth the people out of the camp to meet with God; and they stood at the nether part of the mount. And mount Sinai was altogether on a smoke, because the Lord descended upon it in fire: and the smoke thereof ascended as the smoke of a furnace, and the whole mount quaked greatly.

And when the voice of the trumpet sounded long, and waxed louder and louder, Moses spake, and God answered him by a voice. And the Lord came down upon mount Sinai, on the top of the mount: and the Lord called Moses up to the top of the mount; and Moses went up. (Exodus 19:16–20)

Here we stumble upon an awkward translation that, sadly, dampens what actually happened that day. The Hebrew words *qowl* and *baraq*, represented here as "thunderings" and "lightnings," mean something different than what the English translation suggests.

Qowl, first and foremost, means "voice," "sound," or "noise," and this is the translation it is given almost every time it appears elsewhere in the Word. As one quick example of hundreds: "Did ever people hear the voice [*qowl*] of God speaking out of the midst of the fire, as thou hast heard, and live?" (Deuteronomy 4:33).

Actually, in its 506 appearances in the Bible, *only two instances* are translated "thunderings," and both are right at this spot in Exodus. In a few other places, the Word in English assigns to *qowl* the more generic translation of "thunder," but it's likely that the translators met the same challenge they did here in Exodus, choosing a weather term because it's the closest English terminology they had to pick from.

Here's the problem: In almost every place where "thunder" (or "thunderings," "thundered," etc.) is chosen as the appropriate English swap-out for a Hebrew word that truly means "voice," the setting involves God displaying extreme vocal power from the heavens in a way that can be *seen* with the human eyes. For instance, Exodus 20:18 explicitly states that "all the people *saw* the thunderings [*qowl*]." It's linguistically awkward to "see" a "voice," so the translators, whose job is certainly unenviable at times, chose what they believed was the closest English alternative. Thunder is loud, it comes from the heavens, and it can be terrifying, but because of the rolling clouds and other weather phenomena accompanying it, it can also be *seen*, which makes it at least a decent place-holder when a narrative literally describes something that is indescribable (such as "seeing" a "voice"). Additionally, there is a historical association between "voice" and "thunder" in literature, though it's more poetic than literal. For instance, if you were to read the following sample sentence from a novel—"'That's it! I've had enough! I'm warning you!' the large, angry man thundered"— you would know that "thundered" was being used to describe the character's volume and intensity, obviously not to portray any activity related to weather. This, too, may have played a part in why the translators chose "thunderings" instead of the more accurate reference to speech, because we know that God's shout was more than just a gentle speaking engagement.

This *qowl* was describing a roar so loud, so rushing, and so atmospherically encompassing that there are no one-word trade-outs from Hebrew to English to accomplish accuracy. Imagine screaming at the very top of your lungs, bloody-murder style, and your voice doesn't even register any sound above the intense reverberation of the atmosphere all around you. Your own loudest, blood-curdling shrieks are completely muted under the waves of sound coming from heaven. God's declaration causes the ground under you to rumble, sinks into your skin, and makes you feel as if you will vibrate away, disintegrate, without ever even being touched by any force other than His voice. It's the kind of permeating sound that digs into your very soul and never leaves. It's the voice of the Lord—spoken in a volume so loud and authoritative that it causes earthquakes (Exodus 19:18)—who is about to give His non-negotiable Ten Commandments for you to live by. The sound emitting from heaven is one from a Creator who has the power to crush all of His own creation by a mere shout; this is a sound that says He *will* be taken seriously.

Don't think us to be sensationalizing. The Israelites at the foot of Mt.

Sinai who had just heard God's *qowl* were convinced that they would all be killed if He used His strong voice to speak to them again (Exodus 20:19b: "let not God speak with us, lest we die"). But in addition, we can look at what God's intense, *qowl*-from-heaven shout did in similar circumstances elsewhere, as we read in 1 Samuel 7:10:

> And as Samuel was offering up the burnt offering, the Philistines drew near to battle against Israel: but the Lord thundered [*ra'am*; Hebrew "roar"] with a great thunder [*qowl*] on that day upon the Philistines, and discomfited them; and they were smitten before Israel.

On a purely technical level, this should read: "the Lord roared with a great voice from heaven."

Did you notice, though, that all the Philistines died? The bellow from the clouds, in and of itself, killed them...but just before it did, it caused them to burst into a great fit of hysterics, confusion, panic, and scrambling about in fear.

What's that? You don't remember reading that?

We know, we know. Much of the Word is lost in translation. Oh, how little the English expresses, sometimes!

The Hebrew *hamam*, translated in 1 Samuel 7:10 as "discomfited," is a primitive root word meaning "to put in motion...to disturb, to put in commotion, to put to flight."[44] In other words, the Philistines were nearby, readying their troops for attack against God's people, and God's *qowl* from the sky caused them to both a) run all over the place in terror, and b) lose the war. This was a total annihilation—not one survivor.

The voice, *alone*, accomplished that.

If you "go there" all the way in your imagination, then you're probably taking the same thought journey the translators did when they placed themselves into the narrative in order to choose the most suitable English word for the Mt. Sinai narrative in Exodus. A translator's responsibility isn't just to transfer one word after another from the native to the foreign language, but to understand, study, and respect the *context* in which words or phrases are used throughout the whole work (the Bible, in this case). What else, *in English*, besides the word "thunder" comes from the heavens and is visible, loud, and potentially frightening enough to confuse multitudes and strike entire armies dead? In this case, "thunder" wasn't the worst possible choice.

However, amiability to the translators aside, *it was not the most accurate choice.*

All the Hebrew says about the supposed "thunderings" is that a "voice" came from God, Himself, as He descended on the mountain, and that the Israelites "saw" it.

To be perfectly clear: There is no reason in the Hebrew to believe that thunder was a part of the display of God's power on Mt. Sinai on the day the Law was given!

In the end, as grammatically awkward as it is to say "the Israelites *saw* a *voice*," that is the true meaning, and this will become clear after reflecting upon the larger picture. As to "what the voice *looked* like," put a pin in that thought for a moment while we home in on the "lightnings."

The Hebrew word *baraq* can certainly be used in a sentence to mean "lightning," but only because its root definition is something extremely bright, like a flash of light. By itself, translators may have chosen to say that "bright lights" or "flashes of light" were seen coming from the sky, but because of the word's association with "lightning" elsewhere in ancient Hebrew—*and* because, by now, the translators had probably already agreed to make *qowl* read "thunderings"—it made sense to make this second, observable phenomenon a part of an erratic weather pattern. Again, however, "lightning" doesn't completely capture this thought.

In fact, this same term is used in other passages such as the following that don't have the first thing to do with lightning or storms. In these instances, our *baraq* appears as a flash of light upon a sharp blade: "If I whet my glittering [*baraq*] sword, and mine hand take hold on judgment; I will render vengeance to mine enemies, and will reward them that hate me" (Deuteronomy 32:41); "It is drawn, and cometh out of the body; yea, the glittering [*baraq*] sword cometh out of his gall: terrors are upon him" (Job 20:25). For the word *baraq*, the "light reflecting off of a sword," along with other similar uses, are more abundant throughout the Old Testament than "lightning." Besides just the numerous "sword" or "spear" allusions (see Ezekiel 21:15, 28; Nahum 3:3; Habakkuk 3:11) *baraq* also refers to the brightness of a flame, like from a lamp or torch (Ezekiel 1:13).

Lucky for us, the "lightnings" of Sinai don't solely rely on our ability to analyze just *baraq*.

After the delivery of the Ten Commandments, this supernatural phenomenon was still going on, but in an unexpected and bizarre turn of events, the Hebrew words aren't exactly the same, nor are they quite where we expected them to be: "And all the people saw the thunderings [*qowl*], and the lightnings [*lappiyd*]" (Exodus 20:18).

Wait a second… What is *lappiyd*? Where did that word come from, and why is it being rendered "lightnings" here, when back in Exodus 19:16 "lightnings" was *baraq*? Were the "bright, flashing lights" from before morphed into something new?

First of all, please note that the Hebrew word for "fire"—meaning *any* regular reference to fire—from what belongs on an altar, to what engulfed the burning bush, to what roasts meat, and so on—is *'esh*. Here, suddenly, the "lightnings," or *lappiyd*, refers to a sort of fire, but it's a specific enough kind of fire that the Hebrew author purposely steered around using the most common *'esh*. As noted, *baraq* means a bright flash of light. Here, in the same context as *baraq*, with an identical "lightnings" translation treatment later, the word *lappiyd* describes the evolution from mere flashes of light to bright flashes of fire!

The Hebrew *lappiyd* means "torch" (or "lamp"), which is how it is translated the most in the Old Testament (Genesis 15:17; Judges 7:16, 20; Job 12:5, 41:19; Isaiah 62:1; Ezekiel 1:13; Daniel 10:6). Consider the context of this word as a tool: The Hebrews would have had hundreds of useful purposes for regular fire in the middle of the day in the sunshine, such as cooking, forging, cleansing, etc. However, they wouldn't have had use for a torch in broad daylight. In proper context, a "torch" or "lamp" are tools that burn brighter than their surroundings.

A certain peculiarity about this word, however, appears fairly consistent. Not only does *lappiyd* indicate a fiery flame, *at times* this flame appears to have a life of its own, like a kind of floating, animated symbol, as it does here:

> And it came to pass, that, when the sun went down, and it was dark, behold a smoking furnace, and a burning lamp [*lappiyd*] that passed between those pieces.
> In the same day the Lord made a covenant with Abram, saying, Unto thy seed have I given this land, from the river of Egypt unto the great river, the river Euphrates. (Genesis 15:17–18)

In Judges 15:4–5, Samson ties a crude hunk of burning wood between two foxes over and over again, eventually setting about three hundred foxes with these *lappiyd* "firebrands" into the corn stalks of the Philistine fields. This fiery scene is not the only one that depicts a wild, out-of-control brushfire caused by *lappiyd*. Nahum once compared *lappiyd* torches to pure chaos, when he prophesied that the chariots in the streets of Nineveh would violently rage and thrash about in the streets and "justle one against another in the broad ways: they shall seem like torches [*lappiyd*]" (Nahum 2:4). In Zechariah, the image is that God will "make the governors of Judah like an hearth of fire among the wood, and like a torch [*lappiyd*] of fire in a sheaf; and they shall devour all the people round about, on the right hand and on the left: and Jerusalem shall be inhabited again in her own place, even in Jerusalem" (Zechariah 12:6).

In context within Scripture, *lappiyd* looks almost feral, untamed, unmanageable, *at least* out of human control, and at times even autonomous or self-governing. In other words, the account in Exodus is not talking about a regular, everyday, run-of-the-mill "fire," and it certainly isn't referring to "lightning." According to the Hebrew author, what started as bright, flashing lights (*baraq*) became, by the end of God's delivery of the Ten Commandments, bright, flashing fire (*lappiyd*)!

To sum up what we've looked at so far: This moment in Exodus never actually mentioned thunder at all. The Israelites "*saw* a voice," and it was the one and only powerful voice of God. How they saw a sound has yet to be addressed. Then, we stopped to reflect upon another fact: The lightning they witnessed was never lightning, but a bright, flashing light (*baraq*) that rapidly evolved into a flashing fire (*lappiyd*) sometime between God's arrival at Sinai and His finalizing of the commandments. And, after viewing the context of the words *baraq* and *lappiyd* in other parts of the Bible and studying the descriptions, it's fair to say that this light/fire was probably moving around of its own (God's) will.

At this point, it might look like we have more information about the lightnings that weren't really lightnings than we do about the thunderings that weren't thunderings. What was really going on with the *qowl* shouting from heaven?

Here's the glue. Ready?

When you study the sentence structure of the description of the phenomenon in Exodus 19:16 in Hebrew, *without all the modern English additions for flow*, we arrive at: *boqer qowl baraq*. That's it. That's all the Hebrew says. In a literal, word-for-word, initially nonsensical reading, *boqer qowl baraq* means "morning voice light." It is from these seemingly vague three Hebrew words that we were given the English, "In the morning there were thunderings and lightnings." Similarly, Exodus 20:18: *'am ra'ah qowl lappiyd*. Once again, the literal, word-for-word rendering is, "people saw voice torch." This is where we received, "All the people saw the thunderings and the lightnings."

Please don't miss this:

The Hebrew never suggested the need to include "and" in the original formation of the sentence. The translators inserted the "and" (as well as other words), as they did in countless other locations in Scripture to ensure that the sentence made sense to the English-speaker's ear. It's all a bit Tarzan style of speech—"morning voice light"; "people saw voice torch"—without the smoothing that occurs during translation. Unfortunately, unless the translators are correct, even the tiniest word, like "and," can disjoint the original narrative.

We're not reading about two separate phenomena. The Hebrew doesn't say that the *baraq* and *lappiyd* were "in addition to" the *qowl*; it says that the *baraq* and *lappiyd* "were" the *qowl*. In English, the Israelites didn't "see a voice" and then also "see lights/fires"; they "saw a voice appearing as lights/fires." Go back to the bare-bones, Tarzan-speech version, and imagine inserting not words but just the punctuation that didn't exist back then. It might look like this: "Morning; voice-light." "People saw voice-torch."

The voice manifested as fire!

All this confusion about how a "voice" can be "seen" is finally explained, because we now have the physical manifestation of God's voice as these flickering, bright flames appeared all over the mountainside.

Dr. Juergen Buehler, physicist, chemist, and president of the International Christian Embassy Jerusalem (ICEJ), painted what these authors believe to be a striking word picture of this moment in the Word. The teachings of the rabbis on this area, Buehler explains, is that "every word God spoke that day was like the stroke of a hammer on an anvil. With each stroke on the anvil, which was Mount Sinai, sparks…of fire flew outward."[45] How appropriate a tapestry this weaves between the *qowl*, *baraq*, and *lappiyd*… God's voice, like sparks, shooting out with every reverberating boom of the Law.

But this visual, especially for those who are learning about it for the first time, does present a few intriguing questions: Why would God, Himself, appear as smoke and fire all over the mountain, while His voice—declaring the Ten Commandments for the first time—appeared as flickering, glinting flames that grew in intensity as He spoke, described in such a way as to travel about? Why were these little flame lights so animated…if they even were? And what was the purpose in any of this?

Perhaps some of the earlier Torah commentary experts would be of help to us now.

The Midrash, the most respected Jewish Scripture commentary, compiled by celebrated rabbis between AD 400 and 1200, is alive and well when it comes to the subject of the "thunderings" and the "lightnings." The rabbis observed a great number of related verses in addition to the geographical spread of God's appearance worldwide as outlined in the Word, and they came to a most interesting connection, starting at Mt. Sinai and spreading outward. Observe what the records say in Midrash, *Shemot Rabbah* (Hebrew: "Great Exodus") 5:9, regarding the visible voice of God in Exodus 19:16 and 20:18:

> This is that which is written (Job 37:5), "God thunders wonders with His voice"—what is it that He thunders? When the Holy One, blessed be He, gave the Torah at Sinai, He showed wonders of wonders to Israel. How is it? The Holy One, blessed be He, would speak and the voice would go out and travel the whole world: Israel would hear the voice coming to them from the South and they would run to the South to meet the voice; and from the South, it would switch for them to the North, and they would all run to the North; and from the North, it would switch to the East, and they would run to the East; and from the East, it would switch to the West, and they would run to the West; and from the West, it would switch [to be] from the heavens, and they would suspend their eyes [to the heavens], and it would switch [to be] in the earth, and they would stare at the earth, as it is stated (Deuteronomy 4:36), "From the Heavens did He make you hear His voice, to discipline you." And Israel would say one to the other, "And wisdom, from where can it be found" (Job 28:12). And Israel would say, from where is the Holy One, blessed be He, coming, from the East or from the South? As it is stated (Deuteronomy 33:2), "The Lord came from Sinai, and shone from Seir

(in the East) to them"; and it is written (Habakuk 3:3), "And God will come from Teiman (in the South)." And it is stated (Exodus 20:18), "And all the people saw the sounds (literally, voices)."[46]

Hmm. So, according to this explanation, God's voice "went out" to the north, south, east, and west, all over the world. There was not one area—from Sinai to the opposite point on our round planet—where anyone could escape His message.

Why the multiple light/fires though? God, the Creator of the universe, whose voice can kill entire armies with one utterance, could have just talked really loudly, right?

He could have. But our creative Father chose this method for His *tongues* to reach everyone on the globe…and it wasn't the only time He would do so.

The New Testament Church's Role and Fulfillment

If these Jewish scholars whose commentary paved the way for Old Testament understanding for the last several thousand years are correct, and we *can* see that God's voice manifested all over the globe, then we humbly seek a deeper understanding if we're to believe there is a fulfillment of the Feast of Weeks.

See, it wasn't just a spectacle of voice, lights, and fire. Rabbi Yochanan, a first-century sage, in his Midrash commentary on this moment in Exodus, notes: "The voice would go out and divide into seventy voices for the seventy languages, so that all the nations would hear [and understand]."[47] Maybe when Yochanan wrote this, he was inspired by Psalm 29:7: "The voice of the Lord divideth the flames of fire"!

You caught that, right? It's about being *multilingual*.

If the Midrash is correct: God's voice came from the heavens over Mt. Sinai, manifesting into bright flashes of fiery light, divided into all known languages of the world at that time, and then traveled all over the globe so that all might hear His words and understand them…*all on 6 Sivan*—the first Day of Pentecost, exactly fifty days from the first Passover in Egypt.

Remember, these rabbis are *Jewish*. Their consideration of what is occurring here in Exodus is naturally no respecter of any story in Acts 2 of the New Testament…that is a "Testament" of the Messiah that they don't believe. Far be it for any rabbi contributing to the Midrash commentary to attempt to show through Jewish theology that the Old Testament Mt. Sinai tongues/languages event foreshadowed the New Testament Mt. Sinai tongues/languages event. A Jewish rabbi would likely be more interested in wanting to present the dissimilarities between Jehovah on the mountain and the Comforter Jesus promised to send!

Yet, as most Christians know, the book of Acts, chapter 2, tells us that, on the Day of Pentecost, fifty days after Jesus sat at the Last Supper and instituted Communion instead of Passover, forty-seven days after He became the Great Sheaf on the Feast of Firstfruits, on the same day all the Jews were wrapping up the Counting of the Omer, on the Hebrews' 6 Sivan, the Holy Spirit descended on Christ's followers. When He did, bright, flickering "tongues of flame" descended from heaven and hovered over the men and women there, who proceeded to file out into the streets, speaking in all the known languages of that day…so that all might hear and understand God's words.

This time, unlike the last time, the message wasn't about the Law, but about Jesus Christ, the Messiah who came to fulfill the Law (Matthew 5:17–20).

…And *this* time, unlike the last time, God's words would be directed and received by both Jew and Gentile.

Before we get into that too far, let's read what happened in Acts 2 directly from the Bible. There is, tragically but not surprisingly, some potency lost in translation:

> And when the day [Feast] of Pentecost was fully come, they were all with one accord in one place.
>
> And suddenly there came a sound from heaven as of a rushing mighty wind, and it filled all the house where they were sitting.
>
> And there appeared unto them cloven tongues like as of fire, and it sat upon each of them.

And they were all filled with the Holy Ghost, and began to
speak with other tongues, as the Spirit gave them utterance. (Acts
2:1–4)

To begin, the "sound" mentioned in the words "there came a sound
from heaven" wasn't just a noise. This is the Greek word *ēchos*, which
appears in only a few places in the Word. One, in Luke 21:25, is translated to "roar"! In Hebrews 12:19, it's used in conjunction with *salpigx*
to refer to the very trumpet blast "which signals the Second Coming"![48]
Then, oddly, over in Luke 4:37, after Jesus cast a demon out of the man
in Capernaum, *ēchos* is translated as "fame": "And the fame [*ēchos*] of him
went out into every place of the country round about."

So far, from only within the Bible, it looks like this word could mean
a roar, a blast signal of God's appearance, or the spreading recognition of
God's power. See what we mean? It's *so* much more than just "a sound."

And you know…that's quite interesting, considering the context of
Acts 2:2 in comparison to the Sinai account. Could it be that the "sound
from heaven" that fell upon the great city of Jerusalem on that Feast of
Pentecost day was a terrifically loud roar from the mouth of God, His
own blast signaling the arrival of God in the Person of the Holy Spirit, the
power of His voice going out from Him and ahead of Him, spreading the
word of His imminent, soon-arriving, fame and glory?!

Man, that's beautiful!

Wouldn't it be almost too good to be true if we could find a solid link
showing that the Greek *chos* was used in literature of this time directly
and irrefutably to mean "voice"? Seriously…wouldn't that nail down the
first parallel between God's *qowl* on Mt. Sinai and the sound described
here in Acts?

Actually, that *is* a definition of this word, and proof isn't difficult to
find. Not only is this Greek term and its variants used to mean "voice" by
other writers at the time of Christ—such in as the medical textbook *de
Materia Medica* ("On Medical Material") by the Greek physician Pedanius Dioscorides[49]—thanks to the scholarly authors and editors behind

the *Greek-English Lexicon* by Oxford, we now know that *it referred specifi-cally to the voice of God* in the LXX (Septuagint) Bible translation![50] (In case that's a new translation to some readers, the LXX was the *Greek* Bible studied at the time of Christ.)

Our iron is hot. Let's strike again, shall we?

Next on the list is "rushing," which is the Greek, *pherō*.

Just as "thunder" wasn't necessarily the *worst* word that could have been chosen from the Hebrew for *qowl*, "rushing" isn't necessarily the worst choice for *pherō*, as the immediate context does describe something happening rapidly ("And *suddenly* there came..."). Nevertheless, just as "thunder" wasn't accurate there, "rushing" isn't accurate here. As just about any lexicon or study tool will tell you, *pherō* means "bring," "carry," or "bear."[51]

As just a few of countless examples from the Word, here are four uses of *pherō*, each from one of the four Gospels:

- "He said, 'Bring [*pherō*] them hither to me'" (Matthew 14:18).
- "'Shall we give, or shall we not give?' But he, knowing their hypocrisy, said unto them, 'Why tempt ye me? bring [*pherō*] me a penny, that I may see it'" (Mark 12:15).
- "And bring [*pherō*] hither the fatted calf, and kill it; and let us eat, and be merry" (Luke 15:23).
- "Every branch in me that beareth not fruit he taketh away: and every branch that beareth fruit, he purgeth it, that it may bring [*pherō*] forth more fruit" (John 15:2).

It's quite a leap, from "bring" to "rushing." Right? The latter term is detached from any identifiable driving force and almost sounds random, chaotic, even accidental. There's nobody involved in it. The former, to "bring" or "carry" something, is personal, intentional...it almost rings from the page like a gift. Though either can be interpreted to acknowl-edge the wind as God's handiwork, considering the colossal significance of what was taking place in both the physical and the spiritual realms in that moment, saying God "brought" or "carried" the wind allows for intention and specificity directly from the Divine.

It probably goes without saying by this point, but we'll say it anyway: You have to try, *hard*, to see the distant, detached, impersonal word "rushing" in this place instead of what is more apparently meant here, which is the act of the Holy Spirit carrying something.

What, exactly, is He carrying, though?

Remember how the "thunder and lightning" at Mt. Sinai wasn't really thunder and lightning, and how it wasn't two phenomena but rather one and its corresponding description? Recall that, in English, there likely wouldn't have been any way of knowing that based on how our language bleeds off the page? Well, this moment in Scripture is similar in that it will require readers to be open-minded in challenging some age-old concepts and imagery. It's surprisingly dissimilar, however, in that even the English—*when read carefully*—by itself dispels the most common misinterpretation of this verse in all of Christendom.

Here it is again, Acts 2:2a, in English. Pay attention to every single word:

> And suddenly there came a sound from heaven as of a rushing mighty wind…

If, in that reading, you came up with the Holy Spirit "bringing" or "carrying" anything other than a *sound*, you might want to go back and read it again. Let us explain.

The time-honored, and frankly *gorgeous*, visual of powerful winds is all over the place in our churches' curricula and charts, religious media, historical paintings, books, and even various Christian retail products. We hear about the "rushing mighty wind" from the pulpit with such excitement—how it came bursting through the windows and doors into the Upper Room, swirling around the followers of Christ, whipping about their robes and hair, alerting everyone that something big is coming. Sometimes the retelling even involves the apostles being lifted up from the floor!

As inspiring as it is, however, the "wind" idea we all have isn't what the Greek originally described. If it *were*, then a few issues would have to be addressed. To name only one: The adjective translated into English as "mighty" here is the Greek word *biaios*, which surprisingly means "violent."[52] In other words, if this wind was a literal, physical, and purely natural element, then we are told here that the gentle Comforter sent a "violent" wind to tear through the city on the day He arrived. But imagining the Holy Spirit sending danger to the disciples He's about to bless is odd. For as many words in the Greek language as there are that would have conveyed *both* might (or power) *and* safety in the presence of the Lord, *biaios* sticks out like a "sore thumb" here.

Why not just "mighty" by itself? Why "violent"? If Luke was only attempting to tell the readers that the wind was "strong" or "mighty," he could have used a number of more appropriate terms ...*and* they were part of a vocabulary he already knew and used! Why wouldn't Luke have chosen to use *dynatos*—the Greek word for "mighty" or "powerful"— here, like he did elsewhere (Luke 1:49, 14:31, 18:27, 24:19; Acts 2:24, 7:22, 11:17, 18:24, 20:16, 25:5)? Why did he break character in Acts 2:2 and depict God as the sender of perilous weather conditions?

Actually, scholarly responses to this section of Scripture are fairly unanimous: Luke wrote "violent," and "violent" is precisely what he meant—but he wasn't describing a "wind"; he was describing a "sound." Technically, the wind didn't exist in any way save for a basis of comparison. For many readers, this is a huge surprise. So long has the literal wind on the Day of Pentecost in the New Testament been ingrained in our thoughts that it's hard to let go of the whooshing, sweeping, dust-in-the-air ideas. But *Thayer's Greek Lexicon* is the first of many sources we can point to fairly quickly that will dispel this. According to *Thayer's*, the comparative Greek adverb *hōsper*, translated "as" here in the cluster "a sound from heaven as of a rushing mighty wind," is a word meaning something that simply "stands in close relation to what precedes," therefore representing a direct comparison in Acts 2:2, "i.e., just as a sound is made when a mighty wind blows."[53] Scotland's finest New Testament scholar and former chairman of the Tyndale Fellowship for Biblical and Theological Research, Ian Howard Marshall, acknowledges this in *Acts: An Introduction and Commentary*, pointing out that the grammatical relationship between the Greek *pnoē* ("wind") next to the aggressive *biaios* is "that of analogy—a sound *like* that of wind."[54] Leading academic and Fellowship of the British Academy award-winning professor of divinity at England's University of Durham, Charles Kingsley Barrett, states in *A Critical and Exegetical Commentary on the Acts of the Apostles* that "Luke is confining himself to a vivid *natural* analogy.... There was a noise *like* that made by a powerful wind."[55]

To recap: 1) The disciples of Christ are all together "in one accord"; 2) God personally ushers, carries, and delivers to them the sound of His voice—with a *roar* so powerful and commanding that it sounds to those assembled like a howling, violent wind.

Next: Not only do the followers of Jesus *hear* the voice of God like a wind, they *see* it as it manifests as "cloven tongues like as of fire, and it sat upon each of them." But note that "cloven" here is a bit misleading in English, because of our familiarity with phrases like "cloven hoof," where it refers to one object with a "split" shape in it. The "cloven" reference is from the Greek *diamerizō* ("divided"), which describes when God's voice descended, then split apart into many "tongues" before "each person present was touched with flame."[56] Again, this is the wonder referred to in Psalm 29:7: "The voice of the Lord divideth the flames of fire."

Then, of course, comes the question that scholars have sometimes taken an unexpected turn on. Do the "tongues" here describe the shape of the flames in comparison to the bodily organ, *or* more simply, do they describe languages? Technically, the Greek word *glōssa* is used for both the tongue, the body part, as well as the speech it makes, so it could be either. However, despite the somewhat convincing argument for the former by some astute language experts (that Luke was saying the flames were "tongue-shaped"), it seems the more complicated conclusion to make. The context of the next verse—"and began to speak with other tongues, as the Spirit gave them utterance"—clearly refers to spoken languages, and, generally speaking, no respectable person in academia argues with that. Since the context and application are therefore the same, it's safe to agree with the vast majority of scholars on this one and stick to the following deduction: "Tongues," *both in verse 3 and in verse 4*, refers to "languages," which renders what readers may have, before our reflection on Sinai, thought was awkward: "And there appeared unto them [divided languages] like as of fire, and it sat upon each of them. And they were all filled with the Holy Ghost, and began to speak with other [languages]."

A couple more thoughts on this area of Scripture before we wrap this up: First, the words "all with one accord" have caused varied speculation. What, exactly, are the disciples in harmony about? Most scholars and commentators link this to the mention of "one accord" in Acts 1:14, which provides a direct description of what they are doing together: "These all continued with one accord in prayer and supplication, with the women, and Mary the mother of Jesus, and with his brethren." These authors particularly like the way *Benson Commentary* explains it:

> The word [Greek *homothymadon*], rendered **with one accord,** implies that they were united in their views, intentions, and affections, and that there was no discord or strife among them, as there sometimes had been while their Master was with them. Doubtless, they were also united in their desire and expectation of the baptism of the Holy Ghost, **the power from on high,** which Christ had promised them; and in praying earnestly and importunately for it whenever they met together, which it appears they were in the habit of doing daily.[57] (Emphasis in original)

They were all praying together, but it's likely they were praying *specifically* for the power from God to assist them in the Great Commission, since that's what the Holy Spirit does. Take note of this, because it is a *crucial* point in the Church Age, which is what the Feast of Pentecost represents. And don't misunderstand this to be an argument for speaking in tongues, as these authors believe that matter should be between each believer and God. We want to stress that, just as the Holy Spirit came to the disciples on 6 Sivan in what was likely the year AD 33 with languages of fire, He can come upon any all believers with the "gifts of the Spirit" they're supposed to have for Great Commission work today, as long as every believer is praying in expectation of that.

Second, though we risk once again disturbing some beautiful imagery for believers everywhere by writing this, the words "in one place" don't necessarily have to mean "the Upper Room." Note that the "house" mentioned in verse 2 is the Greek *oikos*, which just means "dwelling place" in many ancient contexts. Actually, though the "Upper Room" is where the apostles tended to meet together, as Acts 1:13 shows, we can't make a solid conclusion that this was the meeting place of Acts 2:1. It's a possibility, certainly, but not a guarantee, as *Barnes' Notes* clarifies:

> In one place—Where this was cannot be known. Commentators have been much divided in their conjectures about it. Some have supposed that it was in the upper room mentioned in Acts 1:13; others that it was a room in the temple; others that it was in a synagogue; others that it was among the promiscuous multitude that assembled for devotion in the courts of the temple.[58]

Consider again Acts 2:1–4 in light of all we've covered. Based on the original languages and contexts, and the consistency of God's nature from the Old Testament, we suggest a contemplative, dynamic wording of this passage as follows:

> And on 6 Sivan, during the Feast of Pentecost, the disciples of Christ were all gathered together in one place, supporting one another and agreeing with one another in prayer [probably for the "power from on high"]. And suddenly there came a voice, roaring from heaven like a violent wind, and the sound filled the dwelling place where they were sitting. And the disciples saw the voice from heaven divide into many languages, looking like fire, and the

fire sat upon each of them. And they were all filled with the Holy
Ghost, and began to speak with other languages, as the Spirit gave
them utterance. (Acts 2:1–4)

Remember that time on Mt. Sinai when God's voice physically manifested as a bright fire, then split up and went out to all the world so that
everyone would know and understand His Law?

Yeah. He did *that* again.

The "fiftieth day" (Pentecost) from the deliverance of Egypt, when the
Law (the *Old Covenant!*) united the nation of Israel under the will of God
while on Mt. Sinai, was a literal, moment-for-moment parallel of the "fiftieth day" (Pentecost) from the death of Christ and deliverance from the
confines of sin, when Jesus fulfilled the Law down to the letter and united
Jew and Gentile (the *New Covenant!*) as a new people under the grace of
God while on Mt. Zion.

Most Christians with little to no familiarity with the feasts will not be
aware of this connection, but once you see it, you can't "unsee" it without
extreme effort. The resemblance between the two events is no coincidence.

Barrett recognizes this comparison without hesitation: "Luke is accu-
mulating features characteristic of theophanies…[like the] descriptions of
the giving of the Law on Mount Sinai: Exod[us] 19:18."[59] Marshall is likewise convinced: "A flame divided itself into several *tongues*, so that each
rested upon one of the persons present.… And again we are reminded of
Old Testament theophanies, especially of that at Sinai (Exod[us] 19:18)."[60]
Dr. Richard Booker of *Celebrating Jesus in the Biblical Feasts* notes this
wonderful Old Testament/New Testament connection as well:

The English translation [of the Sinai event] says all the people witnessed the thunderings and the lightnings. Jewish scholars believe
that the people actually "saw the voice of God" coming out of the
mountain in tongues of fire.…

The first Pentecost was at Mount Sinai when God wrote His
words on tablets of stone. Yet, the Lord promised there would be

a time in the distant future when He would write His laws on the fleshly tablets of their hearts. (See Jeremiah 31:31–34.)…

In His own appointed time, God would come down on the people. Not on Mount Sinai in the desert, but on Mount Zion in Jerusalem.[61]

Let's not leave out a very important rabbi, Southern Evangelical Seminary's pride and Word of Messiah Ministries' president, Dr. Sam Nadler, who also acknowledged in his book, *Messiah in the Feasts of Israel*:

Luke, who wrote the book of Acts, was trained by his mentor Paul to understand the work of God in Messiah from a Biblically Jewish frame of reference. Luke depicts the events of Acts 2 as a second "Mount Sinai experience." When the Law was given, there was fire and noise as God descended on Mount Sinai (Exodus 19:18–20). When the Spirit was given there was fire and noise as well (Acts 2:2–3). The rabbis comment in the Talmud that when the Torah was given at Mount Sinai, "Every single word that went forth from the Omnipotent was split up into seventy languages for the nations of the world." When the Holy Spirit was given, men from every nation spoke in other languages as the Spirit enabled them.[62]

A number of the classic commentators, at the time of their writings (circa 1820–1850 for many), wrote as if God's manifestation in both the Old Testament and New Testament Pentecost was a foreshadowing followed by fulfillment. As one example from *Benson*:

It is computed that the law was given just fifty days after their coming out of Egypt, in remembrance of which the feast of pentecost was observed the fiftieth day after the passover, and in compliance with which the Spirit was poured out upon the apostles, at the feast of pentecost, fifty days after the death of Christ.[63]

It's really no wonder that scholars conclude that the Acts 2 episode was a direct fulfillment of what God started on Mt. Sinai. The parallels are seemingly endless, including many that we haven't covered well enough to do great justice. Take a look at this list, which isn't even close to exhaustive:

- Both demonstrations of God's power involve tongues of fire and multiple languages so that all mankind will hear and understand the message of God.
- Both events took place on the Feast of Pentecost, and on 6 Sivan.
- Both events involved a theophany—that is, a visible manifestation of the Lord.
- Both events marked the delivery of a divine covenant: In Exodus, it was fifty days after the Israelites completed the threshold covenant with the lamb sacrifice; in Acts, it was fifty days after Jesus became the ultimate Lamb sacrifice.
- In Exodus, Israel as a nation was established; in Acts, Christianity was established.
- Exodus 24:13 calls Mt. *Sinai* the "mountain of God." Isaiah 2:3 calls Mt. *Zion* the "mountain of God." Both the Old Testament (Old Covenant) tongues-of-fire event at Sinai and the New Testament (New Covenant) tongues-of-fire event at Zion took place on "the mountain of God," though they are over three hundred miles apart.
- In Hebrew, the word *towrah* ("Torah," the Law), as it derives from the root *yarah*, means "teach." John 14:16 refers to the Holy Spirit as the "teacher."
- In Exodus, we read about the inauguration of the Old Testament Church, as the *Jamieson-Fausset-Brown Bible Commentary* stated earlier; in Acts, we read about the inauguration of the New Testament—and current—Church.

Again, the list goes on. Studying these two occurrences side by side as we have done flags another hundred or so deeply theological parallels that blow the mind. If this book were *just* about the Jewish feasts, these authors would be tempted to devote another hundred pages to Pentecost alone. Alas, we don't have space to accomplish that...but what do you say? One more for the road?

This next one is the *best*!

In Exodus 32, just after the Mt. Sinai Pentecost demonstration when the idolatry-forbidding Mosaic Law had been given to the Israelites, God's chosen people had the audacity to create and worship a golden calf. Moses delegated the tribe of Levi, who had *not* turned their backs upon the Lord like the others, to carry out the unfortunate task of making an example out of the idolaters: "And the children of Levi did according to the word of Moses: and there fell of the people that day about three thousand men" (Exodus 32:28). Could this particular travesty have been in Paul's mind when he called the Law the "ministry of condemnation" (2 Corinthians 3:7–9)?

Flip forward a heavy heap in the Word. Just after the Holy Spirit's Pentecost demonstration, the disciples ran to the streets to preach that "God hath made the same Jesus, [who was] crucified, both Lord and Christ" (Acts 2:36). Here's what happened next:

> Now when they heard this, they were pricked in their heart, and said unto Peter and to the rest of the apostles, "Men and brethren, what shall we do?"
>
> Then Peter said unto them, "Repent, and be baptized every one of you in the name of Jesus Christ for the remission of sins, and ye shall receive the gift of the Holy Ghost.
>
> For the promise is unto you, and to your children, and to all that are afar off, even as many as the Lord our God shall call."
>
> And with many other words did he testify and exhort, saying, "Save yourselves from this untoward generation."
>
> Then they that gladly received his word were baptized: and the same day there were added unto them about three thousand souls. (Acts 2:37–41)

What a glorious, gracious turnaround! At Sinai, three thousand people died under the Old Covenant. In the book of Acts, three thousand were saved because of the message of the New Covenant!

Folks, this *is* the Church Age that fulfills the old Feast of Pentecost. Jesus fulfilled it by sending the Spirit He promised, and now, with the Spirit's gentle, personal, and patient help, we believers are empowered to take God's story to the ends of the earth in every language, just like the followers of Christ did in the book of Acts. What a privilege!

But what about those leavened loaves the Jews waved before the Lord at the feast? How do those fit in?

Two Leavened Loaves: The Church, the Body

Recall that at the opening of this section about Pentecost, we stated that the Pentecost offering was the only two-loaf offering in the Bible. This number seems to come from out of nowhere if one's personal theology stops at the Old Testament. It's hard to find an answer for why the Jews would celebrate the harvest with *two* loaves of bread. Why not three? Why not twelve? Why not offer a half of a loaf and eat the other half?

Once in a while, we stumble upon an explanation in a commentary or in a scholarly analysis, but at best, the "answers" are mere conjecture, and they often raise even more questions. This command of God that the Jews followed for centuries appears to be a curiosity for certain... until the symbolism of the New Testament Day of Pentecost comes into play.

First, let's take a moment to mull over these following verses from both the Old Testament and the New Testament and see what they have in common:

- "One witness shall not rise up against a man for any iniquity, or for any sin, in any sin that he sinneth: at the mouth of two witnesses, or at the mouth of three witnesses, shall the matter be established" (Deuteronomy 19:15).

- "Whoso killeth any person, the murderer shall be put to death by the mouth of witnesses: but one witness shall not testify against any person to cause him to die" (Numbers 35:30).
- "But if he will not hear thee, then take with thee one or two more, that in the mouth of two or three witnesses every word may be established" (Matthew 18:16).
- "This is the third time I am coming to you. In the mouth of two or three witnesses shall every word be established" (2 Corinthians 13:1).
- "It is also written in your law, that the testimony of two [witnesses] is true" (John 8:17).
- "And I will give power unto my two witnesses, and they shall prophesy a thousand two hundred and threescore days, clothed in sackcloth" (Revelation 11:3).

We'll stop this list here, but note that many other verses in the Word of God also make it clear that "two" is the number of witnesses needed to establish the credibility of a claim or reported circumstance. The contexts certainly change—ranging from those who have seen a crime and testify in the court of law to the holy men who oppose the Antichrist in the Apocalypse, among others—and though the Word allows for more, it's clear that "two witnesses" are a symbol of integrity, reliability, and officiation.

Before the time of Christ, Israel was God's "witness" (*both* literally at the foot of Mt. Sinai, as well as of God's nature, character, morality, etc.; see Isaiah 42:6–7; 43:10, 12; 44:8; 49:5–7). On the Day of Pentecost described in the book of Acts, the message of Christ was delivered to the Jews as well as to the "proselytes" (2:10). Today, "proselyte" or "proselytizing" has a pejorative feel due to its historical association with pushy, preachy Christians who don't really care about the lost as much as they do about leading a "prospect" through "the sinner's prayer" so they can "check them off the list" and tell God later that they did their Christian duty. (It's this sort of superficial witnessing that Jesus was referring to when He railed against the pretenders: "Woe unto you, scribes and

Pharisees, hypocrites! for ye compass sea and land to make one proselyte, and when he is made, ye make him twofold more the child of hell than yourselves" [Matthew 23:15].) That unfortunate correlation aside, however, the original Greek word *prosēlytos* means "newcomer," "stranger," "alien," or, in the context of religious affiliation, "one who has come over from a Gentile religion to Judaism [or Christianity]" (see this endnote[64] for a fuller explanation).

Therefore, the tongues-of-fire phenomenon in Acts 2 was seen and experienced by *two early Christian witnesses*: the believing (Messianic) Jew and the believing (proselyte) Gentile. (The Gentiles also received the Holy Spirit; see Acts 10:44–46.) As we all know, when Christ died for us, He also destroyed the spiritual segregation between Jew and Gentile. As many *do not* know, the two loaves of bread presented as a wave offering to Jehovah during every annual Feast of Pentecost was a prophetic symbol of that seismic shift, representing both parties, now identical inside and out, both "waved" before God to be found equally acceptable as the Body of Christ and His New Church.

Remember also that the two loaves to be offered to the Lord had to be baked with only the finest flour (Leviticus 23:17), which the Jews sifted tediously. Because this act removed all of the grain's imperfections and lumps, this is said to be a symbol of righteousness and sinlessness, which characterizes Jesus in His perfection.[65] However, the dough was to involve leaven...which is a peculiar ingredient, considering that grain offerings with leaven were typically forbidden (Leviticus 2:11). Also, as we discussed almost exhaustively in the "Unleavened Bread" section earlier, leaven is a symbol of sin.

Why, for *centuries* before Christ, would the "prophetic" bread imagery involve both "sinless" fine flour and "sinful" leaven?...

Because *we* involve both.

We all have sin in us and the propensity to sadden the Lord with our less-than-ideal choices (Romans 3:23). Until we get to heaven, that's the reality of our current status. We will always be "leavened" in this life. Nevertheless, by accepting Jesus, He comes to live within us like fine flour, overpowering the death effects of sin-leaven and bringing the soul to life anew in righteousness (Romans 8:10).

Combine these ingredients—the Jew, the Gentile, the leaven of human nature, and the fine flour of a Savior—and put them in a refining oven. What does this make? The *perfect*, two-loaf wave offering to represent the Body of Christ being acceptable to the Father.

We are *in* the Church Age, and the harvest is always plentiful.

5

More on Understanding the Mystery and Importance of Pentecost

By Gary Stearman

In Hebrew, the word for "Pentecost" is *Shavuot*, which means "weeks." In the Jewish calendar, the Feast of Weeks is the festival of the wheat harvest in the land of Israel, which is always a metaphor of souls saved being brought into the household of God.

> Seven weeks shalt thou number unto thee: begin to number the seven weeks from such time as thou beginnest to put the sickle to the corn.
>
> And thou shalt keep the feast of weeks unto the LORD thy God with a tribute of a freewill offering of thine hand, which thou shalt give unto the LORD thy God, according as the LORD thy God hath blessed thee. (Deuteronomy 16:9–10)

As first given in Leviticus, it is seen as the culmination of seven weeks, plus one day—the day after the Sabbath. These fifty days are mentioned in the New Testament as *Pentecost*, the Greek word for "fifty."

Of all the observances of the Jewish festival calendar, the Feast of

Weeks is the most mysterious. In modern Judaism, Pentecost is always observed on two days, a mystery in itself. Because it floats on their calendar, it is called, "the festival without a date."

When most Christians think of Pentecost, they don't think of Jewish holidays at all. Quite naturally, their first thought is the book of Acts. This book—the history of apostolic activity in the formative days of the Church—is founded upon the dispensation of the Holy Spirit and the birth of the Church on Pentecost morning. By itself, it is one of the most amazing events in the history of the world.

The book of Acts opens near the end of the fifty-day period that began to be counted after the Feast of Firstfruits—the day that marks the Resurrection of our Lord. Luke opens his narrative in Acts by referring back to his Gospel, calling it "the former treatise." At the end of that "former treatise"—the Gospel of Luke—Jesus ascends into the heavens after meeting with many people. He ended his appearances by saying, "And, behold, I send the promise of my Father upon you: but tarry ye in the city of Jerusalem, until ye be endued with power from on high" (Luke 24:49).

Then, in Acts, after a forty-day gap, Luke writes:

The former treatise have I made, O Theophilus, of all that Jesus began both to do and teach,

Until the day in which he was taken up, after that he through the Holy Ghost had given commandments unto the apostles whom he had chosen.

To whom also he shewed himself alive after his passion by many infallible proofs, being seen of them forty days, and speaking of the things pertaining to the kingdom of God:

And, being assembled together with them, commanded them that they should not depart from Jerusalem, but wait for the promise of the Father, which, saith he, ye have heard of me.

For John truly baptized with water; but ye shall be baptized with the Holy Ghost not many days hence

When they therefore were come together, they asked of him, saying, Lord, wilt thou at this time restore again the kingdom to Israel?

And he said unto them, It is not for you to know the times or the seasons, which the Father hath put in his own power.

But ye shall receive power, after that the Holy Ghost is come upon you: and ye shall be witnesses unto me both in Jerusalem, and in all Judaea, and in Samaria, and unto the uttermost part of the earth.

And when he had spoken these things, while they beheld, he was taken up; and a cloud received him out of their sight.

And while they looked stedfastly toward heaven as he went up, behold, two men stood by them in white apparel;

Which also said, Ye men of Galilee, why stand ye gazing up into heaven? this same Jesus, which is taken up from you into heaven, shall so come in like manner as ye have seen him go into heaven. (Acts1:1–11)

Jesus rose before their wondering eyes, received into a "cloud." Many believe that this event foreshadows the moment when Christians will be caught up to be with Him. During the following ten days, they gathered and prayed until Pentecost:

And when the day of Pentecost was fully come, they were all with one accord in one place.

And suddenly there came a sound from heaven as of a rushing mighty wind, and it filled all the house where they were sitting.

And there appeared unto them cloven tongues like as of fire, and it sat upon each of them.

And they were all filled with the Holy Ghost, and began to speak with other tongues, as the Spirit gave them utterance. (Acts 2:1–4)

Festival of the Harvest

From its earliest days, Pentecost was known as a festival of the harvest. Long ago, the omer was offered by the high priest, who stood before the tabernacle, or later, the temple. It was the token of the Festival of Firstfruits. In Leviticus 23:11, it is called "the sheaf." In its most common sense, an omer was a dry measure that amounted to a little over two quarts. The offering of the omer marked the first day of a fifty-day countdown to Pentecost:

> And ye shall count unto you from the morrow after the sabbath, from the day that ye brought the sheaf [omer] of the wave offering; seven sabbaths shall be complete:
>
> Even unto the morrow after the seventh sabbath shall ye number fifty days; and ye shall offer a new meat offering unto the Lord.
>
> Ye shall bring out of your habitations two wave loaves of two tenth deals: they shall be of fine flour; they shall be baken with leaven; they are the firstfruits unto the Lord. (Leviticus 23:15–17)

The counting of fifty days from Firstfruits to Pentecost is typical of redemption in general. For the Jew, in the observance of the Feast of Weeks (*Shavuot*), it has always represented the maturing relationship between God and Israel.

Think for a moment about the traditions that originated in the first years of the Church. Its central doctrines were handed down through men brought up in the traditions of Jewish history and prophecy. Their lives had literally revolved around keeping the festival calendar. They had heard the teachings of Christ. Some, no doubt, had heard them in person. They had listened to His parable of the harvest, when the good wheat and the tares, which had grown up together would be separated. They knew about the Festival of Harvest (Pentecost).

When Peter preached that historic sermon on the Day of Pentecost, he quoted the prophet Joel, whose entire book is centered around the harvest cycle.

When Joel wrote the prophecy, "I will pour out my Spirit upon all flesh," he set the theme of the harvest. "The field is wasted, the land mourneth" (Joel 1:10); "That which the palmerworm hath left hath the locust eaten" (Joel 1:4). That was a prediction of Israel's exile. The Jews must be scattered from their land, to suffer among the nations.

But that's not all. Joel also spoke of Israel's restoration and linked it to the time of the spring harvest.

> Be glad then, ye children of Zion, and rejoice in the Lord your God: for he hath given you the former rain and the latter rain in the first month.
>
> And the floors shall be full of wheat, and the fats shall over-flow with wine and oil.
>
> And I will restore to you the years that the locust hath eaten. (Joel 2:23–25)

This is a prophecy that began to be fulfilled in 1948. Furthermore, Israel was restored on May 14 of that year, during the season of the harvest cycle. This date, 5 Iyar in the Jewish calendar, was the twentieth day in the counting of the omer.

In Matthew 13:39, Jesus said, "The harvest is the end of the world." He indicated that end-time events would culminate in a great harvest of souls. Pentecost, the day following the seventh Sabbath, marked the end of the grain harvest, at which time two loaves baked with leavening were brought to the temple and held aloft by the high priest. These two loaves symbolize the completed bodies of the redeemed. It seems quite reason-able that one is emblematic of spiritual Israel, while the other represents the Church.

Early and Latter Rains

Once the Holy Spirit was poured out in Jerusalem on the Day of Pentecost, the prophecy of the "early rain" was fulfilled. Someday, the Holy Spirit will be poured out again in Jerusalem. It should be a fulfillment of the promise of a "latter rain." Will it also occur on Pentecost? In Peter's second sermon, he spoke of the ultimate fulfillment of the festival cycle. In Acts 3:19–21, he said:

> Repent ye therefore, and be converted, that your sins may be blotted out, when the times of refreshing shall come from the presence of the Lord;
>
> And he shall send Jesus Christ, which before was preached unto you:
>
> Whom the heaven must receive until the times of restitution of all things, which God hath spoken by the mouth of all his holy prophets since the world began. (Acts 3:19–21)

The prophetic implications of the festival cycle lie in God's promise to restore the earth to the state of glory that He originally intended. So that His people would always remember what He has in mind, He planted this prophetic scenario in their culture. At some future time known only to Him, the story will become a reality. The festival narrative is arranged around events in their calendar that foreshadow their future counterparts.

We find ourselves experiencing another wave of renewed excitement about the near possibility of the Rapture of the Church. Interest in the prophesied culmination of the Church Age has waxed and waned over the years, periodically rising to its present level when world developments seem to signal a radical change. At the moment, an imminent war in the Middle East, coupled with financial collapse on a global scale, have aroused the attention of Christians around the world.

Many years ago, we began to share our studies on the traditions of Pentecost, which demonstrated numerous remarkable connections with the prophetic conclusion of the Church Age. It is the fourth and central feast among the seven feasts of Israel: Passover, Unleavened Bread, First-fruits, Pentecost, Rosh HaShanah, Yom Kippur, and Tabernacles. The first three are spring festivals, representing the blood sacrifice and resurrection. The last three come in the fall, calling forth judgment and the establishment of the Kingdom. At the middle—in summer—is Pentecost. In the Bible, it is represented by two loaves of leavened bread, held aloft by the High Priest. Today's Jews celebrate it in a ceremony called "decorating the bride." Most remarkably, it typifies the catching-away of the Church.

Every year, we are reminded afresh of Pentecost's enormous significance in the panorama of biblical prophecy. Better than any other ancient festival, it embodies the elements that we associate with the catching-away, or Rapture, of the Church. We list them here to refresh your memory concerning the joys of this season and to remind you that the Lord is near, even at the door. Our studies have made it increasingly obvious that the Lord—specifically for latter-day understanding—has inculcated specific memorial elements into the Jewish traditions surrounding Pentecost. As we continue to investigate this important subject, we are repeatedly impressed by the strong connections between Pentecost and the coming change of dispensation that will move the world into the age of the Kingdom.

Watching this festival, we constantly stress that it is the most mysterious of all the Jewish festivals. First called the "Feast of Weeks," it is the major harvest festival. But its associated symbols and metaphors invoke meanings far beyond the mere harvesting of grain.

Among the Jews, this is the festival that celebrates the giving of the Torah, or the Law. This was the time, they say, when Jews gathered at the foot of Mt. Sinai. There, they heard the actual voice of God as He spoke the commandments. The Bible does not seem, at first glance, to make a clear connection between Sinai and Pentecost. Nevertheless, the link is there, if we take the time to look.

Furthermore, this festival presents the ceremony of the marriage between God and Israel. In this context, Passover (which precedes Pentecost by seven weeks) becomes the period of God's courtship of His wife.

The spiritual picture that emerges is the establishment of a faithful and holy household. A bit later, we'll examine it in greater depth.

Judgment of the Fruit of Trees

Traditional Jewish belief holds that Pentecost is the day when the fruit of trees is judged in heaven. Christians throughout the Church Age have believed that the fruit of one's life will be judged following the Rapture. This, of course, is the picture given by the apostle Paul to the church at Corinth in 2 Corinthians 5:10:

> For we must all appear before the judgment seat of Christ; that every one may receive the things done in his body, according to that he hath done, whether it be good or bad.

The Resurrection of Jesus as the omer or offering of Firstfruits began a countdown to the completion of the Body of Christ. The good fruit of the righteous will be reviewed, then will come the judgment of the depraved world.

But there is more to add to this picture. Jewish families observe Pentecost by wearing bright and festive clothing. Homes are decorated with green plants and celebrative foods are prepared.

According to Hayyim Schauss, writing in *The Jewish Festivals*:

> "The custom of decorating the homes and synagogues with green plants is variously explained. One theory is that the day is marked in heaven as the day of judgment for the fruit of the trees." Here is the theme of fruit-bearing, which points to the Judgment Seat of Christ following the rapture and resurrection. In Matthew 7:15–20, Jesus likened true versus false teaching to the fruit of trees:
>
> "Beware of false prophets, which come to you in sheep's clothing, but inwardly they are ravening wolves. Ye shall know them by their fruits. Do men gather grapes of thorns, or figs of thistles?

Even so every good tree bringeth forth good fruit; but a corrupt
tree bringeth forth evil fruit. A good tree cannot bring forth evil
fruit, neither can a corrupt tree bring forth good fruit. Every tree
that bringeth not forth good fruit is hewn down, and cast into
the fire. Wherefore by their fruits ye shall know them" (Matthew
7:15–20).

Jesus teaches that false prophets can be known by their "fruits." The
righteous will bring forth "good fruit." This is the "fruit of the Spirit" spoken of in Galatians 5:22–23: "But the fruit of the Spirit is love, joy, peace,
longsuffering, gentleness, goodness, faith, meekness, temperance: against
such there is no law."

Pentecost, associated with the giving of the Law, is a time for review-
ing one's "fruit." To the Jews, the Law is seen as the way toward such
"good fruit." But the apostle Paul wrote that only through the Resurrection of Christ can we bring forth "fruit" unto God.

Wherefore, my brethren, ye also are become dead to the law by
the body of Christ; that ye should be married to another, even to
him who is raised from the dead, that we should bring forth fruit
unto God. (Romans 7:4)

By His Resurrection, Christ became our "firstfruits." He laid the
"foundation" that made it possible for the Church to bring forth more
"fruit." This principle is clearly stated in 1 Corinthians:

For other foundation can no man lay than that is laid, which is
Jesus Christ.

Now if any man build upon this foundation gold, silver, precious stones, wood, hay, stubble;

Every man's work shall be made manifest: for the day shall
declare it, because it shall be revealed by fire; and the fire shall try
every man's work of what sort it is. (1 Corinthians 3:11–13)

The judgment of the fruit of trees corresponds to the reward of the believer in heaven, here likened to a building. The good fruit of the believer's life will be judged for its final worth. This is exactly the theme seen in the Jewish festival of Pentecost.

Pentecost: Festival without a Date

Remember, Pentecost is called *Shavuot* (or "Weeks") in the Hebrew. It is so named to reflect the nature of its dating. It always falls seven weeks plus one day after the offering of the omer.

Since it is based on counting the seven weeks following the Feast of Firstfruits, the date of Pentecost is fluid. Thus, when the Jewish calendar was still based upon visually marking the appearance of the new moon, Pentecost could fall on fifth, sixth, or seventh of Sivan. The final determination of the date would depend upon whether the months of Nisan and Iyar were full, thirty-day months.

To this day, if one calculates the date of Pentecost as actually instructed in the Bible, its precise timing is always something of a mystery. Symbolically then, it becomes a perfect model of the Rapture, since its date is also beyond reckoning.

According to Schauss, the date for Pentecost cannot be fixed. He calls it the "only Jewish festival for which there is no fixed date." The books of Moses do not state on which day of the month Pentecost is to be observed. They say only that it is to be celebrated fifty days after the offering of the omer [Firstfruits], the first sheaf of the grain harvest, which was to be offered on "the morrow after the Sabbath," as we have already seen in Leviticus 23:15–17, making it a Sunday.

Following the destruction of the second temple in AD 70, it became physically impossible to commemorate either the Festival of Firstfruits or the waving of the loaves at Pentecost. The calendar date for Pentecost then became fixed at the sixth of Sivan—the date upon which it is remembered to this day.

The Trumpet and the Bride

Around the same time, Jews adopted Pentecost as the time to commemorate the giving of the Law. The nineteenth chapter of Exodus relates that the giving of the Law at Sinai came in the third month on the third day of the month. This places the event at the time of Pentecost. They call it, "the revelation at Sinai." This revelation and the symbols of harvest are intertwined to give full significance to the observance of Pentecost.

In the festival, they also commemorate the symbolism of the marriage between God, the Groom, and Israel, the Bride. They view Mt. Sinai as an enormous *ketubah*, or wedding canopy. The two tablets of the Law that Moses brought down from the mountain represent the marriage contract.

As mentioned earlier, this image is developed at Passover, which becomes the time of God's courtship with Israel, and Pentecost comes to represent the marriage itself. In its traditional aspects, Pentecost pictures the catching away of the Bride more clearly than any other festival.

We have noted before that the blowing of the ram's horn on Rosh Hashanah has been suggested as representing the final trumpet of resurrection. But does it really? Is it possible that the trumpet blast on Rosh Hashanah represents instead, a "memorial" of the heavenly Pentecost trumpet?

> In the seventh month, in the first day of the month, shall ye have a sabbath, a memorial of blowing of trumpets, an holy convocation. (Leviticus 23:24)

Dispensational Change

Let's review the part Pentecost has played at the beginning of two dispensations—law and grace. The rabbis say that the dispensation of law began on Pentecost. On that day, a heavenly trumpet was heard at Mt. Sinai. The Jews remember this as a time when their national identity took a new direction: "And when the voice of the trumpet sounded long, and waxed louder and louder, Moses spoke, and God answered him by a voice" (Exodus 19:19).

Many Jews say that this, the first mention of a trumpet blast in Exodus, was regarded by the spiritual leaders of Israel as having occurred on Pentecost. Exodus 19:1 tells us that this event came about in Sivan, the third month.

Furthermore, the trumpet was blown not by a human, but by a heavenly being. It was God's own voice! Moses and the chosen people had gathered at Mt. Sinai, on the third day of preparation, wherein they washed themselves, cleaned their clothes, and were forbidden to touch the mountain. When God came down, a trumpet sounded long and loud, filling the people with awe and terror. On that occasion, the fire of God's glory descended and God gave the Ten Commandments. Here, we find the only heavenly trumpet recorded in the Old Testament. The next such trumpet should sound on the day of Rapture and resurrection, making the day of Pentecost an interesting possibility for that event

> For the Lord himself shall descend from heaven with a shout, with the voice of the archangel, and with the trump of God: and the dead in Christ shall rise first. (1 Thessalonians 4:16)

The Order of the Resurrections

For the Gentile, Pentecost represents the relationship between Christ, the Bridegroom, and His Bride, the Church. As mentioned earlier, the Resurrection of Jesus was a literal firstfruits offering that looked forward to the resurrection of all the faithful:

> But now is Christ risen from the dead, and become the firstfruits of them that slept.
>
> For since by man came death, by man came also the resurrection from the dead.

For as in Adam all die, even so in Christ shall all be made alive.
But every man in his own order:

Christ the firstfruits; afterward they that are Christ's at his
coming.

Then cometh the end, when he shall have delivered up the
kingdom to God, even the Father; when he shall have put down
all rule and all authority and power. (1 Corinthians 15:20–24)

Here, Paul writes about Christ's Resurrection in a specific way. Let's
consider that word, "order." There is a specific order in the Jewish festival
cycle, and there is a well-defined order of resurrections. Paul, an Israelite
of the tribe of Benjamin, had been schooled in the Scriptures at the feet of
Gamaliel. Without a doubt, he was intimately aware of the tiniest details
of the Jewish calendar. Therefore, when he speaks of Christ as the "firstfruits" in the context of an order of events, he knows that the next event
in that sequence is Pentecost.

But of course, this was not the Pentecost at which the Holy Spirit was
given to the infant Church. No, that signal event had already taken place
more than twenty-five years before Paul wrote these words. He must,
then, be referring to a future Pentecost that would conclude the harvest—
Christ's Resurrection being the "firstfruits," and our resurrection coming
at the end of the harvest. Might this possibly occur on a future Pentecost?
Might this be the time when Christ will come to take home His followers?
Remember, Pentecost is the formal conclusion of the grain harvest.

It seems that when Paul used the word "order," he intended the reader
to see the order of the Jewish festival cycle. It is at least possible that he was
suggesting that the resurrection could take place on a future Pentecost.

Apparently the early Church thought so. The *Zondervan Pictorial
Encyclopedia of the Bible* offers the following comment:

The Church Fathers highly regarded Pentecost. Easter was always
on Sunday, so Pentecost was also. Between Easter and Pentecost,
there was to be no fasting. Praying was done standing, rather than

kneeling. During this time, catechumens [new converts] were baptized. Many expected, because the Ascension had taken place near Pentecost, that Christ would return in the same season.

Pentecost was a time of expectation for the early Church. They felt that Christ might come for His own during this period. Why did they believe this? Was it because of its closeness to the time of the Ascension, or was it because of something else they had been taught? Remember, Christ's actual Ascension took place forty days after His Resurrection. Ten days later, the Holy Spirit empowered the Church for its future role in the harvest of souls…the fifty days till Pentecost.

Prophecies of Summer

Biblically, the spring harvest is often seen to typify the "harvest" or catching-away of the Church. As we have seen, this is the season when grain and fruit crops come to maturity. Fruit is judged and stored. Wheat is now safe in the granaries of the land. At Pentecost, a small sample is taken, ground into flour, and baked into two loaves. They are the leavened "test loaves" of the new harvest. As already stated, they typify the two bodies of the redeemed at the end of the age: Israel and the Church.

Bread and fruit are the perfect picture of redemption, blessing, and bounty. But to Israel, at the time of Jacob's trouble, the harvest will not bring satisfaction. Instead, there will be the realization that something drastic has happened. The prophet Micah graphically describes this, as we see in Micah 7:1–6:

Woe is me! for I am as when they have gathered the summer fruits, as the grapegleanings of the vintage: there is no cluster to eat: my soul desired the firstripe fruit.

The good man is perished out of the Earth: and there is none upright among men: they all lie in wait for blood; they hunt every man his brother with a net.

That they may do evil with both hands earnestly, the prince asketh, and the judge asketh for a reward; and the great man, he uttereth his mischievous desire: so they wrap it up.

The best of them is as a brier: the most upright is sharper than a thorn hedge: the day of thy watchmen and thy visitation cometh; now shall be their perplexity.

Trust ye not in a friend, put ye not confidence in a guide: keep the doors of thy mouth from her that lieth in thy bosom.

For the son dishonoureth the father, the daughter riseth up against her mother, the daughter in law against her mother in law; a man's enemies are the men of his own house. (Micah 7:1–6)

Here, the prophet Micah speaks as the voice of Israel in the latter days. The time is set at the end of fruit harvest—late April through early June— the season that begins with Passover and ends with Pentecost.

The summer fruits have been "gathered," or harvested. The Hebrew term *asaph* means "to remove, or take away." But one of its major meanings is "to be gathered to one's fathers at death." This translation easily fits in the context of these verses. The good fruit of the righteous has been harvested and taken for inspection and storage. From Micah's point of view, the friends of Israel have gone away.

As we continue, Micah's distress becomes more clear. He has a deep desire for the fruit that has been removed. What is this fruit? Verse 2 tells us that it is the "good man" who has "perished" from the earth. This fits perfectly with the idea of the judgment of the fruit of trees.

"Perish" is represented by the Hebrew verb *avad*, meaning, "to cause to vanish"! As the picture develops, it is easy to see that Micah's vision perfectly describes the conditions that will prevail when righteous mankind is instantly transported from the earth at the catching-away of the Church.

The unredeemed remainder of humanity left on earth is devoid of morals, scruples, or ethics. Lust and extortion become the basis of human behavior. There are no trustworthy friends; even family members can't be trusted without a suitable bribe.

The Rapture has come. It is an event associated with early summer. And immediately afterward comes a horror that Israel has long dreaded. Verse 4 says, "the day of thy watchmen and thy visitation cometh; now shall be their perplexity." What is this visitation?

Jewish translations of this verse often say, "The day of your visitation from the north has come." The Jerusalem Bible translates it as, "Today will come their ordeal from the North, now is the time for their confusion."

Because of this fact, some ancient Jewish expositions of this passage link it with Ezekiel's prophecy of Gog's invasion of Israel.

This interpretation stems from the fact that the word for "watchman" in Hebrew contains the root word for "north" or "northern." Thus, "watchman" is built around a word that carries the meaning of both "watch" and "north." Hence, ancient expositors see in this verse an invasion from the north. One of the most graphic of all latter-day prophecies is Ezekiel's narrative of Gog's invasion of Israel. It comes from the north:

And thou shalt come from thy place out of the north parts, thou, and many people with thee, all of them riding upon horses, a great company, and a mighty army. (Ezekiel 38:15)

What makes Micah's prophecy most interesting, of course, is that it links the Rapture of the Church with Ezekiel's prophecy of the northern invasion.

First, there is the gathering up of the fruitful righteous. They are "made to vanish" from the face of the earth. Then comes a time of horror, when Israel realizes that she is without friends upon earth. Israel's difficulties begin in earnest, as society becomes totally degenerate.

Apparently, shortly thereafter, the prophesied invasion takes place.

But the sequence begins at the summer harvest. Without a doubt, this is the picture meant to come to our minds when we think of the Rapture. Jesus prophesied His own coming for the Church in this way:

And when these things begin to come to pass, then look up, and lift up your heads; for your redemption draweth nigh.

And he spake to them a parable; Behold the fig tree, and all the trees;

When they now shoot forth, ye see and know of your own selves that summer is now nigh at hand.

So likewise ye, when ye see these things come to pass, know ye that the kingdom of God is nigh at hand.

Verily I say unto you, This generation shall not pass away, till all be fulfilled. (Luke 21:28–32)

What Jesus is talking about here is the very beginning of a long procession of events that will bring the Kingdom to planet earth at last. Preparation is being made for the judgment of the fruit of trees, here, a metaphor of Israel and all the nations in the latter days. This metaphor applies to the change of dispensation that will come with the spring festival calendar.

The Bridegroom and His Bride

Another well-known example of this thought is the coming of the Bridegroom for the bride in the Song of Solomon. He comes for His bride at the time when spring is fully come and the fruit is almost ripe:

The voice of my beloved! behold, he cometh leaping upon the mountains, skipping upon the hills.

My beloved is like a roe or a young hart: behold, he standeth behind our wall, he looketh forth at the windows, showing himself through the lattice.

My beloved spake, and said unto me, Rise up, my love, my fair one, and come away.

For, lo, the winter is past, the rain is over and gone;

The flowers appear on the earth; the time of the singing of birds is come, and the voice of the turtle is heard in our land;

The fig tree putteth forth her green figs, and the vines with the tender grape give a good smell. Arise, my love, my fair one, and come away. (Song of Solomon 2:8–13)

Once again, in another notable Rapture passage, we see that the season is spring. Here, the coming of Solomon for his Shulamite bride is an obvious type of the Lord and His relationship with the Church—the Bridegroom coming for His Bride.

In this picture, the figs and grapes will soon be ready for harvest. The beloved is depicted as skimming across the mountain tops. In other words, he is near, but has not quite yet arrived. The season is late spring. Soon, the fruit will be gathered. This passage implies that the Church will be taken home. The season is that of Pentecost.

Then, according to the prophet Micah, Israel will realize that her best and closest friend has vanished from the earth.

A Chosen Bride from Moab

As earlier noted, grain harvest comes in late spring. It was in this season that Ruth became the wife of Boaz.

Trees are laden with fresh foliage. Flowers are in bloom. The heart of humanity is light and optimistic. Jewish homes are decorated with fresh greenery and floral decoration. Hayyim Schauss says:

Even in school the instruction is festive and breathes the spirit of the holiday. The children are taught the book of Ruth. So clear is the imagery thereof that they are carried back to the days of old, when Jews reaped the harvest of the fields of their own land.

The older children sit around a long table with the teacher and study the Book of Ruth. But their thoughts are not on their studies; they are thinking of Bethlehem, the town where David was born and spent his childhood. They imagine they are standing at harvest time in the fields that surround the town. Gentle breezes blow from the hills of Judah. The fields are filled with freshly-cut sheaves. They hear the whir of the reaping scythe, and the song of the workers in the fields. And everywhere is the pleasing aroma of the newly-fallen gleanings which Ruth is gathering in the field.

Their thoughts are carried still farther afield when the teacher recites, or rather sings, as he interprets "Akdomus" [an eleventh-century poem]. King David is descended from Ruth and Boaz, and from David's seed, it is believed, will come the Messiah. In "Akdomus" is presented vividly a picture of the day when the Messiah will have arrived, the time of eternal bliss on Earth.

Many have said that the book of Ruth is the most beautiful narrative in the entire Bible. Ruth was a Gentile woman of Moab who married into a Hebrew family. At that time, there was a famine in Israel, which the family hoped to escape by emigrating from Bethlehem to Moab. These events took place during the period of time in which the judges ruled the land after the death of Joshua. It was a time of deep moral and spiritual decline.

The husband and both sons died in Moab, widowing Ruth, her mother-in-law, Naomi, and her sister-in-law, Orpah, who soon departed. Naomi elected to return to her home in Bethlehem, urging Ruth to stay with her own people, as Orpah had done. But Ruth faithfully determined to go with her and remain by her side until death separated them.

They arrived in Bethlehem at harvest time. As was the right of the poor, Ruth gleaned in the fields for their food. As a poor foreigner, she had nothing to expect but a future of perpetual widowhood. Yet she found favor in the sight of Boaz, a wealthy landowner. He allowed her to glean even among the sheaves of the field. At Naomi's instruction, Ruth went to the threshing floor and laid down at the feet of Boaz on the night of Pentecost, the festival of harvest. That night, he claimed her and redeemed her as a near kinsman had the right to do. After securing the legal right to marry her, they were united in marriage, and she bore him a son. That son was Obed, the grandfather of David the king.

Ruth: A prophetic picture of the Gentile Bride of Christ

This is the story of a Gentile bride in a strange land who started out with only her faith. She provides a prophetic picture of the Gentile Bride of Christ—the Church. On the very night of Pentecost, Ruth came to lie at the feet of Boaz.

At midnight, startled, he awoke to discover the woman of whom he had earlier taken note as she gleaned in his fields. His acceptance of her set in motion a series of legal steps, which he undertook promptly, in order that he might marry her. Ruth had remained completely faithful to Naomi. Boaz knew of her reputation as a virtuous woman. He completed her righteousness in their marriage, making her an heir to the Messianic promise. A poor woman of Moab was brought into the lineage of the throne of David, from which the Messiah would one day rule over the nations.

According to Michael Strassfeld, writing in *The Jewish Holidays, a*

Guide and Commentary, rabbinical authority calls for the book of Ruth to be read at Pentecost, because:

> [1] The story is set at the time of harvest [2] Ruth's conversion to Judaism is thought to bear a close resemblance to one's voluntary acceptance of the Torah and God's covenant at Sinai, [3] King David, according to tradition, was born and died on Shavuot [Pentecost]. The book of Ruth, of course, ends with a genealogy from Ruth down to King David. And, [4] Reading Ruth means that the totality of the Torah is celebrated on Shavuot, for Ruth is part of the...writings that together with the Torah and the prophets compose the whole Bible.

An Overnight Vigil for Jews

At this point, it is of great interest to note another element of this Jewish festival: The Jews stay up all night in their synagogue's house of study, poring over *tikkun*. This consists of little sections from each book of the Torah and the Talmud, representing all of the most important texts of Judaism. But even this act of staying up all night sets forth the theme of resurrection. Michael Strassfeld writes of this custom:

> A kabbalistic custom emanating from the mystics in Safed (sixteenth century) is to stay up the whole (first) night of Shavuot studying Torah. The *tikkun* —a set order of study—was composed of selections from the Bible, rabbinic literature, and even mystical literature such as the Zohar. In this fashion the kabbalists prepared for the momentous revelation of the following morning.
>
> This practice of staying up all night is in stark contrast to that of the Israelites at Sinai, who according to tradition slept late that morning and had to be awakened by Moses. In atonement for this, Jews nowadays stay awake all night. The sense of preparation for Sinai is heightened by a mystical tradition holding that the

skies open up during this night for a brief instant. At that very moment, we are told, God will favorably answer any prayer. The kabbalists also regard Pentecost as the wedding of God and Israel. Therefore, we stay up all night to "decorate the bride."

What an incredible picture of the Rapture! The opening of the heavens "for a brief instant" corresponds with the message in 1 Corinthians 15:51:

Behold, I show you a mystery: We shall not all sleep, but we shall all be changed, in a moment, in the twinkling of an eye...

Here is the perfect picture of Christ coming to catch away His Bride! And where does He take her? To the marriage supper of the Lamb! This corresponds with Pentecost, when the Jews "stay up all night to decorate the bride."

To an amazing degree, their activities remind us of the catching-away of the Church, the Bride of Christ; Pentecost has many features that are suggestive of the Rapture. It is associated with harvest, marriage, and the taking of a Gentile bride. Its date is variable, picturing the unpredictability of Christ's coming for His own.

Like all the Jewish festivals, it is made up of pictures and ideas that preserve God's truth, even among those whose eyes may be temporarily blinded by unbelief or the rote practices of tradition. Quite significantly, it marks the birth of the Church Age, and before that, the giving of the Law. Each of these events marks the turning to a different dispensation: first to law, and then to grace. In the eyes of God, therefore, Pentecost must be an important festival. To the Jew, it is a vital part of the festival calendar.

Today, observant Jews seek spiritual purification (called *taharah*) on Pentecost night. Their vigil of prayer and study is the culmination of a process that begins every year on Firstfruits, and continues through the counting of the omer. It reaches a climax on this particular night.

From *The Three Festivals* by Josef Stern, we read:

During these days and weeks [between Passover and Pentecost], our personal efforts to cleanse ourselves of spiritual impurities are critical, as the Torah says...you shall count for yourselves. However, if we make sincere efforts during [the counting of the *omer*], we can be assured that Hashem [the Lord] will shower us with an outpouring of *taharah* on the night of *Shavuos*, as the Sages said, someone who comes to purify himself will receive Divine help.

More than just a single night, the Pentecost vigil is said to set the tone for an entire year, if it is taken seriously:

The Zohar also reminds us that the *taharah* that descends on those who immerse themselves in Torah study on this night is a fragile thing. Unless we take active steps to preserve it throughout the year we cannot be assured that it will remain with us.

It is a day laden with rich spiritual types and symbols. Many Jews will stay up all night in the hope of catching that precise moment when the sky opens for an instant. They will read their Scriptures, pray, and "decorate the bride."

Will the Church be called home on a night such as this? Although it is impossible to name this particular night as the time of the Rapture, it is nevertheless a stimulating thought for these last days. What a picture of our blessed hope! There are many precedents for what will happen to all believers on that day. Paul was once taken to heaven:

I knew a man in Christ above fourteen years ago, (whether in the body, I cannot tell; or whether out of the body, I cannot tell: God knoweth) such an one caught up to the third heaven. (2 Corinthians 12:2)

To be *"caught up"* is the blessed hope of faithful Christians everywhere. Scripture makes it quite plain that this is our destiny. In some inexplicable way, the sky will open for a moment, and we shall be gone...vanished without a trace! The language of 1 Thessalonians 4:17 is very similar to the preceding passage:

> Then we which are alive and remain shall be caught up together with them in the clouds, to meet the Lord in the air: and so shall we ever be with the Lord.

This will be the biggest historical event since the Lord's own Ascension into the heavens. And it will certainly be the trigger that sets in motion an increasingly cataclysmic series of judgments. In Paul's second letter to the Thessalonians, the restraining force associated with the presence of the Body of Christ is given as the key factor in the timing of latter-day events. Its removal will provide the environmental changes necessary for evil to advance toward the fulfillment of prophecy.

In other words, as long as we are present and active, the revelation of the wicked one, and wickedness in general, cannot manifest in full power. Pentecost, the festival that has traditionally marked the dispensational change from law to grace, seems ideally suited as the model for this event. Then, a rapid succession of biblical marvels will bring Messianic rule to the earth.

> He which testifieth these things saith, Surely I come quickly. Amen. Even so, come, Lord Jesus. (Revelation 22:20)

6

The Seven Feasts: Part III

Fall

The last three of the seven major feasts—Trumpets, Atonement, and Tabernacles—occur in the fall. The question in this section is not "How *did* Jesus fulfill them?" but "How *will they be* fulfilled in prophecy?" Jesus most definitely interacted with certain elements of these feasts during His time on earth, but their ultimate culmination lies in the future.

We will, in the following pages, deviate slightly from the layout and format that we have followed up to this moment, in order to address theological concepts regarding the future.

Prophetic Passages of Revelation

Studying and understanding the feasts has provided an illuminating way of seeing how much God truly cares about us. He has put detail into every fulfillment in order to show us the precision and intentionality of His plan. The first season of feasts—the spring feasts—have seen their fulfillment in a manifestation of the Messiah: through His life, His sacrifice, His victory over death, and His Resurrection. The summer feast—the Pentecost—represents more than the Church era itself; it mirrors not only the fulfillment of God's plan for His people of all nationalities, it likewise celebrates this intangible icon of His invitation to Gentiles to join His long-term plan.

The third season of feasts—those that take place in the fall—are unique from the first two seasons in that their fulfillment is still forthcoming. While we see partial fulfillment in the way Jesus *has already* interacted with the celebrations, we also see that these are indicative of events that still loom on the horizon.

Currently, we live in an era when the Gentile Church has been invited to partake in God's plan. Since the summer feast is a reflection of this inclusion, we find ourselves in an exciting time when the Gentile Church of today, like its Jewish counterpart, awaits the fulfillment of prophecy. However, our backgrounds aren't necessarily the same. For those of Jewish heritage, much of the teachings and religious edifications derive from the Torah, the Talmud, and other ancient Hebrew sources. The Christian Church, however, pulls its teachings from sources that, at times, are entirely different. For example, we benefit from centuries of Church Fathers and religious philosophers who have developed modern denominational doctrines via careful interpretation of the Old and the New Testament. In this way, both Jews and Gentiles have separate but complementary pools of resources from which to derive information about the upcoming fulfillment of prophecy.

With this in mind, we find it helpful here to address some of the modern Christian doctrines regarding future events.

Even in Christian academia, doctrinal teachings can vary greatly. This wide swing is particularly seen among end-times teachings, since these tell of events that haven't yet taken place and are thus subject to interpretive speculation. Because of this, we will only deviate from our conversation of feasts long enough to truncate the end-times teachings that are the most mainstream. When it comes to prophetic passages, particularly in the book of Revelation, there are typically four views held and taught today:

Preterism: This is the view that the prophecies outlined in the book of

Revelation were fulfilled through the struggles of the early church during the time of Rome's power. The "beast" mentioned throughout the book represent the Caesars who demanded to be worshiped, and it is perceived that this book reached its apex between AD 70 and 500, meaning that while it offers insight to Christian persecution and church history, it isn't relevant today.[66]

Historicism: This view holds that Revelation describes a series of historical events that have by now transpired. The chronological events claimed to be represented within Revelation vary among those who hold this view. Some cite such historical entities as Hitler, Napoleon, the Huns, or even Islam as key players in what they now perceive to be a historical narrative of completed events.[67]

Idealism/Spiritualism: This analysis of Revelation sees its story as metaphorical and its events as holding spiritual principles with meanings pertaining to a general battle of good vs. evil, one which righteousness wins. This view doesn't allow for the events in the book of Revelation to point to specific, literal events that have or will take place on earth.[68]

Futurism: This view holds that the book of Revelation depicts actual events that will take place in the future, and that will usher in end-time events. To be sure, every miniscule detail may not be taken literally— "they do not mean the Antichrist is going to have seven heads and ten horns"[69]—yet the personalities and events represented in the Revelation story are interpreted to point to real people and events that will emerge and occur at the appointed times leading to the end of the earth.[70]

Since the authors of this book subscribe to the futurist view, that is the angle from which we'll present the forthcoming doctrines and passages. Revelation 1:1 readily sets the tone for the upcoming content:

The Revelation of Jesus Christ, which God gave unto him, to shew unto his servants things which must shortly come to pass; and he sent and signified it by his angel unto his servant John. (Revelation 1:1)

At first glance, it's clear that Jesus intentionally revealed this information to John, to share this message with His servants. Few would argue this point. However, within the same passage, the phrase "which must shortly come to pass" is often the source of much debate. Many people interpret this to mean that the manifestation of events outlined in this work would occur within a short amount of time of its authorship. Understanding the term "shortly" in its Greek context helps clarify.

"Shortly" is derived from *en tachos,* with *en* meaning "in, through, or with,"[71] while *tachos* indicates speed over "a brief space (of time)," or "in haste."[72] While some interpret this passage to mean that events outlined will occur soon thereafter, many state that the *true* meaning of this phrase indicates a rapid succession after the onset of trigger events.[73] However, when studying closely, we realize that the events of Revelation, once launched, rapidly escalate to many game-changing events, such as the Rapture of the Church, the rise of the Antichrist, the eventual rebuilding of heaven and earth, and the reuniting of God with His people. If this book were written about events that are behind us, then God's people would be with Him now, and His Kingdom would already be established here with us (see Revelation chapters 21–22). However, these things have not yet occurred, as is apparent with a mere glance around us at the debauchery of our world.

Further, this introduction tells us that the book is the "Revelation of Jesus Christ," *not* the "revelation of a lot of scary events," or "the revelation of a history lesson." While there are indeed some terrifying elements in the narrative, they are puzzle pieces to a larger story, one in which, at the end, our Lord and Savior is revealed to and reunited with us.

Thus, if this chronology had run itself out centuries ago, as some claim, it would have left the saints suspended in a current, earthly type of limbo, as though God simply forgot to trim the chronological ends of His timeline, accidentally leaving centuries attached that serve no purpose in His plan. Not only this, but if we were at the end of this story, the Church would be both unified and filled with only the most biblically sound doctrine. We understand that when we meet Him face to face, there will be no denying who He is:

> That at the name of Jesus every knee should bow, of the things in heaven, and things in earth, and things under the earth; and that every tongue should confess that Jesus Christ is Lord, to the glory of God the Father. (Philippians 2:10–11)

Thus, there can be no denying that, were we currently in the proximity to God that the end of Revelation describes, the Church *certainly* would not be in the shape it's in. These authors, then, see the condition of our world as proof that Revelation's happenings are still forthcoming. We perceive that there are trigger events lurking in the literal, chronological future that are outlined in Revelation and thus initiate the end of the world as we know it, and that will lay the groundwork for the reign of Jesus Christ in His Kingdom here on earth.

This is the blessed hope anticipated through the celebration of the Fall Feasts.

Many views and interpretations render varying timelines regarding the Rapture. Likewise, the passion with which believers argue these points of view can escalate, causing the debate to become a divisive element among brethren. For this reason, many speakers and ministers avoid the topic. In a room filled with those who would argue for such positions as Rapture being scheduled to occur "pre-Tribulation," "mid-Tribulation," "pre-wrath (similar to mid-Tribulation)," and even "post-Tribulation," these authors have often seen those who wish to remain neutral borrow the phrase "pan-Tribulation" to describe their position. By this, they mean that, regardless of timing, God is in control, and it will all "pan out" in the end.

What Is the Rapture?

The Rapture is an event believed to take place in the end-times; it is a moment when Jesus will take all Christians back to heaven with Him.

According to the doctrine of the Rapture, the faithful, deceased believers will be resurrected first and taken to meet the Lord in the air. Then the living who have accepted Him as their Savior will be caught up as well; after that, we will all spend eternity with Him.

> For the Lord Himself shall descend from heaven with a shout, with the voice of the archangel, and with the trump of God: and the dead in Christ shall rise first:
>
> Then we which are alive and remain shall be caught up together with them in the clouds, to meet the Lord in the air: and so shall we ever be with the Lord. (1 Thessalonians 3:16–17)

Most theological schools of thought agree that the Rapture will be a sudden event, and even Jesus made it clear that only the Heavenly Father knows the timing:

> For yourselves know perfectly that the day of the Lord so cometh as a thief in the night. (1 Thessalonians 5:2)

> But as the days of Noah were, so shall also the coming of the Son of man be.
>
> For as in the days that were before the flood they were eating and drinking, marrying and giving in marriage, until the day that Noe entered into the ark,
>
> And knew not until the flood came, and took them all away; so shall also the coming of the Son of man be.
>
> Then shall two be in the field; the one shall be taken, and the other left.
>
> Two women shall be grinding at the mill; the one shall be taken, and the other left.
>
> Watch therefore: for ye know not what hour your Lord doth come. (Matthew 24:37–43)

But of that day and hour knoweth no man, no, not even the angels of heaven, but my Father only. (Matthew 24:36)

Imminence

The notion of "imminence" regarding the Rapture indicates that the event will be unforeseen and sudden. Recall earlier that we mentioned Revelation 1:1 and that many scholars view the translation of "shortly" (*en tachos*) as meaning a rapid succession of events that will be kicked off by a trigger happening. Considering this in conjunction with the passages we looked at establishing that the Rapture will be sudden and unexpected, its imminence has understandably made its way into mainstream end-time teachings. Many—usually those who subscribe to the pre-Tribulation view of the Rapture—even regard it as *the* trigger event that will launch us into a quick succession of end-time prophetic happenings because it will mean the "restrainer" will have been removed (more on this in a bit).

It's important to understand how this distinction plays out in prophetic teachings because, whereas some people think that Revelation is based on events that have already occurred the doctrine of imminence indicates that the timeline *could begin* at any moment. In other words, one God-ordained occurrence could launch this series of end-times events at any time.

The concept of imminence may appear to introduce a problem for those who hold a mid-Trib Rapture position. After all, how can a happening be sudden and unforeseen if prophetic "stars" have aligned to indicate its approach? Mid-Tribulationism requires a series of events to occur before the world is "ready" for the Rapture.

Consider this: If we ask a pre-Tribber, "Could God come today?" the answer will be "Yes!" A mid-Trib believer, on the other hand, may begin to answer the question by referring to recent newspaper headlines, prophetic tutorials, or timelines displaying critical events that must first occur. So how is the question of imminence—which

Scripture establishes as true—reconciled in the mid-Tribulation perception?

Those who argue the mid-Trib case explain that, to them, "imminence" is in a different context. They state that this is why the Bible so clearly emphasizes the importance of vigilantly watching (Matthew 24:42), of not being deceived (Revelation 2:3–12), and of remaining faithful until the end (Revelation 2:10). The Rapture's element of surprise to the world, they assert, is because "the love of many will wax cold" (Matthew 24:12), and that except for the fact that God Himself will cut time short, "even the elect would be deceived" (Mark 13:22).

In other words, the imminence and suddenness of the Rapture refers to the way in which those who are not carefully watching—in what Scripture explains will be an *unprecedentedly deceitful time*—will remain completely unaware of what is happening around them, and thus will be taken by surprise when the event occurs. The "imminence" of the event is because people (even believers) will be spiritually asleep; the Rapture will "sneak up" on them. First Thessalonians 5:2–6 reinforces this:

> For yourselves know perfectly that the day of the Lord so cometh as a thief in the night.
>
> For when they shall say, Peace and safety; then sudden destruction cometh upon them, as travail upon a woman with child; and they shall not escape.
>
> But ye, brethren, are not in darkness, that that day should overtake you as a thief.
>
> Ye are all the children of light, and the children of the day: we are not of the night, nor of darkness.
>
> Therefore let us not sleep, as do others; but let us watch and be sober.

Accountability

We've mentioned that those who believe the Rapture is imminent will always answer "yes" to the question, "Could the Rapture happen today?"

Those who are watching for kick-start events that must happen before the Rapture can occur will answer, "Well, no, because first we have to see (insert prophetic event here) take place." This point becomes another premise often used in defense of a pre-Tribulation Rapture position, in that the design should keep saints living in a high level of accountability, never letting them "get too comfortable" with how much time they have on earth.

Consider Matthew 24:43–44:

But know this, that if the goodman of the house had known in what watch the thief would come, he would have watched, and would not have suffered his house to be broken up.

Therefore be ye ready: for in such an hour as ye think not the Son of man cometh."

In this passage, God acknowledges the very point we are making: If we know exactly when Rapture will happen, we will live according to that timing and not in a constant state of preparedness.

The Restraining Force

Since the Rapture is believed to be imminent, some state that the restraining force referred to in 2 Thessalonians 2:3–8 offers a clue about its timing:

Let no man deceive you by any means: for that day shall not come, except there come a falling away first, and that man of sin be revealed, the son of perdition;

Who opposeth and exalteth himself above all that is called God, or that is worshipped; so that he as God sitteth in the temple of God, shewing himself that he is God.

Remember ye not, that, when I was yet with you, I told you these things?

And now ye know what withholdeth that he might be revealed in his time.

For the mystery of iniquity doth already work: only he who now letteth will let, until he be taken out of the way.

And then shall that Wicked be revealed, whom the Lord shall consume with the spirit of his mouth, and shall destroy with the brightness of his coming.

Many people interpret the phrase "he who now letteth will let" to indicate a force that restrains the one who "might be revealed in his time," and whose "mystery of iniquity doth already work." Thus, this thinking goes, the source of evil, iniquity, and the one who will bring about end-times manifestations already occupies this earth, awaiting his opportunity to act, while the restraining force holds this malevolence at bay "until he be taken out of the way."

Many say that Holy Spirit and/or the Church are the restraining force alluded to here, and as long as these two entities are on the earth, the Antichrist cannot rise to power. This is the basis for viewing the Rapture as a trigger that opens the door for end-times events; the removal of the restrainer allows evil to culminate and clears the path for Antichrist.

According to many who believe in a pre-Tribulation Rapture, the Church is the restraining force, while others assert that it is the Holy Spirit. If the latter is true, then the argument arises: without the Holy Spirit, no one could come to God during the Tribulation, that terrible time that will befall those who are left on the earth following the Rapture. Nor would those who are "left behind" have the spiritual intuition to deny the Mark of the Beast that Antichrist will implement during the Tribulation. Yet, it seems reasonable when reading Revelation to perceive that God accepts repentance throughout the catastrophic happenings, and that there will be a number of people who refuse to take the Mark. In fact, there are plenty of indications throughout Revelation that people will be given opportunities to atone for their sins (see Revelation 9:20, 11:1–14, 14:6). It also appears that mankind will have the option to surrender to God's will all the way until the very end of the earth as we know it, which seems impossible without the Holy Spirit's presence.

For this reason, many believe that the restraining power that is removed is the Church, but that the Holy Spirit remains on earth until the end of the Tribulation. This concept is reinforced in that the imminence of the Rapture is fortified by Christians' inability to even pinpoint the Antichrist's identity or watch him rise to power; *they themselves*, merely by being on earth, obstruct his very ability to surface.

In another point of view, the "restrainer" is merely a spiritual force God sets in place, one that will remain until the preordained point on His timeline when the Antichrist comes to power.

Church Not Referenced; Israel Back in Focus

Throughout the New Testament, Jesus and His messengers made it a point to broaden the eligibility for salvation to people of all races and nationalities (see Galatians 3:28–29). In Revelation, however, we see that references to the Church are paused (from Revelation 4–22 we see no mention of the Church being here on earth), while the focus on Israel begins to increase.

Interestingly, in Revelation 1:20, the churches are called candlesticks:

The seven stars are the angels of the seven churches: and the seven candlesticks which thou sawest are the seven churches.

Revelation 4:5 later describes the throne room of God:

And out of the throne proceeded lightnings and thunderings and voices: and there were seven lamps of fire burning before the throne, which are the seven Spirits of God.

For some, these two passages correlate to show that, around the time of the events described in Revelation 4, the Church has been taken to heaven.

In the meantime, while references to the Church seem to be put on hold, the emphasis on the nation of Israel, for the first time since the Old Testament, once again becomes heavy. To name just a few of the highlights of Israel's part in the storyline of Revelation:

- The Israelites are "sealed" (Revelation 7:4): "And I heard the number of them which were sealed: and there were sealed an hundred and forty and four thousand of all the tribes of the children of Israel."
- The nation of Israel is said to be represented by a woman travailing in childbirth (Revelation 12:1): "And there appeared a great wonder in heaven; a woman clothed with the sun, and the moon under her feet, and upon her head a crown of twelve stars."
- When this woman is endangered by the dragon, she flees to a safe place prepared by God for her (Revelation 12:4): "And the woman fled into the wilderness, where she hath a place prepared of God, they should feed her there a thousand two hundred and threescore days."
- The story culminates with God destroying earth as we know it and rebuilding a new heaven and a new earth, which will be the new Jerusalem (Revelation 21:2): "And I John saw the holy city, new Jerusalem, coming down from God out of heaven, prepared as a bride adorned for her husband."

While the theme of Israel's role in end-times prophecy is the topic of many interesting books, for our research here, suffice to say that around the time described in Revelation 4, the theme of Scripture seems to shift abruptly from emphasizing all-inclusive salvation (Galatians 3:28) to highlighting the importance of Israel's role.

Essentially, the argument becomes that this period is about giving Israel a second chance to recognize Jesus, and that the Church is removed because the Church Age has come to an end; this period of time is simply not about us.

This belief is drawn from those who interpret Daniel 9:24 to be a sentence made by God outlining a time when this nation would be oppressed:

Seventy weeks are determined upon thy people and upon thy holy city, to finish the transgression, and to make an end of sins, and to make reconciliation for iniquity, and to bring in everlasting righteousness, and to seal up the vision and prophecy, and to anoint the most Holy.

The same scholars then turn to on Daniel 12:7 for further illumination:

And I heard the man clothed in linen, which was upon the waters of the river, when he held up his right hand and his left hand unto heaven, and sware by him that liveth for ever that it shall be for a time, times, and an half; and when he shall have accomplished to scatter the power of the holy people, all these things shall be finished.

Deliverance from Wrath

Regardless of one's belief about the timing of the Rapture, few debate that it *will* occur before the wrath of God is poured out on the earth. Several biblical passages fortify this position. For example, Jeremiah 30:7 states:

Alas! for that day is great, so that none is like it: it is even the time of Jacob's trouble [another term for the Tribulation, or God's wrath], but he shall be saved out of it.

Some believe this refers to Israel (as it would align with the context of the entire chapter of Jeremiah 30), and that the hiding place prepared for the woman in labor (Revelation 12:6) is the way Jacob's seed will be protected. Others assert that this is a guarantee that Christians won't be required to endure the wrath of God. Since the New Testament places such emphasis on Gentiles being welcomed into the fold, these individuals now perceive such passages to refer generically to God's people of all nations.

There are other scriptural references to the Lord protecting His people from His wrath. First Thessalonians 1:10 states:

And to wait for his Son from heaven, whom he raised from the dead, even Jesus, which delivered us from the wrath to come. (See also 1 Thessalonians 5:9, Romans 5:9, and Revelation 3:10.)

Further, we see a correlation between historical outpourings of God's wrath and pre-deliverance of His people. For example, Matthew 24:37–39 states that "as the days of Noah were…so shall the coming of the Son of man be." Those who rebelled against God did not see the impending judgment, yet Noah and his family were spared (Genesis 6–9). Passages such as this are most often interpreted to mean that God intends to remove His people from the earth *before* His wrath is poured out upon it. In fact, in this case, *God Himself* shut Noah's family into the ark before allowing His destructive judgment to fall on the earth, killing every other living thing (Genesis 6:16, 21).

The account of Noah is referenced in Luke 17:26–30, where it is also compared to the situation with Sodom and Gomorrah, alongside God's rescue of Lot and his family. We are again told that we can expect the future events to play out similarly:

And as it was in the days of Noe, so shall it be also in the days of the Son of man.

They did eat, they drank, they married wives, they were given in marriage, until the day that Noah entered into the ark, and the flood came, and destroyed them all.

Likewise also as it was in the days of Lot; they did eat, they drank, they bought, they sold, they planted, they builded;

But the same day that Lot went out of Sodom it rained fire and brimstone from heaven, and destroyed them all.

Even thus shall it be in the day when the Son of man is revealed.

Bearing this in mind, the element of timing takes on the dimension not merely of when tragedy occurs on this earth, but when persecution of the Church, international or global war, escalating evil, and natural disasters such as earthquakes and plagues—which have gone on for centuries—transition from being acts of nature or mankind the Lord allows to become the *intentional wrath of God poured out upon the land in His righteous judgment.* Thus, it becomes necessary to try to understand *when,* in the chronology of Revelation, it becomes the wrath of God from which calamity pours. When we determine this, we can safely bet that we have defined the latter segment of the window of time in which the Rapture may occur.

While it is outside the scope of this book to provide a detailed outline of each event foretold in Revelation, it is pertinent here to understand the timing of certain ones as they pertain to God's wrath. For this reason, we'll highlight some key points in the book of Revelation that *some* perceive to be the appearance of God's wrath. The roster of events discussed in the coming pages is not exhaustive; there are many good books that can illuminate the topic for the curious reader who wishes to study further.

The first reference to God's wrath in Revelation is in chapter 6:16–17. Earlier in the same chapter, we saw six "seals" unleash a variety of hardships—including plagues, earthquakes, pestilence, war, disease, famine, and likely even cosmic upheaval—upon the earth. These certainly fit the description of the happenings Jesus warned His followers about in Matthew 24. However, while we're shown in Revelation 6 that it is God who is sending such trials to the earth, Scripture doesn't indicate that they are necessarily enactments of God's wrath. The wording indicates that the "wrath" is actually mentioned out by people of the earth who suffer these calamities. While the "wrath" they speak of could point to the wrath of God, it could also be that the term is used speculatively by people who fearfully acknowledge that they have encountered the power of a Supreme Being. (Much later, in Revelation 9:20, we see that mankind "repented not" of their evil deeds, which indicates that, at the point we're now at in the timeline, people could still repent, should they choose.)

We also see in Revelation 7:3 that God "seals" His people in their foreheads, showing that *some* are still here (as mentioned previously, some argue that the Church will have been been removed from the earth at this point, and that these are Israelites who remain). In Revelation 7:14, saints appear in the throne room who "came out of great tribulation"; many say this indicates that the Rapture has occurred somewhere near this point. In 8:1, we see that the seventh seal is opened, an event so somber that all of heaven is silent for a half hour. In 8:5, an incense offering made of the prayers of the saints is sent to the earth, likely causing cosmic disturbances. Immediately thereafter, seven angels, each carrying trumpets, appear, ready to sound their instruments. The first four do so, bringing celestial wreckage upon the earth that corrupts the waters, destroys foliage, and even darkens the sky (8:7–12).

Then, something interesting occurs. An angel flies through the midst of heaven, repeating the word "woe" (Revelation 8:13). Taken from the Greek *ouai*, a quick definition of this word appears to indicate "a primary exclamation of grief."[74] Yet, further investigation shows that it "must be regarded either as an accusative of exclamation…[or] genitive of the evil the infliction of which is deplored." The same word, used in 1 Corinthians 9:16 in the phrase "woe is unto me," is defined as "divine penalty threatens me."[75] With this in mind, this is another point at which some say God's wrath enters the scene. If this *is* the case, then the notion of imminence is supported as well, since this view is somewhat obscure and wouldn't stand out as a likely candidate for the timing of God's wrath. Thus, its timing would certainly be unexpected.

If it is true that "woe" is the moment of the commencement of God's wrath, then it could explain why, in the next verse, 9:1, the occurrences take on a distinct element of spiritual warfare. Locusts are unleashed upon the earth; Abaddon/Apollyon is named the people's leader; four angels are freed from the Euphrates with their terrifying armies of horsemen; and we are brought to chapter 10, where the angel clothed with a cloud (discussed previously) stands on land and sea, declaring there is no more time.

Notice that Revelation 10:7 states:

But in the days of the seventh angel, when he shall begin to sound, the mystery of God should be finished, as he hath declared to his servants the prophets.

We mentioned earlier that God Himself refers to the Rapture as a mystery (1 Corinthians 15:51–52). This *could* mean that it occurs at the seventh trumpet, which sounds in Revelation 11:15 (a commonly held perception).

In the meantime, we two witnesses enter the scene, prophesying in sackcloth for "a thousand two hundred and threescore days" (Revelation 11:3). Right after these men are killed by the beast, lie dead for three days, and then arise (Revelation 7–11), a great earthquake occurs on earth, and the seventh trumpet sounds. Since we are given the timeline regarding these witnesses as three and one-half years (there's that number again), many use this as an argument for a mid-Tribulation Rapture.

Later in the same chapter, we see the indubitable appearance of the wrath of God. If we couldn't be certain that the previous catastrophic events of Revelation were definitely not the outpouring of God's wrath, all ambiguity is lost at this point. The elders in the throne room praise God, saying, "We give thanks, O Lord God Almighty…because thou hast taken to thee thy great power, and hast reigned. And the nations were angry, and thy wrath is come, and the time of the dead, that they should be judged." We likewise see a new dynamic element unfold as the temple of God in heaven is opened, the Ark of the Covenant appears, and there even more cosmic disturbances occur (Revelation 11:17–19).

At this point in the timeline, the woman in travail and her flight from the dragon becomes a focus (Revelation 12), followed by the rise of the Beast and his image (Revelation 13). By the time we reach chapter 14, few could doubt that the days of God's wrath are upon the earth:

And the third angel followed them, saying with a loud voice, If any man worship the beast and his image, and receive his mark in his forehead, or in his hand,

The same shall drink of the wine of the wrath of God, which is poured out without mixture into the cup of his indignation; and he shall be tormented with fire and brimstone in the presence of the holy angels, and in the presence of the Lamb. (Revelation 14:9–10)

And another angel came out from the altar, which had power over fire; and cried with a loud cry to him that had the sharp sickle, saying, Thrust in thy sharp sickle, and gather the clusters of the vine of the earth; for her grapes are fully ripe.

And the angel thrust in his sickle into the earth, and gathered the vine of the earth, and cast it into the great winepress of the wrath of God.

And the winepress was trodden without the city, and blood came out of the winepress, even unto the horse bridles, by the space of a thousand and six hundred furlongs. (Revelation 14:18–20)

Unless one believes the Rapture and the Second Coming are the same event (which we will discuss in upcoming pages), most will agree that, by this point, since God's wrath is now the driving force of the calamities bludgeoning the earth, the Rapture of the Church has occurred.

Western Society and Escapism

Some argue that the pre-Tribulation Rapture position is popular among evangelicals because it "tickles the ears" of those who want to believe that they will never face persecution. In this way, the stance—often referred to as "escapism"—is accused of being popular only because it is conducive to Western culture. The logic behind this argument is that throughout history, in nearly every culture, Christians have been—and are still being—persecuted, often to death. Thus, these argue that the notion of God rapturing His Church to help them escape martyrdom is contradictory to what we see taking place every day. Western society gets picked on a bit via this point of view, because countries such as the United States have, so far, been immensely blessed in that we have not had to stand against such adversity. So, when a preacher says, "We will not be martyrs; we aren't going to be here when that happens," those frustrated with escapist mentality point to the places across the world where such travesties are already occurring. Their evidence contradicts this theological position. In turn, Christians suffering across the globe see Western-culture Christians as asserting such doctrines in order to appease their own sense of dread regarding persecution.

The key principle to keep in mind in responding to this argument is that the Rapture—according to Scripture—is designed to remove God's people from the earth before He pours out His wrath on it. (While *people* persecute each other, the end times will be characterized by an outpouring of *God's* wrath that escalates as well).[76] Likewise, the doctrine of the Rapture is meant to be a comfort, not a cop-out regarding the level of diligence that Christians should live out each day. Thus, some are frustrated when Christians show nonchalance about the hardships that will be faced by those who are left behind.

Jesus Himself placed a lot of emphasis on saints being prepared for and vigilant about the end times (see Matthew 24, Mark 13, Luke 17 and 21). He even pointed out signs that would indicate that a particular generation *would* see the end of times. He warned that it would be a difficult period, and He admonished people not to be deceived. While He promised *protection* from God's wrath, He never guaranteed that there would not be adversities. Instead, He said to be vigilant in watching for signs, and to be ready to flee if necessary. He even warned the generation alive at the time of the end-days to be prepared for martyrdom.

Many ask, "Why would He do this if the Church wasn't going to be here?" But, Scripture also reminds us of the blessed hope: the beautiful day when—suddenly, without warning—these trials will all be over.

This isn't to say that the Rapture couldn't happen before God's wrath befalls the planet. It could be that that the blessed event will occur far before things have escalated to that degree. These authors would love to believe that one day, long before such hardships have struck, we will suddenly find ourselves in the presence of our Creator. Similarly, some subscribe to a pre-Tribulation Rapture view not because they are afraid of hardship or because their faith/relationship in God lacks depth, but rather, this is their *honest* assessment of what the Bible says. As stated previously, these authors see both views (pre-Tribulation and mid-Tribulation) compellingly argued. To say that people latch onto a pre-Trib view because it "tickles their ears" isn't necessarily a fair or objective analysis of their motivation. For those who would fault pre-Tribulationists, accusing them of merely wanting to dodge the terrifying events that are prophesied, we suggest you their spiritual fruit. Sure, some who think such travesties simply are not their problem may be looking toward the future with a sense of escapism. Others, however, may be storing up food, supplies, or other essentials and collecting "what to do if you're left behind" or "how to survive the Great Tribulation" literature for others should the need someday arise. These folks may honestly believe that though they won't personally be here, they can still show compassion for those who will remain.

The Trumpet Debate

First Corinthians 15:51–52 has been mentioned earlier, but now we'll revisit it in a different context:

> …at the last trump: for the trumpet shall sound, and the dead shall be raised incorruptible, and we shall be changed.

This passage clearly indicates that at the time of the Rapture, the "last trump" will sound. For many, this easily places the Rapture at the seventh trumpet of Revelation 11:15, well into mid-Tribulation timing. We also see just after that, in Revelation 11:18, that the time of the wrath of the Lord is upon the earth. Thus, this timing *does* align with the notion that saints are removed *before* the outpouring of wrath. (That is to say, *unless* the seals referenced earlier in Revelation are to be interpreted as part of

God's wrath.) However, some state that this trumpet is different than the one mentioned in Matthew 24:31, which says that the Lord will send His angels at the sound of a trumpet to "gather His elect from the four winds." For these scholars, the earlier mention of Tribulation events causes them to state that this *must* be a different trump than the one sounded in Revelation 11. The argument, then, is that one of these trumpets announces judgment, while another announces the Rapture.

Parousia

The notion that saints will be "caught up together" in the air to meet the Lord comes from the combination of Greek words *parousia*, meaning, "a personal arrival or coming," which refers to Christ's arrival, with the word *harpzado*; meaning "to snatch away by force."[77] These words, used with each other and in consideration of the general message of the preceding passages, fortify the general doctrines involving the Rapture. However, many confuse the Rapture (combined *parousia* and *harpzado*) with the Second Coming (combined *parousia* and *epiphaneia* or *ephanes*). While both of these events portray Jesus Christ's personal arrival, the context in which He arrives and the circumstances of each event are distinct. Confusion about these two events usually further convolutes the conversation of Rapture timing. Thus, it helps to clarify that these are viewed by many scholars as two distinctly separate events.

The Rapture of the Church, as mentioned, is outlined in such Scriptures as 1 Corinthians 15:51–52 and 1 Thessalonians 4:16–17. Notice that the latter passage specifies that we will be called up to meet the Lord in the air. Since verse 17 uses the Greek term *harpazdo* in conjunction with *parousia*, it denotes a sudden taking-up of the saints who arise to meet Jesus us in the air—but notice that *His feet never touch the earth's surface* in such passages.[78] Instead, saints ascend to join Him and are then taken to heaven with Him.

The Second Coming, however, refers to the second time He will make an appearance during end-times events. In this instance, *parousia*, is used in conjuction with *epiphaneia,* which means "brightness" or "splendor."[79] Passages that combine these terms (for example, 2 Thessalonians 2:8; *ephanes,* meaning "glorious"[80] in Acts 2:20) change the trajectory and notoriety of the *parousia* visitation from that of a sudden and secretive "snatching" to that of a public appearance that demands recognition and worship. These distinctions reveal an elevated and triumphant status of Jesus' return, showing that the world will then recognize Him for who He is. His entry will be visible to all in glory and splendor.

Between the Rapture and the Second Coming will be a period that will last for either *part* of the seven-year Tribulation period *or for its entirety,* depending on whether the Rapture occurs before the beginning of the Tribulation or just before the wrath of God is poured out (as discussed previously). However, it is important to note, again, that the Second Coming is understood as being a separate event from the Rapture. In passages describing the Second Coming, Jesus' appearance is described as a visitation wherein He will descend *completely to earth* and reveal Himself to the kingdoms of earth as King of Kings and Lord of Lords as He rules with an iron scepter. This arrival is described in Revelation 19:11–16, with elements distinguishable from that of the Rapture: Heaven will open and Jesus will ride a white horse. He will be recognized as faithful and true while He simultaneously takes charge of the earth's kingdoms, both judging and making war with them. The armies of heaven, also riding white horses, follow Him. Jesus is clothed with robes dipped in blood, which establishes Him as the sacrifice who atoned for our sins. This, in conjunction with the iron scepter, the sword of His Word, and the winepress of His wrath, shows that this will be a just but fear-inciting day of reckoning as He comes to establish His Kingdom on earth.

Pre-Trib Doctrine Is Older Than You Think...

Many people state that the doctrine of a pre-Tribulation Rapture is only a couple hundred years old, and that the Church Fathers fully expected to live through the entire Tribulation, should it occur during their lifetime. Furthermore, rumors circulate that the entire idea was dreamt up by, of all people, a fifteen-year-old girl in Scotland, far removed from the theological origins of our faith (more on this later). However, this isn't entirely true. Several Church Fathers are said to have held a pre-Trib view and even taught it in their writings.

Ephrem the Syrian (AD 338–373) said:

> For all the saints and elect of God are gathered, prior to the tribulation that is to come, and are taken to the Lord lest they see the confusion that will overwhelm the world because of our sins. And so, dear brothers, it is the 11th hour, and the end of the world comes to the harvest, and angels, armed and prepared, hold sickles in their hands, awaiting the Empire of the Lord. And we think that the world is completely blind to this, arriving at its downfall early. Commotions are happening, wars of diverse peoples, battles, incursions of the barbarians threatened, and countries are being desolated. We seem neither afraid when hearing the rumors of wars nor seeing them appear. We should repent! If we are afraid of them it is because we do not wish to be changed; we need to repent of that too![81]

Similarly, Irenaeus' (AD 130–202) work has been established over the centuries as vital to Christian doctrine. He was a student of Polycarp, who knew the apostle John.[82] In fact, Polycarp was even said to be John's student,[83] making Irenaeus a "theological grandson" of the Great Revelator. Irenaeus, then, would likely have some authority on prophetic Scripture, considering his proximity to the author of the book of Revelation. He stated in his work *Against Heresies*:

> And therefore, when in the end the Church shall be suddenly caught up from this, it is said, There shall be tribulation such as has not been since the beginning, neither shall be.[84]

Further, he spoke against allegorizing such things, viewing the events as being both *real* and *forthcoming*:

> In the Resurrection we will have fellowship and communion with the holy angels, and union with spiritual beings. The new heavens and earth are first created and then the new Jerusalem descends. These are literal things, and Christians who allegorize them are immature Christians. (*Against Heresies 5.35*)

As mentioned, a widely circulated rumor states that the concept of a pre-Tribulation Rapture is a "new" doctrine, borne from a fifteen-year-old girl in the early 1800s in Scotland. This would be good reason for some to find it suspect. However, knowing that this notion dates back as far as those who immediately followed the apostle John lends credibility to the view. While the concept wasn't as widely circulated before the 1800s, it *did* have a revival in the early part of the nineteenth century, especially in evangelical circles.

The Revival of the Pre-Tribulation View

The study of Rapture timing could—and has, on many occasions—be the topic of its own book. We have shown that early in church history, at least some prominent Church Fathers who believed the Rapture would precede the Tribulation. However, as in modern times, there were differing views in that era as well. Some perceived the Rapture and the Second Coming to be one and the same event, and these folks fully expected to endure the hardships of the Tribulation, should those days to dawn during their time here on earth. During the following centuries, views that stated believers would be here to face at least part of—if not all—of the Tribulation circulated with more mainstream popularity than the pre-Tribulation view enjoyed. But one day, in early 1830, a fifteen-year-old girl named Margaret MacDonald from Port-Glasgow, Scotland, changed that. Soon, the notion of a pre-Tribulation Rapture became repopularized, which is how the common belief that the doctrine is only a couple hundred years old came about.

Margaret McDonald claimed that God had granted her visions of an imminent Rapture: one that would happen *before* the Great Tribulation. Her vision showed a two-phase Rapture that would be divided between a pre-Tribulation, partial Rapture and a second harvest, which would occur at the Second Coming of Christ.[85] After confiding in John Darby, who visited her in her home shortly thereafter, it is said that he "tweaked" her assessment of a two-phase Rapture according to his own perspective, modifying it to state that *all* believers would be taken at the same time.[86] "Within a few months, her distinctive prophetic outlook was mirrored in the September, 1830 issue of *The Morning Watch* and the early Brethren Assembly at Plymouth, England."[87]

For many, this cleared up the theological ambiguity that occurred when one must reconcile the Scriptures promising the Church deliverance from God's wrath against doctrines having them endure the entire Tribulation.

John Nelson Darby (1801–1882) originally asserted many theological theories that would later become known as dispensationalism, futurism, and even the imminence of the Rapture. During many religious conferences held during the nineteenth century, prophetic interpretations of the Bible took on a new point of interest, as dispensationalist and futurist points of view grew in popularity. Alongside these views, the pre-Trib and mid-Trib Rapture doctrines grew in popularity as well. (Before this, some vagueness had lingered regarding the two contexts of the term *parousia*,[88] which left believers interpreting these events interchangeably). This was only one of many scriptural distinctions upon which the pre-Trib Rapture was revisited and revitalized.

Prophecy conferences trended throughout the end of the nineteenth century and the early parts of the twentieth. These gatherings provided a place for frontrunners of modern doctrine to exchange information and set a new precedent for theological circulation. (There was the Niagara Bible Conference in New York, to mention one,[89] which was "founded in 1875, [and] became a prototype for others" like it in subsequent decades.[90]) Many of these gatherings featured transmission of information on such hot, "modern" topics as dispensationalism, futurism, and the newly reexamined idea of a pre-Tribulation Rapture.

In addition to the theological material being exchanged at such events was the fact that many frontrunners of doctrinal development in that era made it a point to attend. These notable individuals latched onto the pre-Trib Rapture theology and began to spread its teaching. Among these were Cyrus Scofield (who perpetuated the doctrine at the Sea Cliff Bible Conference in Long Island and through his influential Scofield Reference Bible, which entered production in 1909), and D. L. Moody, of Moody's Bible Training School, later known as Moody Bible Institute.[91] Naturally, such well-known men with resources for perpetuating their doctrinal beliefs were in a position to circulate the notions they picked up at such conferences. *And,* the reintroduction of pre-Trib Rapture was readily embraced, not only because of its appeal (no one wants to face the Great Tribulation!), but likewise, because of the theological "question marks" (such as the seeming "disappearance" of the Church from the picture in Revelation 4–22) that these individuals felt the doctrine cleaned up.

As a result, pre-Tribulation commentary circulated via materials such as Bible commentaries and theological training publications put out by these influential conference attendees, nudging the pre-Trib theology into acceptance alongside Scripture in many mainstream evangelical circles. Other theologians involved in sharing the teachings included R. A. Torrey, superintendent of Moody's school; A. C. Gaebelein (1861–1945); a prominent Methodist minister and public speaker; L. S. Chafer; Dr. H. Ironside; and James Gray. These men, also known as movers and shakers in the world of theology, made a strong impact through vehicles such as their printing/publishing endeavors, public speaking, and biblical and theological training centers. Thus, their endorsement of pre-Trib doctrine was quickly spread and widely accepted during the twentieth century.

At the end of the day, the authors of this book believe that God has intentionally left the topic of the timing of the Rapture to be mysterious. Jesus Himself stated in Matthew 24:36, "But of that day and hour no one knows, not even the angels of heaven, but My Father only." *Even Jesus Himself does not know.* Thus, we should simply identify the important principles of each doctrine and do our best to live in the way that God would have us to live. In a nutshell: We should be wary of deception; live as though Jesus could come back any moment; and make earthly preparations as though we expect to endure the long haul. If the Rapture occurs before the Tribulation and stockpiled supplies are left abandoned, it's a win/win situation. Those who are in heaven will not give so much as a sigh for the "wasted" resources put into earthly preparation, and they may provide necessities to one left behind who attempts to avoid the economic trade system that will be implemented by the Beast.

The three fall feasts are tied together in a forward-looking theme of prophetic events. They are the Feast of Trumpets (Rosh Hashanah), the Day of Atonement (Yom Kippur), and the Feast of Tabernacles (Sukkot). The first is Trumpets, which brings on a ten-day period of repentance and penitence. This period ends with the Day of Atonement, the day of obtaining forgiveness for wrongdoings. Five days after this, the Feast of Tabernacles begins, which is a celebration of redemption and deliverance. Sounds simple enough, right? For many, the face-value explanations of these feasts provide ample reason to observe and celebrate them. However, deeper exploration reveals many details that point toward the future and show that even as God planned and fulfilled the first feasts with meticulous intent through the First Advent of Christ, as examined earlier in this work, He intends to complete some similar and dynamic work through the prophetic events linked to the fall feasts as well. Let's dig in…

Trumpets

Scripture Reference

And the Lord spake unto Moses, saying, Speak unto the children of Israel, saying,

In the seventh month, in the first day of the month, shall ye have a sabbath, a memorial of blowing of trumpets, an holy convocation.

Ye shall do no servile work therein: but ye shall offer an offering made by fire unto the Lord. (Leviticus 23:23–25)

Observations and Prophetic Implications

On the first day of the seventh month each year, Israelites were instructed to watch the sky for the new moon, which would provide confirmation that the awaited new month was upon them. This particular day, called Rosh Hashanah, was the marker of day one in the Hebrew month Tishri, which falls in the September and October range of the today's Gregorian calendar. When workers saw that the new moon had arrived, they were to blow trumpets to summon all workers to come in from the fields and enjoy a day of rest. These instruments were also known as *shofars*, made of the horn of a ram, in remembrance of the substitute ram that was sacrificed in Isaac's place in Genesis 22.

Tishri was the first month on the Jewish calendar, so this is also the Jewish Civil New Year. As mentioned, this day is also known as Rosh Hashanah, which means "Head of the Year."[92] The day called everyone to begin to prepare for the Day of Atonement, which commenced ten days afterward. This may have been the first month of the year, but it was the seventh and *final* month in the religious season, meaning that these Jews would soon make the pilgrimage to Jerusalem for the Feast of Tabernacles, which would be the final trek to the Holy City required for *that year*. They wouldn't return until Passover of the next year.

The Rosh Hashanah feast, as mentioned earlier, launched a ten-day preparation period for the Day of Atonement (more on this later). This time of getting ready was known as the "Awesome Days," "Days of Awe," "High Holy Days," or the "Ten Days of Repentance." Jewish tradition holds that on the first day of this prep period, the Jews would participate in the *Tashlich*,[93] a cleansing of their sins by wading into a river or stream while saying the prayer of Micah in 7:18–20:

> Who is a God like unto thee, that pardoneth iniquity, and passeth by the transgression of the remnant of his heritage? he retaineth not his anger for ever, because he delighteth in mercy.
>
> He will turn again, he will have compassion upon us; he will subdue our iniquities; and thou wilt cast all their sins into the depths of the sea.
>
> Thou wilt perform the truth to Jacob, and the mercy to Abraham, which thou hast sworn unto our fathers from the days of old.

It was customary in that day for shofars to be blown on the first of the month, so that people would know the new moon—thus the new month—had arrived, but on the first of *Tishri* the instruments were sounded louder and longer than at any other time of the year..[94] Then, the shofars would be left silent until the Day of Atonement. During the ten-day period, people would reflect on their deeds over the past year and attempt to right any wrongs they may have done, knowing that the day of judgment was upon them.[95]

Trumpets, throughout Scripture, are used to signal victories for the Lord or His people. We see examples of this in Joshua 6, where the trumpet blasts called Jericho's city walls to come tumbling down, giving the Israelites triumph, and in King David's reference to God as his "horn of salvation," indicating spiritual victory (Psalm 18:2). In prophetic events, the sound of the trump signals Jesus' returns in power and glory (Revelation 19). Since Jesus holds all the supremacy of God's army and is the Lamb behind the redeeming power of the horn of salvation, we know that at His return, the trumpets will sound, proclaiming His complete authority rendering all power from on high.

Prophetically, we see that the shofar also initiates catastrophic events (Revelation 9). The Day of the Lord will be announced using a trumpet (Joel 2:1) and the seventh trumpet in Revelation 11 will call for worship of God for His triumph. This indicates that the shofar is often used to announce warfare, and each time it is used at God's command, He and His people are victorious. The vision of Jesus' return painted in Revelation 19 shows the King of Heaven leading His holy army and coming to make warfare against the evil of the ages.

Consider the war hero who returns after a victorious battle: He comes through the city gate as instruments (often shofars) hail his arrival. The streets are lined with cheering onlookers who recognize their champion, and the captives of warfare are imprisoned or otherwise dealt with as part of the triumphant warrior's victory. Then, the king, queen, or supreme governmental authority presents the hero with the key to the city or kingdom. This gesture denotes that the warrior now has a position of premium honor and authority; he can come and go as he pleases, and no areas within the kingdom are off-limits him. He is awarded ultimate dominion and power throughout the kingdom because he is the reason the victory has been won.[96]

Thus, Jesus' return will carry all the splendor of a hero who returns triumphant from a victorious battle: trumpets will announce His arrival and the streets will be lined with excited onlookers who recognize their Champion's homecoming as He stands in His Kingdom and *finally* receives the recognition He is due. Everyone will bow before Him and confess His majesty (Philippians 2:10–11). The spoils, or captive principalities and powers, will be justly dealt with once and for all (Colossians 2:14–15). He will be holding the keys to hell and death (Revelation 1:18), and will reign in ultimate authority at the right hand of God (1 Peter 3:22).

This is the parallel of the Feast of Trumpets. First, it reminds that we should live in preparation of the Day of Judgment. This observance will be partially fulfilled when Jesus comes as our Champion to take us to heaven, and will be even further achieved at His Second Coming: "Jewish tradition teaches that God blew one of the ram's horns at Mount Sinai at Pentecost and will blow the other ram's horn at the coming of Messiah."[97]

This has been foreshadowed in Jesus' entry into Jerusalem during His time here on earth on Palm Sunday. The streets were filled with those who waved branches before Him and shouted, "Hosanna to the son of David: Blessed is he that cometh in the name of the Lord; Hosanna in the highest" (Matthew 21:9). However, the full time of prophecy had not yet been fulfilled, so He did not receive the full recognition he deserved. Through the subsequent battles He won through His Crucifixion and Resurrection, Jesus obtained the victory and will one day make His triumphant return as the Champion.

In addition to the Feast of Trumpets pointing to Jesus' return, we see a parallel regarding the laborers who watched for the new moon, then announced its appearance to the community via the shofar. These were folks who could very nearly predict the arrival of the new moon based on a lifetime of experience in watching the skies. Yet, they could only very closely calculate the arrival of the cosmic turn based on signs. As believers, we are in a similar position: We're told to watch for the signs (Matthew 24:42), yet we're also aware that we can't know the exact day of His arrival (Mark 13:35). Thus, we are to be like those who awaited the arrival of the new moon. We can conclude that the time is nearing based on signs we see around us, but it's not until we hear the sound of the trumpets that we'll know our Savior has arrived. Upon, that sound, those whose sins are atoned will be called into a time of rest; but for those who are unprepared, the Day of Judgment will be impending.

The Day of Atonement

Scripture Reference

> And the Lord spake unto Moses, saying, Also on the tenth day of this seventh month there shall be a day of atonement:
>
> it shall be an holy convocation unto you; and ye shall afflict your souls, and offer an offering made by fire unto the Lord.
>
> And ye shall do no work in that same day: for it is a day of atonement, to make an atonement for you before the Lord your God.
>
> For whatsoever soul it be that shall not be afflicted in that same day, he shall be cut off from among his people.
>
> And whatsoever soul it be that doeth any work in that same day, the same soul will I destroy from among his people.
>
> Ye shall do no manner of work: it shall be a statute for ever throughout your generations in all your dwellings.
>
> It shall be unto you a sabbath of rest, and ye shall afflict your souls: in the ninth day of the month at even, from even unto even, shall ye celebrate your sabbath. (Leviticus 23:26–32)

Observations and Prophetic Implications

According to Leviticus 23:26–32, the tenth day of the seventh month, Tishri, was to be known as Yom Kippur, or the Day of Atonement. (As stated, this is the closing of the Days of Awe.) This was also known as the Day of Judgment.[98] On this day, men were to abstain from working, "afflict" their souls, and make offerings by fire to the Lord. This was a national day of cleansing and repentance from sin. "It was on this day that God judged the sins of the entire nation. In view of this, the Day of Atonement became known as the Day of Judgment."[99] You may think you know nothing of the Day of Atonement, but you've likely heard much about it, as you'll recognize it as the day the high priest would enter the Holy of Holies after sprinkling the mercy seat with the blood from the atoning sacrifice. Because this sacrifice was presented by an individual whom the Lord deemed "fit/suitable" and because it was carried out on a divinely appointed day, the sins of the nation Israel during the past year were covered (in fact, the word "atone" means "to cover"). This was an annual custom, so remission of sin was put on hold throughout the year until the Day of Atonement arrived.

Contrition, sadness, humility, confession of sins, and fasting were markers of the Day of Atonement. While many calendars refer to it as a "feast day," alluding to the notion that plentiful food is offered/consumed, it is actually, for the Israelites, a biblically required day of fasting. Some within Jewish tradition believe it is on this day that the "final judgment and accounting of the soul would come."[100] Thus, some even believe that this holy day would provide the chronology for the Great White Throne Judgment: Each person's eternal destination would be "sealed, and the gates of heaven would be closed" on this day.[101] The Talmud teaches that on Rosh Hashanah, all people are sorted and listed by God, according to their deeds, in "one of three books. The righteous go into the Book of Life, the evil go into the Book of Death, and those in-between have judgment suspended until Yom Kippur."[102] This third category provides motivation for many to attempt to right wrongs during the Days of Awe, since most people, when viewing themselves with honesty, perceive themselves to fall somewhere between fully good or bad.[103]

As mentioned, Rosh Hashanah's trumpet blast ushered in a period of repentance wherein the Israelites would focus on getting their affairs straight, doing good deeds, mending relationships, and spending much time in prayer to forgiveness for sins they had committed since the Yom Kippur of the previous year. It's more than lip service when the Jews greet each other with the sincere phrase, "May your name be inscribed in the Book of Life."[104] At the end of the Day of Atonement, the shofar is blown; this is the first time it's heard since the evening of the announcement of trumpets.[105] On Yom Kippur, or the Day of Atonement, it is believed that

God will then pass judgment on each individual, and those whose names are found in the Book of Life will be saved until the following year's Yom Kippur, when the process will be repeated.

Observation of this feast also included reading the book of Jonah. This narrative, for those who don't believe that Jesus is the Redeeming Messiah, is the strongest and most distinct illustration of God's all-inclusive mercy and grace. Thus, on the day that they seek forgiveness of their own wrongdoings, the words of the book of Job offer a reminder that the Lord is merciful and just toward *all* people.

Jesus partially fulfilled this feast during His life on earth, because once His own blood was shed, He tore the curtain restricting entry into the Holy of Holies, allowing all people, at all times, to enter the presence of God. Further, through Jesus, we receive something better than atonement, because to "atone" means "to cover." But, the gift we receive is a blanket that *hides* our sin from God's view with a blood offering. Our sins are *washed away* by the precious, redeeming blood of the Lamb of God, who was slain for our sins (John 1:29 and 36).

The Scapegoat

The term "scapegoat" is known by many to mean a general substitute that carries culpability for another's wrongdoings, but few realize that its origins are found in the Day of Atonement. Leviticus 16 describes the process by which Israel's sins were atoned. The high priest would present two goats to the Lord, and a lottery-style drawing was held to designate which of the animals would be offered to the Lord at the temple as a sacrifice for a sin offering. The other goat would be led into the wilderness to "be presented alive before the Lord" as a living sacrifice that would "make atonement with the Lord" (Leviticus 16:10). In other words, a man whom God found to be fit or suitable took this second goat to a cliff, where he led the animal off the edge to its death to atone for the sins of Israel. Tradition holds that a scarlet-colored wool cord was cut in half on this day; one part was tied to the temple door and the remaining part was wound upon the goat's horns. When the goat plummeted over the bluff, it is said that the cord on the temple door turned white, pointing to Isaiah's words in Isaiah 1:18: "Though your sins be as scarlet, they shall be as white as snow; though they be red like crimson, they shall be as wool." This color change indicated that God had received and approved of Israel's sacrifice, allowing them atonement for another year.[106]

God no longer requires a scapegoat to cover our sins. Jesus is the Ultimate Lamb who was slain to remove, not just cover, our sins (John 1:29). However, we are called, in turn, to be living sacrifices (Romans 12:1) who daily die to our own flesh (Romans 11; 1 Corinthians 15:31) and seek the things of heaven (Hebrews 12:14). The Feast of Trumpets is a call to repentance that reaches its apex on the Day of Atonement, but on the day that the last trumpet sounds, the fates of all people will be sealed. Thus, it is necessary to accept the gift of salvation *now* and live the life that God requires of us.

Saints in Revelation

In Revelation 6, we see martyred souls who await vengeance beneath the altar. It is poetic and beautiful that these believers are placed in this location. First of all, there is a correlation between this altar and the Day of Atonement, observed via the altar located in front of the Holy of Holies; which would bear a sacrifice both of blood and incense for the cleansing of sin. Yet, the heavenly throne room's altar has much more precious blood upon it. John 1:29 shows us that Jesus is the Lamb; Hebrews 9:22 tells that without the shedding of blood there is no remission of sins. It is true that Jesus is the Lamb who was slain for our sins so that we can obtain the ultimate atonement and redemption. Thus, this symbolism indicates that, upon the heavenly altar, Jesus' blood was offered in the spiritual realm for our sins before the throne of God. Now, as we view this heavenly altar, we see the saints *beneath* it. This means that they are covered by the blood of Jesus; He holds them in redemption beneath the provision of His sacrifice.[107] Thus, heaven commemorates the fulfillment of the ultimate Day of Atonement.

Further, we see in Revelation 14:2–3 that saints in heaven sing a new song—one that no one else can sing. This song is said by some scholars to parallel those from Exodus 15:1 and Deuteronomy 31–32; because they boast of God's deliverance of the righteous and judgment of the wicked. The melody that described in Revelation 14 is sung by those "redeemed from the earth." The tune will be a prophetic fulfillment, because it will celebrate the permanent liberation from sin and evil. Just as the Israelites were able to sing that the "horse and rider had been thrown into the sea," these will sing that God has triumphed over malevolence and that His end-time victory draws nigh.[108]

The Great White Throne Judgment

The final, prophetic fulfillment of this feast will take place at the Great White Throne Judgment: the final Great Day of Atonement. Revelation 20:11–12 tells us that all of "the dead, small and great…[will stand] before God…And the dead…[will be] judged according to their works, by the things which…[are] written in the books." This is the moment when the eternal destination of every individual will be forever established. This court session will likewise settle final judgment upon Satan, the Beast, and the False Prophet (Revelation 20:10).

But the righteous have nothing to fear on this day, because of Jesus' provision for *removal*, not just *coverage*, of their sins. This was foreshadowed in Leviticus 25:1–4 and 8–10, which explain that on the fiftieth year, beginning on the Day of Atonement, the Lord ordered a Year of Jubilee to be consecrated. This year "was a year full of releasing people from their debts, releasing all slaves, and returning property to who owned it…. This year was also dedicated to rest."[109] Thus, on this Great and Final Day of Atonement, the Final, *Forever* Year of Jubilee will begin! Once and for all, the captive will be set free; property (our souls, along with undisputed recognition of majesty and praise) will be returned to the rightful owner (God). And, we will be brought into the Ultimate Season of Rest.

Just as the Feast of Trumpets culminates into the Day of Atonement, events surrounding the Rapture and the coming of our Lord will pave the way for the Great White Throne Judgment and the Ultimate Year of Jubilee.

Then, we will all join in the final celebration of the Feast of Tabernacles.

Tabernacles

Scripture Reference

And the Lord spake unto Moses, saying, Speak unto the children of Israel, saying, The fifteenth day of this seventh month shall be the feast of tabernacles for seven days unto the Lord.

On the first day shall be an holy convocation: ye shall do no servile work therein.

Seven days ye shall offer an offering made by fire unto the Lord: on the eighth day shall be an holy convocation unto you; and ye shall offer an offering made by fire unto the Lord: it is a solemn assembly; and ye shall do no servile work therein.

These are the feasts of the Lord, which ye shall proclaim to be holy convocations, to offer an offering made by fire unto the Lord, a burnt offering, and a meat offering, a sacrifice, and drink offerings, every thing upon his day:

Beside the sabbaths of the Lord, and beside your gifts, and beside all your vows, and beside all your freewill offerings, which ye give unto the Lord.

Also in the fifteenth day of the seventh month, when ye have gathered in the fruit of the land, ye shall keep a feast unto the Lord seven days: on the first day shall be a sabbath, and on the eighth day shall be a sabbath.

And ye shall take you on the first day the boughs of goodly trees, branches of palm trees, and the boughs of thick trees, and willows of the brook; and ye shall rejoice before the Lord your God seven days.

And ye shall keep it a feast unto the Lord seven days in the year. It shall be a statute for ever in your generations: ye shall celebrate it in the seventh month.

Ye shall dwell in booths seven days; all that are Israelites born shall dwell in booths: That your generations may know that I made the children of Israel to dwell in booths, when I brought them out of the land of Egypt: I am the Lord your God.

And Moses declared unto the children of Israel the feasts of the Lord. (Leviticus 23:33–44)

Observations and Prophetic Implications

The Feast of *Succot*, or Tabernacles, occurs on the fifteenth day of Tishri, falling at the end of the harvest season. It is also sometimes known as the Feast of Booths, Festival of Shelters, or even the Festival or Feast of Indwelling, because during this feast the people stayed in temporary shelters or "booths," made of "citron, myrtle, palm, and willow."[110] This was a celebration of the year's final harvest, a time for laborers to enter a season of rest. Recall that it was earlier mentioned that this feast was the final of the religious season; it was the *seventh* feast, and *seven* is God's number of completion. For this observation, God's people were called to take a Sabbath day. Then, each day for seven days, they were to make offerings by fire to the Lord, followed by an eighth day, which was another day of rest. (Placing these two Sabbaths on Tishri 15 and 22).

In addition to celebrating the end of a particular year's harvest—thus recognizing God supplying their physical needs— this was a time of memorializing His ongoing, reliable providence. This is why people were ordered to dwell in booths for seven days: a remembrance of when God had given them temporary dwellings to occupy when He had delivered them out of the land of Egypt. He had given them manna to eat (Exodus 16:4), a pillar of cloud during the day and one of fire to light their way at night (Exodus 13:21), and laws to follow (Exodus 20). He had even eventually led them to the Promised Land—despite their disobedience

(Joshua 1:4). By building and living in these temporary shelters for this feast, God's people show that they *still* lean on Him for all of their needs, both physical *and* spiritual. Likewise, they show their recognition that we still live a nomadic and temporary existence, not one wherein we reside in our permanent home. This reinforces our awareness that the delay in our reaching our permanent home is brought about by our own disobedience, lack of faith, or even idolatry—just as was the case for the Israelites in that day (Deuteronomy 1:35). However, present-day observation of the Feast of Booths reaffirms that we only live an existence of temporariness and wandering until we fully learn to trust in Him *and* that even while times such as this occur in our lives, God will provide our needs and bring us to a permanent dwelling if we put our faith in Him. This what Deuteronomy 1:33 states: He "[goes] before you, to search you out a place to pitch your tents in, in fire by night, to ... [show] you by what way ye should go, and in a cloud by day."

Most importantly, the brevity of the booth-dwelling during this feast reminds God's people that this world is not our home; He has a permanent home for us in a future place. We are to occupy this space while watching for another home in heaven:

> By faith Abraham obeyed when he was called to go out to the place which he would receive as an inheritance; and he went out, not knowing where he was to go.
>
> By faith he dwelt in the land of promise as in a foreign country, dwelling in tents with Isaac and Jacob, the heirs with him of the same promise.
>
> For he waited for the city which has foundations, whose builder and maker is God. (Hebrews 11:8–10)

While God's people live as nomads and outcasts here on earth, we have assurance that our situation is as temporary as the booths in which the Israelites dwelt during their journey to the Promised Land. Jesus Himself has guaranteed us a home where we really belong—our *forever home*:

In my Father's house are many [rooms-tents]: if it were not so, I would have told you. I go to prepare a place for you.

And if I go and prepare a place for you, I will come again, and receive you unto myself; that where I am, there ye may be also. (John 14:2–3)

When Jesus spoke those words, His Hebrew followers would have immediately caught the connection between the Feast of Tabernacles and His Second Coming (or the Rapture), for the annual feast was one of the occasions requiring the Israelites to make a pilgrimage to the wilderness tabernacle and, later, the temple in Jerusalem to appear before God. This is the event that will be transpiring on earth exactly three and a half years before Apophis-Wormwood crashes into this planet. Is this mere coincidence, or does it point to an imminent pre-Tribulation Rapture?

Additionally, considering that Jesus was the Tabernacle of the Lord God who came to earth in the flesh, and since He left with us the Holy Spirit who lives in our bodies (John 14:16, 1 Corinthians 6:19); each of us is *also* a partial fulfillment of this feast. After all, we are now the temples (tabernacles) of the Spirit. The spiritual symbolism is inspiring and reassuring. However, Jesus interacted with this feast in a very bold, outspoken, and *literal* way during His earthly life.

Pouring the Water

When Jesus walked the earth, on the last day of the Feast of Tabernacles, also called *Hoshanah Rabbah* ("The Day of the Great Hosanna"), the ritual of water-pouring took place.[111] This was a petition for God to send the Messiah to save/deliver them. The water-pouring was also an act of faith, as the rainy season had not yet arrived. Thus, this offering expressed faith that God would send adequate rain in the coming months. On a deeper level, it was a supplication for the forthcoming Messiah and the life-saving deliverance He would bring with Him. The ritual consisted of one priest using a golden receptacle to retrieve water from the Pool of Siloam, which he then delivered to the high priest in the temple. The contents would then be emptied into a basin that sat below the altar to signify the Messiah's coming.

Meanwhile, nearby priests blew shofars as onlookers waved palm leaves and sang the praises of the Most High God. These traditions draw from Isaiah 12:3 and 44:3: "Therefore with joy shall ye draw water out of the wells of salvation"; "For I will pour water upon him that is thirsty, and floods upon the dry ground: I will pour my spirit upon thy seed, and my blessing upon thine offspring."

While the feast itself holds a future-facing thrust, it has already been mentioned that Jesus addressed it (and this tradition in particular) in His own lifetime on earth. It was on *Hoshanah Rabbah* that "Jesus stood and cried, saying, If any man thirst, let him come unto me, and drink. He that believeth on me, as the scripture hath said, out of his belly shall flow rivers of living water" (John 7:37–38). In other words, while those in the temple poured water in petition to God to provide the blessing of rain in the upcoming seasons and to send the Delivering Messiah, Jesus stood in the midst of them and explained that the answer to their prayers had *already* arrived. Likewise, this was His way of saying that while the waters of this earth (even those drawn from the Pool of Siloam) were temporary and fleeting, His was the true Water of Life that would forever satisfy.

Unfortunately, we see in the following verse that only some *truly* heard Jesus' message: "But this spake he of the Spirit, which they that believe on him should receive: for the Holy Ghost was not yet given; because that Jesus was not yet glorified" (John 7:39). Of those who understood, many began comparing prophetic lineages and birth origins to what they knew of Him in attempt to discern His true identity. Jesus, later (that is to say, later the same day on a *Hebrew* calendar, but what, by modern Gregorian day-counts, would be considered the afternoon of the following day), *also* took ownership of another unique aspect of this feast's elements.

The Lighting of the Temple

Another element associated with this feast was the temple lighting. Because people would make a pilgrimage to Jerusalem from miles around and then reside in temporary booths that had been built on-site for the week of this feast, the entire area would be lit with tens of thousands of burning torches, which illuminated the city. The temple was filled with golden, glowing lampposts, and other lighting was located throughout the town. All of this radiance signified the Light of the forthcoming Messiah (Isaiah 49:6). The glow provided an ambience that became known as the "lighting of the temple." Also, the entire city bore the luminosity of the torches of large numbers of incoming travelers,. Jesus, after a night spent amongst these burning torches, said to those around Him, "I am the light of the world. He who follows me shall not walk in darkness, but have the light of life" (John 8:12). Many of today's readers overlook the significance of Jesus' statements about being the water and the light because they don't catch their implications the feast's cultural setting. This, often causes them to miss that Jesus essentially stood among the populace and told them that He was *the very answer they were looking for*—the cool drink to quench all thirst and the brilliance that would never leave them in the darkness.

When studied alongside end-times prophecy, the Feast of Tabernacles not only represents the Rapture and Second Coming, but the Millennial Reign of the Messiah here on earth as well. During this time, Satan will be bound and the curse of sin will be defeated. Jesus' Kingdom will be established here on earth, and we will reign with Him (Revelation 20). The restful season of the Feast of Tabernacles foreshadows the rest God's people will experience during this time. Further, we will finally be with our Heavenly Father, where we eternally belong. *And,* in contrast to the earthly "booths," we'll be approaching the building of our final, permanent home.

Zechariah 14:1–19 tells us that at the time of His return, Jesus will appear in power and glory; the mountains will divide; living waters will flow from Jerusalem; He "shall be king over all the earth"; those who stood against Jerusalem will perish; and all people will honor the "feast of tabernacles of tabernacles," lest the Lord smite them with drought, plague, and famine. This passage illustrates that this is an important feast to God. However, it is symbolically celebrated in Jerusalem, and the phrase "tabernacle of tabernacles" indicates that the final observation of this celebration is to commemorate the *Final* tabernacle: The New Jerusalem.

Thus, this passage makes prophetic correlation to the wedding supper of the Lamb. When Jesus comes to reign in glory and to make war with those who opposed Him, we will be invited to this event. Those inside Jerusalem will celebrate together over this feast, while those who stood against God's armies will perish outside the gates:

> And I heard as it were the voice of a great multitude, and as the voice of many waters, and as the voice of mighty thunderings, saying, Alleluia: for the Lord God omnipotent reigneth.
>
> Let us be glad and rejoice, and give honour to him: for the marriage of the Lamb is come, and his wife hath made herself ready.
>
> And to her was granted that she should be arrayed in fine linen, clean and white: for the fine linen is the righteousness of saints. (Revelation 19:6–8)

22 Tishri, The Great Sabbath

22 Tishri (the eighth day/second Sabbath of the Feast of Tabernacles) is observed as an especially "holy convocation" (Leviticus 23:36). The glorious status of this date is particularly elevated in Jewish tradition, even beyond the preceding days of the festival. In prophecy, this day is considered to be a *special*, Ultimate Sabbath. This represents the time that God will welcome us to a new heaven and a new earth. He will build a New Jerusalem that is a permanent structure. In the fulfillment of the prophetic eighth day of the Feast of Tabernacles, we will enter the Ultimate Sabbath in a sublime new world with the Lord who loves us. He will be our God and we will be His people. He will personally wipe the tears from our eyes and will tell us that all pain is a thing of the past. He will be the only Light we need, the only home we could ever long for. And on that great day, He will declare that "it is done":

> And I saw a new heaven and a new earth: for the first heaven and the first earth were passed away; and there was no more sea.
>
> And I John saw the holy city, new Jerusalem, coming down from God out of heaven, prepared as a bride adorned for her husband.
>
> And I heard a great voice out of heaven saying, Behold, the tabernacle of God is with men, and he will dwell with them, and they shall be his people, and God himself shall be with them, and be their God.
>
> And God shall wipe away all tears from their eyes; and there shall be no more death, neither sorrow, nor crying, neither shall there be any more pain: for the former things are passed away.
>
> And he that sat upon the throne said, Behold, I make all things new. And he said unto me, Write: for these words are true and faithful.
>
> And he said unto me, It is done. I am Alpha and Omega, the beginning and the end. I will give unto him that is athirst of the fountain of the water of life freely....
>
> And I saw no temple therein: for the Lord God Almighty and the Lamb are the temple of it.
>
> And the city had no need of the sun, neither of the moon, to shine in it: for the glory of God did lighten it, and the Lamb is the light thereof. (Revelation 21:1–6 and 22–23)

A Timing Correlation?

In Genesis 22, God tested Abraham by ordering him to take Isaac to the land of Moriah and offer him as a burnt sacrifice to the Lord. The journey was three days, and at the last minute God provided a ram to offer instead. However, because of Abraham's complete obedience to God, he was promised that his seed would be multiplied as the stars in heaven.

For those who haven't heard this story, it is worthwhile to note that God did this not to encourage human sacrifice, but to test Abraham's obedience (verse 1); Abraham *knew* God would provide a substitute (verse 8); and, as a very worst-case scenario, God would resurrect Isaac (Hebrews 11:19). This incident was used by God to teach Abraham a lesson that ran counter-cultural to his own experience and pagan religious surroundings: God is big enough to provide His *own* sacrifice, thus would *never* demand a human sacrifice. See author Carl Gibbs' comment regarding this below:

> In the cultural setting, the reader needs to understand that it was a common practice among pagan worshipers to offer their firstborn sons as human sacrifices. Such sacrifices were customary in Abraham's day. Certainly it was a command Abraham would understand. At the same time God's intention was not to teach him the merit of human sacrifice but to teach that only He could provide a sacrifice for sins. Abraham could offer only his faith.
>
> In this text the truth taught is obedience to God, not human sacrifice. In fact, the story stands out as an apologetic against the pagan practice of appeasing a god with a sacrifice, for it teaches that God provides the sacrifice, not humankind.[112]

Returning to the parallels between this account and that of Jesus' crucifixion: during a three-day interim, a spiritual work of providence was being done. But the timeline is a curious element to explore as well.

Biblical scholars place the date of Abraham's journey with Isaac at approximately two thousand years after Creation (approaching the third millennium), and two thousand years before Christ: between 2100–1770 BC. Similar scholars (and historical documents) place Jesus' time on earth at 6 BC–AD 2033, two thousand years after Abraham and Isaac's pilgrimage and two thousand years ago from our present day (entering the fifth millennium). (To be sure, there are many who would debate the date of Creation, or even the Creation theory, but let us set aside that point for the moment, since our number correlation pertains to time as it is referenced from the era of the first biblically recorded man, which is Adam). The way these numbers align indicates that after the first two thousand years into His interaction with mankind, God was establishing His covenant with Israel. Two thousand years after that, He was establishing the Church and a New Covenant that invited Gentiles into the fold. And now, here we sit, two thousand years later (approaching the seventh millennium), awaiting His next move…

It would seem as though each group has likewise been reflected by the feast seasons as well (as has been stated). The spring season pertains to the nation of Israel: those whose covenant with God occurred around the two thousandth year. The summer feast season—observed through Pentecost—applies to the Gentile Church and was formed two-thousand years after the Abrahamic Covenant. As we round the corner on the *next* two-thousandth year (which from the Crucifixion ranges from the Apophis-Wormwood dates of 2029–2033), it will be interesting to see if the *third* feast season—that which features a future-facing, prophetic time of manifestation—becomes fulfilled.

It is an interesting and exciting time to be alive and watch events unfold. Now, as we approach the relative year 6000 (thus entering the seventh millennium), we near what could very well be the opening of the third feast seasons: the prophetic feasts. Up to now, we can see God using a chronological pattern that, if continued at the established pace, could line us up for end-time events soon. It could be that He soon will establish His Kingdom here on earth to reign for a Millennium with all those who He calls His own. It may seem like a sensationalistic statement, but believe it or not, there are authorities even in antiquity who believed this very notion to be plausible.

Church Fathers' Teaching Regarding the Rapture

The Church Fathers are often referred to and remembered as men of old who divided, debated, and interpreted Scripture. Many wrote letters, doctrinal dissertations, and theological teachings regarding their analysis of God's Word. While it's easy for people today to take scriptural inter-pretation for granted, many of these men were executed for their beliefs, their work, and their stubborn refusal to denounce what they stood for theologically. Thus, they didn't make careless statements; rather, the things they said and taught were the products of *extreme* conviction. Surprisingly, many of these men perceived the early parts of the seventh millennium to usher in end-time events. This notion is taken from the way they chose to interpret a few key passages, listed here:

- "For a thousand years in thy sight are but as yesterday when it is past, and as a watch in the night" (Psalm 90:4).
- "But, beloved, be not ignorant of this one thing, that one day is with the Lord as a thousand years, and a thousand years as one day" (2 Peter 3:8).
- "And on the seventh day God ended his work which he had made; and he rested on the seventh day from all his work which he had made. And God blessed he seventh day, and sanctified it: because that in it he had rested from all his work which God created and made" (Genesis 2:2–3).

Saint Barnabas (AD first century, approx. 70–130), taught that the Second Coming of Christ could very possibly be placed at the early phases of the seventh millennium. The reader has probably already connected the logic behind this conclusion based upon the aforementioned Scrip-tures: Since a day is as a thousand years to the Lord, then this would mean that in the seventh day, God intends to usher in the Ultimate Sabbath and rest.[113] Barnabus taught that the sixth millennium would be the end of this earth's era as we know it, and that the seventh millennium would bring on the Kingdom of Christ:

> "He finished in six days." This implieth that the Lord will finish all things in six thousand years, for a day is with Him a thousand years.... Therefore, my children, in six days, that is, six thousand years, all things will be finished. "And He rested on the seventh day." This meaneth: when His Son, coming [again], shall destroy the time of wicked man, and judge the ungodly, and change the sun, and the moon, and the stars, then shall He truly rest on the seventh day.[114]

Ireneaus (AD 130–202) taught similarly:

> For in as many days as this world was made, in so many thousand years shall it be concluded. And for this reason the Scripture says: Thus the heaven and the earth were finished, and all their adornment. And God brought to a conclusion upon the sixth day the works that He had made; and God rested upon the seventh day from all His works (Genesis 2:2). This is an account of the things formerly created, as also it is a prophecy of what is to come. For the day of the Lord is as a thousand years; (2 Peter 3:8) and in six days created things were completed: it is evident, therefore, that they will come to an end at the sixth thousand year. (*Against Heresies*, 5.28)[115]

Hippolytus (cir. 170–236) reinforced this notion held by early Church Fathers *and* shared his belief that the Ultimate Sabbath would occur during the seventh millennium:

> For the first appearance of our Lord in the flesh took place in Bethlehem, under Augustus, in the year 5500; and He suffered in the thirty-third year. And 6,000 years must needs be accom-

plished, in order that the Sabbath may come, the rest, the holy day "on which God rested from all His works." For the Sabbath is the type and emblem of the future kingdom of the saints, when they "shall reign with Christ," when He comes from heaven, as John says in his Apocalypse: for "a day with the Lord is as a thousand years." Since, then, in six days God made all things, it follows that 6,000 years must be fulfilled. And they are not yet fulfilled, as John says: "five are fallen; one is," that is, the sixth; "the other is not yet come."[116]

Victorinus (AD 240) said:

Satan will be bound until the thousand years are finished; that is, after the sixth day. (*Commentary on Revelation* 20.1–3)[117]

Better still, Methodius (AD 290) connected this potential six-thousand-year countdown to the final feast season when He wrote:

In the seventh millennium we will be immortal and truly celebrate the Feast of Tabernacles. (*Ten Virgins* 9.1)[118]

Many other Church Fathers held the notion that the seventh millennium would usher in the Ultimate Sabbath; in which the Lord would reign on earth for a thousand years. Additional fathers who asserted these views included (but were certainly not limited to) Commodianus, AD 240, and Lactantius, AD 304.

Jewish Tradition Regarding Bringing on Sabbath

If it is true that we are approaching the time when God will initiate the Ultimate Sabbath, some may be tempted to claim (based on *when* they place the beginning of the world) that the day has either already passed to no avail, or that it is projected so far into the future that the expiration lies beyond one's lifetime, making the matter irrelevant to them. However, understanding Sabbath initiation helps us see that there is room for variation in its timing. Since the early calendar saw the transition from one day to the next at *sunset*, the actual timing could be thrown off one way or another, depending on the season, cosmic alignment, and location. Bear with us while we explain.

As mentioned, some believe that the world is currently more than six thousand years old—and that we rapidly approach the entrance of the seven-thousandth year, which many Church Fathers placed around AD 2030–2060. Interestingly, Jewish tradition holds a similar notion (more on this in a minute). Many also perceive the beginning of the seven-thousandth year to be the grandiose, Ultimate Sabbath: the millennial reign of Christ. Since we're currently in Jewish year 5780, many scholars place the Jewish year 6000 at approximately AD 2239–2240 on the Gregorian Calendar. If this theory is correct, then this logic could place these years to be among the *last* days that Jesus may return. These dates may seem so far off that we need not worry about them; however, it is said that He could decide to return sooner, since we are entering the last millennium. To some, this would merely be as simple as Jesus exercising His "prerogative of ushering in early on Friday afternoon."[119] What does this mean? This is the variation by which Sabbath can be initiated early during times of the year that waiting for sunset would mean that Sabbath rituals cannot begin until extremely late at night. In such cases, Jewish tradition, via the Talmud, makes provision for an early Sabbath.

On this matter, Rabbi Baruch Davidson states:

The Talmud tells us that this world, as we know it, will last for six thousand years, with the seventh millennium ushering in the cosmic Shabbat, the Messianic Era. Six days a week we work, and on the Shabbat we rest and enjoy the fruits of our labor; the same is true with millenniums.[120]

Jews were prompted to pray three times daily as their routine. These prayers are modeled by various devout followers of God throughout the Old Testament. The morning prayer was called the Shacharit prayer, the midday prayer was Mincha, and the evening prayer was called Maariv. Typically, the Jewish Sabbath started at sundown. However, when the sun wouldn't set until very late, Sabbath rituals became impeded. With this in mind, many synagogues would say the evening prayer before the actual sundown, which would initiate Shabbat during the afternoon or evening that Sabbath was expected, but before actual sundown.

In these cases, the timing of the Mincha was varied, which allowed the Plag Haminchah (the midpoint prayer) to be followed directly by the Maariv prayer, which traditionally took place at nightfall, but could be spoken earlier to bring on an early Sabbath:

> By praying the Minchah (afternoon) prayer before the 'Plag Haminchah,' which is 1 1/4 halachic hours [explained in a moment] before sunset, it is permitted to pray Maariv and accept the Shabbat [Sabbath] any time after the Plag Haminchah.[121]

(A halachic hour isn't a sixty-minute period as we consider it. It is, rather, one of twelve segments of a given day, divided evenly based on solar activity on that particular day. These were made up of twelve equal increments of sunlight on a given day, so a longer day meant longer halachic hours. This means the length of this increment can vary from forty-five to seventy-five minutes, depending on the season and other cosmic elements.)

The rituals altering the timing of the Minchah to bring Sabbath on earlier in the evening are complicated. (Two schools of thought have for centuries debated allowing this modification; some correlate this prayer with the afternoon sacrifice, while others move according to the offering of incense). Because the subject is really outside the scope of this work, we won't elaborate here. However, we will say that we can see each side of the debate as pre-Rapture criteria that will have been met by the time the Ultimate Sabbath is ushered in. We quickly see the parallel between Jesus and the sacrifice. That has been done. "It is finished" (John 19:30). When we look for a spiritual connection to the offering of incense, we see that in Revelation 8:4, just before the angels sound the seven trumpets, there is an offering of incense. So, unless one believes the Rapture will happen *far* in advance of these events, this criterion is met regardless of which event the early Ultimate Sabbath must correlate to.

The implications of what such principles may have in prophecy are fascinating. It could be that the link between the two-thousand-year increments, the teachings of certain Church Fathers, and Jewish historical tradition culminate to make a similar near-future assertion. *And,* it is interesting that during certain periods of the year (since the onset of Sabbath is based on sundown), the afternoon and evening prayers are spoken earlier so that Sabbath comes in at the right *time* of the night rather than in its proper timing at *sundown*. With this in mind, there is room for variation regarding the arrival of the Ultimate Sabbath.[122]

That said, many of the Church Fathers placed this occurrence closer to the two-thousandth anniversary of Christ's time on earth, which is the era in which we are living. In fact, scholars place Jesus' crucifixion between AD 29–33, which means that the perfect manifestation of this time window occurs while Apophis will be just overhead, flying too close for comfort.

7

The Messenger Apophis and the Terrible Gods Coming with It

One of the many surprising aspects of asteroid Apophis is the supernatural timing of its arrival. The Jet Propulsion Laboratory at Cal Tech, which tracks Near Earth Objects (NEOs) for NASA, tells us that it "will cruise harmlessly by Earth, about 19,000 miles (31,000 kilometers) above the surface" on April 13, 2029.[123] Why is this interesting? The date has intriguing connections to the annual feasts God decreed to Moses in the wilderness.

Assuming for the moment that Apophis is biblical Wormwood (we're not certifying that or setting dates here), and that 2029 would thus represent a period sometime around the middle of the Great Tribulation period when the trumpet judgments begin, Monday, October 13, 2025 (April 13, 2029, minus three and a half years), would be the approximate start date of the seven years of Tribulation foreseen in Scripture (see Matthew 24:21, Revelation 7:14, and Daniel 12:1). For evangelical dispensationalists (and some Catholic prophecy believers), this timing may seem an ominous sign that a Rapture of the Church is soon to occur (the eschatological event, as we've described earlier, when all true Christians who are alive will be transformed into glorious bodies in an instant and joined by the resurrection of dead believers, who ascend with them into heaven).

Depending on one's position, this would place the last possible date for a pre-Tribulation Rapture sometime around October 13, 2025.[124]

October 13, 2025, is 21 Tishri on the Hebrew calendar, the seventh day of the annual Feast of Tabernacles (Sukkot, literally "Feast of Booths"), one of the annual festivals God directed the Israelites to keep when He gave the Law to Moses.

Sukkot is a seven-day festival that begins on 15 Tishri, the seventh month of the Hebrew calendar. That puts it exactly six months after the Feast of Unleavened Bread, a seven-day festival that follows Passover, which falls on the evening of 14 Nisan, the first month of the year. Those two, along with *Shavuot*, the Feast of Weeks (Pentecost), were the annual pilgrimage festivals that required Jewish men to appear before God at the tabernacle and, later, the temple in Jerusalem.[125]

The pagan religious calendar in the ancient Near East likewise featured festivals in the spring and fall called the *akitu*. This rite dates back at least to the middle of the third millennium BC.[126] For many years, scholars thought the *akitu* was a new year festival held each spring at Babylon to honor the chief god, Marduk. More recent discoveries, however, have shown that there were two *akitu* festivals, one in the spring, the harvesting season, and the other in the fall, the planting season, and many cities performed the ritual to honor their patron deities. For example, the earliest *akitu* known to scholars was at Ur in Sumer, the home city of the moon-god, Sîn.[127]

The *akitu* began on the first of Nisan and first of Tishri, close to the spring and fall equinoxes. Although the length of the festival changed over the years, it appears it generally lasted eleven[128] or twelve days.[129] So, the Feasts of Unleavened Bread and Tabernacles began a few days after the pagan neighbors of the Hebrews finished their annual harvest and planting rituals.

Sukkot is a seven-day festival. The sheer number of sacrificial animals required suggests that this was the preeminent festival in the Jewish calendar, and it's especially interesting because they were bulls. Numbers 29:12–34 spells out the requirements:

Day 1: 13 bulls, 2 rams, 14 lambs, 1 goat
Day 2: 12 bulls, 2 rams, 14 lambs, 1 goat
Day 3: 11 bulls, 2 rams, 14 lambs, 1 goat
Day 4: 10 bulls, 2 rams, 14 lambs, 1 goat
Day 5: 9 bulls, 2 rams, 14 lambs, 1 goat
Day 6: 8 bulls, 2 rams, 14 lambs, 1 goat
Day 7: 7 bulls, 2 rams, 14 lambs, 1 goat

So, a total of seventy bulls were sacrificed over the seven days of Sukkot. The Feast of Unleavened Bread, also a seven-day festival, required only one ram and seven lambs each day. But the biggest difference between the two feasts is that only two bulls were sacrificed each day during the Feast of Unleavened Bread.[130] In fact, none of the other festivals God decreed for Israel required the offering more than two bulls per day.[131]

So, Sukkot was unique in the annual calendar. It was so important that it was sometimes simply called "the festival" or "the feast."[132] But why? Why were so many bulls required at this feast? One thing, at least, is certain: It wasn't about the beef.

Bovid imagery was commonly used to describe the pagan gods of the ancient world. For example, the name of the old gods of the Greek pantheon, the Titans, derives from an ancient tribe of the Amorite people, the Tidanu (or Ditanu, depending on where and when it was inscribed onto clay tablets).[133] This was a semi-mythical group from which the Amorite kings of Babylon (including Hammurabi the Great), northern Mesopotamia, and Ugarit claimed to descend.

By the time of the judges in Israel, the tribe had passed into history. The Ditanu lived on in Amorite religion, however, venerated as gods of the underworld. Religious texts linked the Ditanu to the Rephaim, who were well known to the pagan Amorites. It appears that Amorite kings aspired to join the "council of the Ditanu" after death, and royal gardens were set apart to venerate the departed kings, presumably to help them join the company of their mighty ancestors in the afterlife.[134]

The relevant point is that the Ditanu/Tidanu derived their name from *ditânu*, the Akkadian word for "bison" or "bull."[135] This probably meant the aurochs, a primitive strain of cattle from which modern domesticated breeds descend. Aurochs bulls were black, weighed about a ton, stood more than six foot at the shoulder, had nasty-looking horns, and were not a beast that an inexperienced hunter wanted to engage on his own.[136]

And this was how the pagan neighbors of the ancient Hebrews described their creator-god.

> The bovid sense of the form Ditanu/Didanu is particularly intriguing in view of other tauromorph elements in the tradition. Thus, **the prominent Titan Kronos was later identified with El, who is given the epithet _tr_, "Bull," in Ugaritic and biblical literature.** Apart from this explicit allusion, we may well ask whether the name El (Akkadian and Ugaritic _ilu_) does not already itself have a bovine sense…. Does it perhaps mean "Bull", (perhaps more generically "male animal"), so that the epithetal title tr is in effect a redundant gloss on it?…
>
> Furthermore, the name Kronos may well carry the same nuance, since it may be construed as referring to bovine horns (Akkadian, Ugaritic _qarnu_, Hebrew _qeren_), which feature prominently in divine iconography in the Near East.[137] (Emphasis added)

References to "Bull El" are common in Ugaritic texts, but if you read the above carefully, you may have been surprised to learn that scholars find those references in the Bible as well. For example, in the book of Hosea, the prophet recalled the idolatry of Jeroboam, who led the rebellion against Solomon's son, Rehoboam, to establish the breakaway northern kingdom of Israel:

> I have spurned your calf, O Samaria.
> My anger burns against them.
> How long will they be incapable of innocence?
> For it is from Israel;
> a craftsman made it;

it is not God.
The calf of Samaria
shall be broken to pieces. (Hosea 8:5–6)

The phrase, "For it is from Israel," comes from the Masoretic Hebrew text, *kî miyyiśrāʾēl*, which literally means, "for from Israel."[138] That makes no sense in Hebrew or English. The verse as published in our English Bibles represents the best guess of translators trying to "fix" a sentence they don't understand.

But scholars of Hebrew have found that separating the characters differently yields *kî mî šōr ʾēl*, which changes verse 6 from "for it is from Israel" to this:

For who is Bull El?[139]
a craftsman made it;
it is not God.
The calf of Samaria
shall be broken to pieces. (Hosea 8:6, modified; emphasis added)

Jeroboam had drawn the northern tribes back into the worship of the creator-god of the Canaanites by erecting the golden calves at Bethel and Dan. By reading "Bull El" in Hosea 8:6, instead of "Israel," the verse becomes a polemic directed not just at the idols of Jeroboam, but against the head of the Canaanite pantheon as well. It fits the context of the passage better than the common English rendering.

And, interestingly, this isn't the only place in the Bible where that substitution comes closer to the meaning of the original Hebrew.

The epithet has also been identified recently in a perceptive study of Deuteronomy 32:8 by Joosten, in which he proposed a similar consonantal regrouping in the expression *bny yśrʾl* (*běnê yiśrāʾēl*) to read (*běnê šōr ʾēl*). Since LXX (ἀγγέλων θεοῦ, some mss υἱων θεοῦ), and one Qumran text, 4QDeut j (*lmspr bny ʾlhym*), already read a divine reference here, rather than the "Israel" of MT, this proposal has much to commend it:

yaṣṣēb gĕbulōt ʿammîm He set up the boundaries of the nations
lĕmisparbĕnê šōr ʾēl in accordance with the number of the sons of
Bull El.[140]

Here is why we're pursuing this rabbit trail: The Amorite neighbors of
ancient Israel believed that El held court on the summit of Mount Hermon[141] with his consort, Asherah, *and their seventy sons.*[142]

The number seventy in the ancient Near East was symbolic. It represented completion, totality, the full set; not one left out.[143] For example,
in accounts of violent transfers of power, the number of the losers put to
death was usually seventy.[144] It described total destruction.

Cases in point: The seventy sons of Gideon killed by Abimelech[145] and
the seventy sons of Ahab slaughtered by the usurper Jehu.[146] Did Ahab and
Gideon really father seventy sons each? Probably not. Similar accounts
outside the Bible from the same time period confirm that what was meant
was that *all* of their sons had been killed (except, of course, Gideon's lone
surviving son, Jotham; in his case, seventy represented all *except* him).

Now, you probably noticed that "Bull El" had the same number of
sons as the number of bulls slaughtered during the Feast of Tabernacles.
Excellent! You see where this is going.

But it's more than just symbolic. There is supernatural significance to
those seventy sons.

Let's circle back to Deuteronomy 32:8, which we cited above. It's safe
to say that you won't find an English translation that renders the end of
that verse "sons of Bull El." However, there are a number of newer translations, such as the English Standard Version and New English Translation,
that are similar.

When the Most High gave to the nations their inheritance,
when he divided mankind,
he fixed the borders of the peoples
according to the number of the sons of God.
(Deuteronomy 32:8, emphasis added)

The translators of the NET were even more precise in what they believe was intended by the original Hebrew:

When the Most High gave the nations their inheritance,
when he divided up humankind,
he set the boundaries of the peoples,
according to the number of the heavenly assembly.
(Deuteronomy 32:8, NET; emphasis added)

Most English translations read "sons of Israel" at the end of the verse. Again, this is an example of translators making their best guess at a difficult phrase.

There are a couple of reasons to favor "sons of God" over "sons of Israel." First, in the passage, Moses referred to God's reaction to the Tower of Babel incident. He confused the language of the people at Babel and then "dispersed them over the face of all the earth."[147] Israel—that is, Jacob—was at least fifteen hundred years in the future when God disrupted Nimrod's pet building project.

Second, and more important: The oldest and best text evidence supports the "sons of God" reading. A copy of Deuteronomy found among the Dead Sea scrolls clearly reads "sons of God," and the Septuagint translation, which was rendered into Greek from Hebrew more than two hundred years before the birth of Jesus, adopts a similar meaning:

When the Most High distributed nations
as he scattered the descendants of Adam,
he set up boundaries for the nations
according to the number of the angels of God.
(Deuteronomy 32:8, Lexham English Septuagint; emphasis added)

Here is the key point for this section: When we read the list of the descendants of Noah in chapter 10 of Genesis, the Table of Nations, we find seventy names. In other words, when God divided the nations after

Babel, He created a balance between the number of nations and the "sons of God," "angels of God," "heavenly assembly," "heavenly court,"[148] or "heavenly beings."[149] Why? Judgment. God decreed that the earth would no longer be under His direct authority but would report to His subordinates, the "sons of God."

> And beware lest you raise your eyes to heaven, and when you see the sun and the moon and the stars, all the host of heaven, you be drawn away and bow down to them and serve them, **things that the Lord your God has allotted to all the peoples under the whole heaven.**
>
> But the Lord has taken you and brought you out of the iron furnace, out of Egypt, to be a people of his own inheritance, as you are this day. (Deuteronomy 4:19–20; emphasis added)

God allotted "the host of heaven" to the nations as their gods, but Israel He reserved for Himself.

> But the Lord's portion is his people,
> Jacob his allotted heritage. (Deuteronomy 32:9)

Babel was an attempt to build an artificial mountain—a portal, if you will, to bring the gods to earth.[150] God's punishment was to give humanity what it wanted, an epic example of "be careful what you wish for."

Just to be clear: We're not pointing out these differences in translation to pick nits with the accuracy of the Bible. Reading "sons of Israel" in Deuteronomy 32:8 doesn't change the Bible's overall message of sin and salvation by grace through faith in Jesus Christ. What we get with the correct reading, "sons of God," is a fuller understanding of the depth and intensity of the supernatural war going on around us.

Were there exactly seventy angels who became the gods of the pagan world? Probably not. Remember, seventy in the ancient world meant "all of them." In other words, God allowed the nations to follow these lesser spirit beings, but reserved Israel for Himself.

The concept that each nation had its own patron deity was widely accepted in the ancient world, and it's evident in the Bible. For example, consider the following, when Jephthah addressed the king of Ammon:

> So then the Lord, the God of Israel, dispossessed the Amorites from before his people Israel; and are you to take possession of them?
>
> Will you not possess what Chemosh your god gives you to possess? And all that the LORD our God has dispossessed before us, we will possess. (Judges 11:23–24)

The point here is that much of what's in the Bible has a deeper meaning than we've been taught because the consensus view of Scripture by most Christian theologians since the time of Augustine in the fifth century AD is that the entities called "gods" were imaginary. That happens not to be the case, and many things in Scripture, such as the Feast of Tabernacles, make more sense—or *only* make sense—when we understand that God meant what He said when He called these beings "gods."

Another case in point: A pagan festival similar to Sukkot was performed in Emar, a city in what is today northern Syria. This annual rite, called the *zukru*, is documented in texts from the time of the judges, the fourteenth through twelfth centuries BC.

> It was celebrated in Emar on the first month of the year, called SAG.MU—namely, the "head of the year". On the first day of the festival, when the moon is full, the god Dagan—the supreme god of Syria—and all the other gods in the pantheon were taken outside the temple and city in the presence of the citizens to a shrine of stones called *sikkānu*....
>
> The first offerings of the *zukru*-festival were sacrificed on the fourteenth of the month of the "head of the year":

On the month of SAG.MU (meaning: the head of the year), on the fourteenth day, they offer seventy pure lambs provided by the king...for all the seventy gods [of the city of] Emar.[151]

There were seventy lambs for the seventy gods of Emar, headed up by the chief god of the pantheon, Dagan, who was the same deity as El and Kronos but known by a different name.[152] The seventy lambs were sacrificed over seven days during a festival "when the moon is full," just like at Sukkot.

The pagans who surrounded ancient Israel believed that their creator-god—variously called El, Dagan, Enlil, and Ashur—fathered *all* of the gods that controlled their world. Similarly, the Hebrews understood that the pagan gods of their neighbors were lesser *elohim*, fallen angels, who had rejected God's authority. The seventy bulls sacrificed to Yahweh represented those small-*g* "gods," which may also have been a message to those fallen angels that their days are numbered. So, the Feast of Tabernacles was a reminder to God's people that He would rescue them from all of the gods of the pagan nations of the earth.

If the arrival of the approaching asteroid named for the ancient Egyptian god of chaos does coincide with the midpoint of the seven-year Great Tribulation, it is not too much to suggest that God may rescue His Church through the prophesied Rapture on or about October 13, 2025—at the end of Sukkot, the annual feast celebrating His victory over the gods of the nations.

There is another fascinating connection between the arrival of asteroid Apophis and an event of huge significance for the Jews, and thus for Christians as well. Let's travel back in time to the year 539 BC.

At that point, exiles from the kingdom of Judah had been in Babylonia for more than fifty years, since Nebuchadnezzar's first siege of Jerusalem in 597 BC. Among them was the prophet Ezekiel, who was among the first wave of exiles and probably died around 570 BC.[153]

By the time of this story, Nebuchadnezzar had been dead for more than twenty years. Nabonidus had been king since about 556 BC, when he led a coup against Nebuchadnezzar's young grandson, Labashi-Marduk, who was apparently deemed unfit to rule.

The last king of Babylon, Nabonidus, is a fascinating character. He might have been remembered as one of the great pagan rulers of the ancient world if he hadn't picked the wrong side in the long supernatural war.

Nabonidus, whose name means "Nabu is praised" (Nabu being the Mesopotamian god of wisdom, literacy, and scribes), wasn't Chaldean like Nebuchadnezzar. His background is somewhat fuzzy, but Nabonidus was probably Assyrian based on his origin in Harran. That's in modern-day Turkey, near the border with Syria. It was home to a major temple to the moon-god, Sîn, where his mother served as a priestess.

He was a competent military leader, but Nabonidus might also be history's first known archaeologist.[154] Nabonidus may have been wrapping himself in the past to please the home crowd, aligning himself with Babylon's glory days, or maybe he just genuinely loved history. Whatever his reasons, Nabonidus dug up artifacts all over Babylonia and displayed his finds in museums, the first person in history that we know of to do so. He also located and restored the ancient temples of Shamash, the sun god, and Ishtar, the goddess of sex and war, in the city of Sippar, and his mother was surely pleased when Nabonidus rebuilt the sanctuary of the moongod at Harran that had been constructed more than fifteen hundred years earlier by the great Akkadian king Naram-Sîn.

The most interesting aspect of Nabonidus' life for this study was his devotion to the moon-god. That's probably not a surprise, considering his mother's lifetime commitment to Sîn. What's unusual is the degree to which Nabonidus took it. While scholars aren't completely agreed about this, evidence suggests he tried to replace the chief god of Babylon, Marduk, at the top of the pantheon with the moon-god. In addition, Nabonidus spent most of his seventeen-year reign outside of Babylon, living for ten years at Tayma,[155] an oasis in the Arabian desert probably named for one of the sons of Ishmael.[156] Not surprisingly, Tayma was a center of moon-god worship.[157]

Why was Nabonidus there? Some scholars suggest he was mainly after wealth. Tayma was on a trade route, the easternmost branch of the ancient incense road.[158] Like any king needing to balance the royal budget, Nabonidus may have felt that his presence was necessary to control the lucrative trade from south Arabia to Mesopotamia, especially when it became clear that his neighbors to the north and east, the Medes and Persians, had become an existential threat.

There may be another explanation. A prayer attributed to Nabonidus found among the Dead Sea scrolls, an Aramaic text called 4Q242, suggests that his long stay at Tayma may have been for his health.

1. The words of the p[ra]yer which Nabonidus, king of [Ba] bylon, the great king, pray[ed] when he was stricken]
2. with an evil disease by the decree of G[o]d in Teman. [I Nabonidus] was stricken with [an evil disease]
3. for seven years, and from [that] (time) I was like [unto a beast and I prayed to the Most High]
4. and, as for my sin, he forgave it.[159]

The similarity of this text to the story of Nebuchadnezzar's madness in the fourth chapter of the book of Daniel is obvious. Some scholars believe Daniel's account may have inspired the text at Qumran.

On the other hand, there is evidence that Nabonidus' ten-year sojourn at Tayma was not medicinal, but spiritual. The oasis is believed to have been a center of moon-god worship as far back as the Bronze Age,[160] at least five hundred years before Nabonidus ascended to the throne of Babylon. Tayma was in the heart of what was the land of Midian in the days of Gideon and his three hundred men, which was probably within a couple decades of 1200 BC. The book of Judges records that the kings of Midian and their camels were adorned with crescent ornaments,[161] which were in all probability in honor of the moon-god.

So, Nabonidus, born in Harran, the northern Mesopotamian city of the moon-god, settled in the Arabian oasis sacred to the moon-god for reasons beyond its strategic importance. It may be that he was waiting for a message from the god—a prophecy or sign of some sort. While he stayed at Tayma, his son Belshazzar ruled as regent in Babylon. He's the king we know from chapter 5 of the book of Daniel.

Belshazzar was in a delicate situation. There were certain religious duties that the king of Babylon was expected to perform. The king played a key role in the annual spring festival for the chief god Marduk called the *akitu*. If the king wasn't in Babylon to "take the hand of Bel" (Marduk), the rites couldn't be performed and the city, it was believed, wouldn't receive the blessing of its patron god. And Nabonidus was outside of Babylon, living at Tayma in the Arabian desert, for ten years.

Nabonidus didn't seem to feel that this was a problem. Scholars take this as evidence that his goal was to replace Marduk as the chief god of Babylon with Sîn, the moon-god. That couldn't have made Nabonidus popular with the ancient priesthood of Marduk or religious conservatives in Babylon.

On that fateful night in 539 BC, Belshazzar, the son and coregent of Babylon's king Nabonidus, hosted a drunken party at the palace. During the festivities, he ordered his servants to bring out the gold and silver vessels that had been plundered from the temple in Jerusalem to serve wine to the Chaldean nobles, and his wives and concubines.

And then:

Immediately the fingers of a human hand appeared and wrote on the plaster of the wall of the king's palace, opposite the lampstand. And the king saw the hand as it wrote.

Then the king's color changed, and his thoughts alarmed him; his limbs gave way, and his knees knocked together. (Daniel 5:5–6)

So, Daniel was summoned to interpret the sign. It was bad news for Belshazzar and Babylon.

You have lifted up yourself against the Lord of heaven. And the vessels of his house have been brought in before you, and you and your lords, your wives, and your concubines have drunk wine from them.

And you have praised the gods of silver and gold, of bronze, iron, wood, and stone, which do not see or hear or know, but the God in whose hand is your breath, and whose are all your ways, you have not honored.

Then from his presence the hand was sent, and this writing was inscribed. And this is the writing that was inscribed: MENE, MENE, TEKEL, and PARSIN.

This is the interpretation of the matter: MENE, God has numbered the days of your kingdom and brought it to an end;

TEKEL, you have been weighed in the balances and found wanting;

PERES, your kingdom is divided and given to the Medes and Persians. (Daniel 5:23–28)

All of this you probably know. The story is popular with all ages, from Sunday school children through adults. It's an easy moral for a sermon: *Don't get too big for your britches*. But there's a lot more to it just under the surface.

First, we need to explain why we're taking you down this rabbit trail. There is a solid connection between the Babylon of old and the end times. The link is through the people who founded ancient Babylon and the gods they served.

The Antichrist's church of the last days is called "Babylon the great," but Mystery Babylon is the name that's stuck. After two thousand years, scholars still can't agree completely on what it represents.

Here's what we know: The Babylon of John's vision is a religion and a city. Ezekiel gave us important clues that modern prophecy scholars have missed because they haven't considered the history and religion of the people who lived in the ancient Near East.

Chapter 27 of Ezekiel is a lament over the city of Tyre. The great trading city was founded by the Phoenician descendants of the Amorites who settled along the eastern shore of the Mediterranean. This lament has a clear parallel in Revelation. It not only cements the connection between the visions of Ezekiel and John, it shows that the iniquity of the Amorites, mentioned by God during His covenant with Abraham,[162] is still with us today.

> The word of the LORD came to me: Now you, son of man, raise a lamentation over Tyre, and say to Tyre, who dwells at the entrances to the sea, merchant of the peoples to many coastlands, thus says the Lord GOD:
>   O Tyre, you have said,
>   "I am perfect in beauty."
>   Your borders are in the heart of the seas;
>   your builders made perfect your beauty.
>   They made all your planks
>   of fir trees from Senir;
>   they took a cedar from Lebanon
>   to make a mast for you.
>   Of oaks of Bashan
>   they made your oars;
>   they made your deck of pines
>   from the coasts of Cyprus,
>   inlaid with ivory. (Ezekiel 27:1–6)

Tyre was the most powerful commercial empire in the Mediterranean for centuries. Even after the city's influence began to fade, its colony in north Africa, Carthage, grew so powerful that its most famous general, Hannibal, nearly destroyed Rome. At the peak of Tyre's power, in Ezekiel's day, the prophet linked the strength of Tyre, its ships, to Mount Hermon and Bashan.

Senir was the Amorite name for Hermon, the mount of assembly ruled by the creator-god of the western Amorites, El. But the Amorites were history by Ezekiel's day, at least under the name "Amorite." By the time of David and Solomon, about four hundred years before Ezekiel, the lands once ruled by Amorite kingdoms were under the control of their descendants, the Arameans, Phoenicians, and Arabs. So, why did Ezekiel use the archaic Amorite name for Mount Hermon?

Here's why: The prophet deliberately linked Tyre to the spiritual wickedness of the Amorites connected to Hermon and the land around it. Not only was Senir/Hermon the abode of El, where the Rephaim spirits (i.e., the spirits of the Nephilim destroyed in the Flood)[163] came to feast,[164] it towered over Bashan, which was believed to be the literal entrance to the netherworld.[165] By calling the mountain "Senir" instead of "Hermon," Ezekiel specifically connected Tyre to the Amorites, whose evil was legendary among Jews.

Here's the important link between the past and future: Babylon was founded by Amorites. Hammurabi, of the ruling house that established the ancient kingdom of Babylon, was an Amorite from a long line of Amorites. When we use the word "Babylonian," we're simply using a geographic term to distinguish the Amorites of eastern Mesopotamia from the Canaanites, who were the Amorites of western Mesopotamia.

The Phoenicians, descended from Amorites who settled in what is now Lebanon, made Tyre the foremost commercial empire of the ancient world. The key link between Tyre in the sixth century BC, the time of Ezekiel, and Mystery Babylon at some as-yet unknown time in the future is the lament over its destruction:

> At the sound of the cry of your pilots
> the countryside shakes,
> and down from their ships
> come all who handle the oar.
> The mariners and all the pilots of the sea
> stand on the land
> and shout aloud over you
> and cry out bitterly.

They cast dust on their heads
and wallow in ashes;
they make themselves bald for you
and put sackcloth on their waist,
and they weep over you in bitterness of soul,
with bitter mourning.
In their wailing they raise a lamentation for you
and lament over you:
"Who is like Tyre,
like one destroyed in the midst of the sea?
When your wares came from the seas,
you satisfied many peoples;
with your abundant wealth and merchandise
you enriched the kings of the earth.
Now you are wrecked by the seas,
in the depths of the waters;
your merchandise and all your crew in your midst
have sunk with you.
All the inhabitants of the coastlands
are appalled at you,
and the hair of their kings bristles with horror;
their faces are convulsed.
The merchants among the peoples hiss at you;
you have come to a dreadful end
and shall be no more forever." (Ezekiel 27:28–36)

Now, compare that section of Ezekiel's lament over Tyre to John's prophecy of the destruction of Babylon the Great in Revelation 18.

After this I saw another angel coming down from heaven, having great authority, and the earth was made bright with his glory. And he called out with a mighty voice,
Fallen, fallen is Babylon the great!

She has become a dwelling place for demons,

a haunt for every unclean spirit,

a haunt for every unclean bird,

a haunt for every unclean and detestable beast....

and the kings of the earth, who committed sexual immorality and lived in luxury with her, will weep and wail over her when they see the smoke of her burning. They will stand far off, in fear of her torment, and say,

"Alas! Alas! You great city,

you mighty city, Babylon!

For in a single hour your judgment has come."...

The merchants of these wares, who gained wealth from her, will stand far off, in fear of her torment, weeping and mourning aloud,

"Alas, alas, for the great city

that was clothed in fine linen,

in purple and scarlet,

adorned with gold,

with jewels, and with pearls!

For in a single hour all this wealth has been laid waste."

And all shipmasters and seafaring men, sailors and all whose trade is on the sea, stood far off and cried out as they saw the smoke of her burning,

"What city was like the great city?"

And they threw dust on their heads as they wept and mourned, crying out,

"Alas, alas, for the great city

where all who had ships at sea

grew rich by her wealth!

For in a single hour she has been laid waste." (Revelation 18:1–2, 9, 15–19)

Let's compare some key phrases from these chapters.

Tyre (Ezekiel 27)	Babylon (Revelation 18)
"enriched the kings of the earth" (Ezekiel 27:33)	"kings of the earth...lived in luxury with her" (Revelation 18:9)
Lamented by mariners, pilots of the sea, merchants, and kings (Ezekiel 27:28–36)	Lamented by kings, merchants, shipmasters, and seafaring men (Revelation 18:919)
"'Who is like Tyre, like one destroyed in the midst of the sea? ...with your abundant wealth and merchandise you enriched the kings of the earth.'" (Ezekiel 27:32–33)	"'What city was like the great city... where all who had ships at sea grew rich by her wealth!'" (Revelation 18:18–19)

The parallels here have been noted by Bible scholars for generations, but God hinted at this almost four thousand years ago when He established His covenant with Abraham. He told the patriarch that his descendants would be afflicted for four hundred years in a land that wasn't theirs, "for the iniquity of the Amorites is not yet complete."[166]

Ezekiel gave us the clues. He pointed to Mount Hermon, Bashan, and the neighbors of ancient Israel who worshiped the gods who called that region home. Those neighbors, the Amorites, were the people who established the wicked occult system of Babylon. The connection between Mystery Babylon and the Amorites is key. Spiritual wickedness connected to an unparalleled maritime trading empire are the two main features of Mystery Babylon.

Then one of the seven angels who had the seven bowls came and said to me, "Come, I will show you the judgment of the great prostitute who is seated on many waters, with whom the kings of the earth have committed sexual immorality, and with the wine of whose sexual immorality the dwellers on earth have become drunk."

And he carried me away in the Spirit into a wilderness, and

I saw a woman sitting on a scarlet beast that was full of blasphe-
mous names, and it had seven heads and ten horns.

The woman was arrayed in purple and scarlet, and adorned
with gold and jewels and pearls, holding in her hand a golden cup
full of abominations and the impurities of her sexual immorality.

And on her forehead was written a name of mystery: "Babylon the great, mother of prostitutes and of earth's abominations."

And I saw the woman, drunk with the blood of the saints, the
blood of the martyrs of Jesus. (Revelation 17:1–6)

"Sexual immorality" is a euphemism for spiritual rebellion, like Israel's
"whorings" with the gods of the pagan nations against which the prophets
of the Old Testament thundered. And the fall of ancient Babylon may
hold a clue to the timing of its future destruction.

The festival hosted by Belshazzar, described in chapter 5 of the book
of Daniel, was not a random event. This was not simply an excuse for
Belshazzar to show off in front of his friends. This party had spiritual
significance.

The tradition of the festivities might reflect historical fact. According
to the chronicle, Babylon was taken on the sixteenth of Tašritu. Accepting
that Nabonidus imposed new features of the cult of Sîn in the capital after
his return from Teima, it is conceivable that festivals linked with the cult
of Sîn at Harran were transplanted to Babylon, perhaps even the *akitu*
festival. This festival started on the seventeenth of Tašritu. As Babylon
was captured on the eve of the seventeenth, the festivities mentioned by
Herodotus and the Book of Daniel may have been those of the Harran
akitu festival, as celebrated in the capital by the supporters of Nabonidus.[167]

The *akitu* was an annual festival celebrated in the ancient Near East for
the patron gods of the cities of Mesopotamia. In Uruk, for example, the
akitu was celebrated for Inanna (Ishtar), the goddess called the Queen of
Heaven in the book of Jeremiah (and, sadly, whose cult has been absorbed
into the Roman Catholic Church).[168]

The oldest celebration documented *akitu* dates to about 2500 BC in Ur.[169] The ancient city was sacred to Sîn, the moon-god. The festival is usually described as a new year celebration because the best-known *akitu* in the ancient world was held at Babylon on the first of Nisan, the first month of the year. Even today, Nisan 1 is the first day of the religious year on the Hebrew calendar.

Akiti, the Sumerian form of the word, refers both to the festival and the special building used during the celebration.[170] Unlike Babylon's festival for Marduk, which was held only in the spring, the *akiti* at Ur was also held in the seventh month around the time of the autumn equinox. The festival involved the idol representing the god traveling by boat from the city to the *akiti*-house, and then returning to the city with great fanfare.[171]

The autumn festival at Ur was the more important of the two. Why? The fall *akitu*, which lasted at least eleven days into the month,[172] took place as the waxing moon grew larger and larger, symbolizing the god's reentry into his city just as the days were getting noticeably shorter and the moon asserted his dominance in the sky over Utu, the sun-god.[173] As it happened, the Babylonian calendar had been tweaked under Nabonidus so that the fall *akitu* was specifically timed to coincide with either the Harvest Moon or the Hunter's Moon:

> The seventeenth of Tašritu always fell during one of the two periods of the year that the moon had an unusually prominent place at night. It should also be remembered that the Harvest Moon and Hunter's Moon, by a curious trick of perception, are popularly believed to be unusually large and luminous. It is therefore singularly appropriate that the *akitu* festival in honor of the moon god Sîn should take place on the seventeenth of Tašritu, when the lunar deity, several days after full moon, retained its sway throughout the night.[174]

This is the key point. Because most Christians are not very familiar with the festivals of Yahweh, we will spell it out: The last Jewish feast of the year, and the most important on the annual calendar, is Sukkot, the Feast of Tabernacles—and it begins every year on the fifteenth of Tishri (the Babylonian month of Tašritu).

So, the night of Belshazzar's party on 16 Tishri, 539 BC, was a kick-off event for the *akitu* festival to honor the moon-god, a Mesopotamian religious rite at least two thousand years old. Meanwhile, the most important annual festival of Yahweh, Sukkot, had begun the day before, on 15 Tishri. And then Belshazzar, for reasons unknown, decided to liven up the party for his god, Sîn, by ordering the wine served in sacred utensils that were consecrated for use in the Temple of Yahweh.

Why did Belshazzar do it? What inspired him? More important, why was he hosting a party with an army of invading Medes and Persians outside the city walls?

It's impossible to say. Accounts of the last night of Babylon are somewhat contradictory. Some sources place Nabonidus at the battle, others don't. It seems unlikely that Cyrus could have marched an army into Babylonia without word reaching the king. Maybe Nabonidus and his son considered the *akitu* feast too important to postpone, even for an invasion. Maybe they believed the invasion made holding the festival imperative, to win the favor of the moon-god so Sîn would protect the city. Maybe Belshazzar's decision to bring out the Temple utensils was meant to demonstrate the power of the moon-god over the God of the exiles from Judah.

Whatever his reasons, it was a big mistake. *Boom.* Lights out. Babylon was done. On the sixteenth of Tishri, the second day of the annual Feast of Tabernacles.

If the fall of the ancient kingdom of Babylon foreshadows the destruction of the end-times church of the Antichrist, then the date may be significant. Tishri 16 in 2025 is October 8, just a few days ahead of our speculative "last possible date for a pre-tribulation rapture."[175]

Looking ahead to the date of the asteroid's fly-by, we find another conflu-
ence of dates that may be significant. And, like the fall of Babylon, this
also has a connection to the moon-god.

We should emphasize that the moon-god was one of the most popular
and important in ancient Mesopotamia. Perhaps that's not surprising in a
dry, desert land where daytime temperatures during the summer months
often exceed 100 degrees Fahrenheit (38 Celsius). Although Marduk was
the chief god of Babylon, who was elevated to the top of the Mesopotamian pantheon as Babylon became the dominant political power in
the region, the great King Hammurabi credited the moon-god Sîn with
establishing his dynasty and creating him personally.

The moon-god was the first-born son of Enlil, who was king of the gods
before the rise of Marduk. In Sumer, where he was called Nanna, Sîn was
one of the "seven gods who decree," with Anu, the sky-god; Enlil, the king;
Ninhursag, mother of the gods; Enki, the god of wisdom; Shamash (also
called Utu), the sun-god; and Ishtar (or Inanna), the goddess of sex and war.

Calendars in Mesopotamia were based on the thirty-day cycle of the
moon. Undoubtedly, there was a fertility aspect to this; in a culture that
depended on the health of flocks and herds, that was important. In fact,
the moon-god's name, Sîn, was represented in cuneiform by the symbol
for the numeral 30. This link between the fertility of the herd and the
moon, and the similarity of the shape of the crescent moon and the horns
of a bull, led to Sîn being described in Mesopotamian texts as the "frisky
calf of Enlil" or "frisky calf of heaven."[176]

Even though Enlil was still considered the king of the gods during the
Old Babylonian period (the time of Abraham, Isaac, and Jacob), a text
fragment translated in 2011 describes the moon-god Nanna/Sîn as ruling over the Mesopotamian divine assembly, which was called the Ubšu-
ukkina. Anu and Enlil, whom we would expect to be the presiding deities,
are there only as advisors, along with the other "gods who decree."[177]

You, who stand before him to sit in the Ubšu-ukkina

An, Enlil, Enki, Ninhursag, Utu, and Inanna sat in assembly for the king

They advised him there.

Nanna sets the holy...in order....

The great gods were paying attention to....

Suen [Sîn], his assembly's decision, his speech of goodness, abundance....

for Suen, they implement abundance in heaven and earth properly(?)

The king suitable for holy heaven, the barge in the midst of heaven.[178]

"The barge in the midst of heaven" is the crescent moon. Besides resembling the horns of a bull, it also looks like a reed boat sailing across the night sky. Even though bits of the tablet are missing, it's clear that Sîn was "the king" in the Mesopotamian divine assembly, with the other "great gods" in subordinate roles. (And note that Marduk isn't even mentioned!) This supports the theory that the Amorite founders of Babylon, even though they hailed from the city sacred to Marduk, considered the moon-god, Sîn, their patron.

It's also important to remember that to Mesopotamians, the Ubšu-ukkina was a physical place. The assembly of the gods took place in Nippur, inside the temple of the chief god Enlil, which was called the *E-kur*, or "Mountain House." We'll explain why that's significant in a moment.

Christians familiar with the Old Testament may have the impression that the chief spiritual enemy of God before the birth of Jesus was Baal. The confrontation between Elijah and the prophets of Baal on Mount Carmel was spectacular, after all, and the slaughter of the priests who'd been eating at the table of Queen Jezebel was serious business. But a closer reading of Scripture shows that until the time of Gideon, maybe two hundred years or so after the Exodus, the pagan deity who was the focus of God's attention was the moon-god.

Our first clue is in the account of the Israelites' escape from Egypt:

They set out from Elim, and all the congregation of the people of Israel came to the wilderness of Sin, which is between Elim and Sinai, on the fifteenth day of the second month after they had departed from the land of Egypt.

And the whole congregation of the people of Israel grumbled against Moses and Aaron in the wilderness, and the people of Israel said to them, "Would that we had died by the hand of the LORD in the land of Egypt, when we sat by the meat pots and ate bread to the full, for you have brought us out into this wilderness to kill this whole assembly with hunger." (Exodus 16:1–3)

Nothing in the Bible is there to fill space. So, why did Moses specifically note the arrival at the wilderness of Sin on "the fifteenth day of the second month"? In the ancient Near East, calendars were set to the phases of the moon, with the new moon starting the month. The fifteenth day, then, was during the full moon, a time when the moon-god was believed to be at full strength. That's precisely when the people of Israel "came to the wilderness of Sin"—the wilderness of the moon-god. That undoubtedly had something to do with the grumbling of the people— they believed they were entering the territory of a god they did not serve when he was at full strength.

The conflict with the moon-god continued at Mount Sinai, which, you have surely noticed, is also derived from the name of the lunar deity.[179] While Moses' encounter with Yahweh in chapter 3 of the book of Exodus is described as taking place at "the mountain of God," the fact that it was named for the moon-god suggests that the Hebrew *har elohim* in Exodus 3:1 could just as well be translated "mountain of the gods." Yahweh must have chosen this place as a message aimed at the entity who masqueraded as the moon to the pagan Amorites of Mesopotamia.

This also suggests a deeper meaning for the golden calf fashioned by Aaron when Moses was too long on the mountain for the Israelites. Perhaps they thought that since they were at the mountain of Sîn, in the middle of the wilderness of Sîn, fashioning a golden idol to represent the "frisky calf of heaven" was a good way to win the favor of the god who ruled the region.

It's difficult for modern American Christians to grasp, but the prophets and apostles understood full well that the pagan gods of their neighbors were real, and that they controlled certain specific territories. This belief continued in Israel for centuries. On one of the many occasions that David escaped from King Saul, he lamented:

> Now therefore let my lord the king hear the words of his servant. If it is the LORD who has stirred you up against me, may he accept an offering, but if it is men, may they be cursed before the LORD, for they have driven me out this day that I should have no share in the heritage of the LORD, saying, "Go, serve other gods." (1 Samuel 26:19)

David understood that Israel belonged to Yahweh. If he was driven out, he would be outside of the territory of Yahweh and would be compelled to serve the gods of the lands where he found refuge. Although this is a strange idea to us today, it was the common understanding of the spirit realm in the ancient Near East.

To the Israelites following Moses, Yahweh was one of many entities in the spirit realm. Yes, He had freed them from Egypt (and delivered manna six days a week like clockwork), but as far as they knew, they were on the moon-god's turf.

Here is where this is leading: Forty years later, as the Israelites finally crossed the Jordan into Canaan, the first target of their war to claim their inheritance was the city of Jericho—another center of the moon-god's cult. The city's name is derived from the Amorite name of the moon-god, Yarikh.

And here's where it gets really interesting. Note the timing of the attack on the city:

While the people of Israel were encamped at Gilgal, they kept the Passover on the fourteenth day of the month in the evening on the plains of Jericho. (Joshua 5:10)

This terrified the people of Jericho. The Bible records that the city was "was shut up inside and outside because of the people of Israel. None went out, and none came in."[180] The significance is that the ancient Mesopotamian *akitu* festival would have been held on or around 1 Nisan, the first day of the new year. While we don't have evidence for such a festival at Jericho, if it was held according to Mesopotamian custom, the celebration would have lasted eleven days, with a grand procession out of the city on the first day of the festival to carry the idol representing the god to the special *akitu*-house. After days of feasts, prayers, and rituals, the god would have returned to his temple inside the city on day seven.

Assuming that this was an annual rite at Jericho (remember, the oldest known *akitu* was documented a thousand years before the Exodus at Ur, the moon-god's city in the land of Sumer), the Bible tells "none went out, and none came in"—there was no celebration for the moon-god that year with the army of Israel camped outside the gates!

Then, Israel celebrated the Passover, which always begins on the evening of 14 Nisan. This is one of the three pilgrimage festivals, along with Shavuot (Feast of Weeks, or Pentecost) and Sukkot, the Feast of Tabernacles we described earlier.

The Israelites would have celebrated this festival for seven days on the plain outside Jericho, in full view of the Amorites inside the city's massive defensive walls. Jewish tradition holds that the march around the city, commanded by the Captain of the Lord's Army (Jesus in the Old Testament), began after Passover, on 22 Nisan.

Then Joshua rose early in the morning, and the priests took up the ark of the LORD.

And the seven priests bearing the seven trumpets of rams' horns before the ark of the LORD walked on, and they blew the trumpets continually.

And the armed men were walking before them, and the rear guard was walking after the ark of the LORD, while the trumpets blew continually.

And the second day they marched around the city once, and returned into the camp. So they did for six days.

On the seventh day they rose early, at the dawn of day, and marched around the city in the same manner seven times. It was only on that day that they marched around the city seven times.

And at the seventh time, when the priests had blown the trumpets, Joshua said to the people, "Shout, for the LORD has given you the city. And the city and all that is within it shall be devoted to the LORD for destruction. Only Rahab the prostitute and all who are with her in her house shall live, because she hid the messengers whom we sent. But you, keep yourselves from the things devoted to destruction, lest when you have devoted them you take any of the devoted things and make the camp of Israel a thing for destruction and bring trouble upon it. But all silver and gold, and every vessel of bronze and iron, are holy to the LORD; they shall go into the treasury of the LORD."

So the people shouted, and the trumpets were blown. As soon as the people heard the sound of the trumpet, the people shouted a great shout, and the wall fell down flat, so that the people went up into the city, every man straight before him, and they captured the city. (Joshua 6:12–20)

There are two things to note here. First, God knocked down the walls of the city so that He and His people could enter *on the seventh day* of marching, a mockery of the ancient festival held in honor of the moon-god (and other pagan deities in Mesopotamia) for more than a thousand years.

Second, and more relevant for us in the not-too-distant future, is that the walls of Jericho came tumbling down on 28 Nisan.

Asteroid Apophis arrives at planet earth on April 13, 2029—which, on the Hebrew calendar, falls on 28 Nisan.[181]

One final observation about Revelation 8, the chapter that includes the famous Wormwood prophecy. This is the judgment that accompanies the blowing of the third trumpet, when "a great star" falls from heaven, "blazing like a torch."[182] The judgment prior to that, after the second angel sounds his trumpet, is just as ominous:

> The second angel blew his trumpet, and something like a great mountain, burning with fire, was thrown into the sea, and a third of the sea became blood.
>
> A third of the living creatures in the sea died, and a third of the ships were destroyed. (Revelation 8:8–9)

It's well known that stars in the Bible often represent angels. But mountains, and specifically burning mountains, also denote supernatural beings in ancient Jewish thought.

Earlier we mentioned that the temple of Enlil, the chief god of Mesopotamia before the rise of Babylon and Marduk, was called the *E-kur*, or "Mountain House." One of the god's main titles was "Great Mountain."[183] Derek Gilbert showed in chapter 8 of his book *Bad Moon Rising* that Enlil was identified across the ancient world as the deity who was the king of the second generation of gods, inheriting (or taking) kingship from the sky-god before eventually turning it over (or losing it) to a storm-god.

To simplify, the generations looked like this:

	Babylonia	Syria	Hittites/ Hurrians	Canaan	Greece/ Rome
Generation 1 Sky-god	Anu	Anu	Anu	Ilib	Ouranos/ Caelus
Generation 2 Grain(?)-god	Enlil	Dagan	Kumarbi	El Hadad (Baal)	Kronos/ Saturn
Generation 3 Storm-god	Marduk	Hadad (Baal)	Tarhunt/ Teshub		Zeus/ Jupiter

As noted earlier, the "Great Mountain" Enlil was the same entity known elsewhere as El, Dagan (Dagon to the Philistines), Kronos, and Saturn. This entity is linked to both mountains and the underworld in all his incarnations. In fact, the word *kur* in Sumerian means both "mountain" and "netherworld," which means that the "Mountain House" of Enlil carries the double meaning of "Underworld House."

Elsewhere, the Amorites of western Mesopotamia believed that Enlil's alter ego, El, dwelt on Mount Hermon. The Hurrian incarnation, Kumarbi, created a giant stone monster, Ullikummi (essentially a sentient mountain), to battle the storm-god, Teshub. One of Dagan's epithets along the Euphrates in Syria, where he was worshiped as the supreme god, was *bēl pagrê*—"lord of the corpse," or "lord of the funerary offering."[184] And you are probably familiar with the story of the rebellion of Zeus/Jupiter and the Olympians against the Titans, led by Kronos/Saturn, and the latter's imprisonment in Tartarus after losing the war.

The link between Enlil/El/Dagan/Kronos and the abyss is one of the reasons we connect the Titans of Greek mythology, whose king was Kronos, to the "sons of God" of Genesis 6 and the Watchers of the Book of 1 Enoch. Peter specifically described the punishment of the angels who sinned, referring to the Genesis 6 event, as *tartaróo*—literally, "thrust down to Tartarus."[185] It's important to note that *tartaróo* is used only once in the Bible, and it is not interchangeable with Hades (hell). Tartarus—the abyss—was a separate place, "as far beneath Hades as heaven is above Earth."[186]

Peter knew this. By his day, the Jews of Judea had been under Greek and Roman control, and exposed to their religion, for three and a half centuries. There is ample evidence in the Septuagint, the Greek Old Testament translated by Jewish scholars more than two hundred years before the birth of Jesus, that religious Jews understood very well the connection between the Titans, the Watchers, and the Nephilim.[187] And besides, Peter wrote under the influence of the Holy Spirit.

All of this—Greek tales of the monstrous Titans of old and the burning mountains of Revelation—may have its origin in older stories preserved in the Book of 1 Enoch. During his travels with the archangel Uriel as his guide, Enoch is shown "pillars of fire descending," which he's told are "angels who mingled with the women."[188] From there:

> I traveled to where it was chaotic. And there I saw a terrible thing; I saw neither heaven above, nor firmly founded earth, but a chaotic and terrible place. And **there I saw seven of the stars of heaven, bound and thrown in it together, like great mountains, and burning in fire.** Then I said, "For what reason have they been bound, and for what reason have they been thrown here?" Then Uriel said to me, one of the holy angels who was with me, and he was their leader, he said to me, "Enoch, why do you inquire, and why are you eager for the truth? These are the stars of heaven that transgressed the command of the Lord; they have been bound here until ten thousand years are fulfilled—the time of their sins."[189] (1 Enoch 21:1–5; emphasis added)

In the passage above, the seven "stars of heaven" refer to angels, just as they often do in the Old Testament. And, just like the chief Sumerian god Enlil, they are also described as "great mountains." Other verses that refer to angels as burning mountains are found in 1 Enoch 18:13 and 24:1.

Given our modern understanding of the concept of hell and punishment, we can be forgiven for thinking that the burning is part of their punishment. Not necessarily. The angels who transgressed in 1 Enoch were bound, and that appears to be the principal burden of their sentence. The mountains are aflame simply because that is their nature.

The root word behind "seraphim," *saraph*, derives from a Hebrew verb that means "to burn."[190] Hence, "seraphim" may be roughly translated as "burning ones." And that clarifies a section of Scripture from Ezekiel:

> You were an anointed guardian cherub.
> I placed you; you were on the holy mountain of God;
> **in the midst of the stones of fire you walked.**
> You were blameless in your ways
> from the day you were created,
> till unrighteousness was found in you.
> In the abundance of your trade
> you were filled with violence in your midst, and you sinned;
> so I cast you as a profane thing from the mountain of God,
> and I destroyed you, O guardian cherub,
> **from the midst of the stones of fire.**
> (Ezekiel 28:14–16; emphasis added)

Some Bible scholars speculate that these verses are evidence of the destruction of a planet that once occupied the orbit of the rocks that float between Mars and Jupiter in the asteroid belt, perhaps during an angelic rebellion before the creation of Adam. Allow us to suggest another explanation.

The seraphim of Isaiah 6 serve as guardians of the throne of God, like the "guardian cherub" of Ezekiel 28 (and the cherubim described in Ezekiel chapters 1 and 10). Thus, the cherubim and seraphim may well be the same type of angel. In fact, Ezekiel wrote that the cherubim of his vision "sparkled like burnished bronze" (or "brass"), and "their appearance was like burning coals of fire, like the appearance of torches moving to and fro among the living creatures. And the fire was bright, and out of the fire went forth lightning."[191]

It's safe to say that "burning ones" is a fair description of these entities.

We know from Mesopotamian texts that the title "Great Mountain" referred to one of the most prominent gods of the ancient world, Enlil. Both terms—"burning" and "mountain"—were used to describe angels in 1 Enoch. And what are burning mountains but "stones of fire," the phrase used in Ezekiel 28?

This suggests an alternate interpretation of the trumpet judgments of Revelation 8: Perhaps what appear to be prophecies of natural disasters— destructive weather, stars and burning mountains falling from heaven, the sun and moon dimmed in the sky—are actually the consequences of angelic beings who are sent to earth to execute God's judgment on an unrepentant world.

In fact, we suggest that all seven of the trumpet judgments may refer to both asteroids and accompanying supernatural entities. We'll summarize them briefly:

The first trumpet (Revelation 8:7). Hail and fire follow the sounding of the first trumpet, echoing the plague against Egypt described in Exodus 9:22–25. What Moses would have known, and so we assume John would have been aware of this as well, is that "hail" and "fire" were known deities in the ancient world that are *specifically* described as angelic beings by the psalmist Asaph:

> He gave over their cattle to the **hail**
> and their flocks to **thunderbolts**.
> He let loose on them his burning anger,
> wrath, indignation, and distress,
> **a company of destroying angels**.
> (Psalm 78:48–49; emphasis added)

"Hail" was *Barad*, a god known from the northern Syrian city of Ebla as much as a thousand years before the Exodus whose names roughly translates as "(big) Chill."[192] The Hebrew word translated as "thunderbolts" is even more interesting: *reshephim* is derived from the name of a well-known Near Eastern deity, Resheph, who has had a long and prominent career among pagan pantheons.

Resheph was a plague-god worshiped in western Mesopotamia, the Levant, and Egypt at least as early as the middle of the third millennium BC. He was depicted as an archer who could spread disease with his arrows, which may explain the occasional links between Resheph and lightning in the Old Testament.[193] (Or, this could be another descriptor for angels who appear as "burning ones.") The use of the plural form of his name suggests that *reshephim* was a class of supernatural being, perhaps a type of warrior angel. This concept was apparently known to the pagan neighbors of ancient Israel; in Sidon, a city on the Phoenician coast, an inscription from the fifth century BC mentions that an entire quarter of the town was named "land of the Reshephs."[194] So, it appears that the *reshephim* were sent out with Barad as a "company of destroying angels," wielding lightning and hail to execute God's judgment on Egypt. And it will happen again on a global scale when the first trumpet sounds.

The second trumpet (Revelation 8:8–9). A "great mountain, burning with fire," is thrown into the sea, destroying a third of the ships and a third of the life in the sea. As you might guess from the above, this may well be a reference to a powerful angel connected to a meteorite or asteroid. More evidence for this theory comes from a vision given to the prophet Zechariah:

> Then he said to me, "This is the word of the LORD to Zerubbabel: Not by might, nor by power, but by my Spirit, says the LORD of hosts. **Who are you, O great mountain?** Before Zerubbabel you shall become a plain. And he shall bring forward the top stone amid shouts of 'Grace, grace to it!" (Zechariah 4:6–7; emphasis added)

Zechariah's vision occurred around 520 BC.[195] At that point in history, the "Great Mountain" Enlil had been eclipsed by Marduk in the Mesopotamian pantheon because of the emergence of the Babylonian kingdom of Nebuchadnezzar. However, Enlil had been king of the gods for at least two thousand years, and he continued to be worshiped into the Christian era by the Romans and Phoenicians as Saturn and Baal-Hammon. (Note that the great winter festival at Rome was Saturnalia, not Jupiteralia, even though Jupiter was king of the Roman pantheon.)

Contrary to many Bible commentaries that interpret Zechariah's vision as a symbol of overcoming great obstacles, we believe it was a message directed at an ancient entity who led the rebellion of the Watchers at Mount Hermon.

Now, the burning mountain of the second trumpet judgment is probably not the same entity. Peter and Jude wrote that the rebellious angels of Genesis 6 are chained in darkness until the judgment.[196] Zechariah's vision simply adds weight to the testimony of Enoch, who saw angels as "burning mountains" in the netherworld, and the references to the "stones of fire" on the mountain of God, Eden, in Ezekiel 28.

Whoever it is, the burning mountain of Revelation 8:8-9 is joined to a destroying angel of great power, and he will bring unprecedented destruction to those on the sea and in it.

The third trumpet (Revelation 8:10–11). Not much needs to be said here since Wormwood is the focus of our study. Suffice it to say that while the "great star" named Wormwood may be a physical object from space, the evidence is just as strong that this may be carrying another supernatural entity tasked with carrying out God's judgment—perhaps by manipulating the asteroid that intersects earth's orbit on April 13, 2029.

Another star from heaven arrives when the fifth trumpet sounds, and that star is unquestionably an angel. Wormwood may be one as well.

The fourth trumpet (Revelation 8:12). A third of the sun, moon, and stars is "struck," or "smitten," so that "a third of their light might be darkened." Of all of the seven trumpet judgments, this one is least obviously connected to the angelic realm. Still, there is scriptural evidence to support the idea.

Early in Israel's history, God gave Moses this warning:

> Beware lest you raise your eyes to heaven, and when you see the sun and the moon and the stars, all the host of heaven, you be drawn away and bow down to them and serve them, things that the LORD your God has allotted to all the peoples under the whole heaven.
>
> But the LORD has taken you and brought you out of the iron furnace, out of Egypt, to be a people of his own inheritance, as you are this day. (Deuteronomy 4:19–20)

The sun, moon, and stars have been worshiped as deities for millennia. It was common practice among Israel's pagan neighbors. God warned the Israelites not to fall into that deception. In our modern world, we might assume that God's warning was because those lights in the sky were imaginary gods, but God's message to Moses was to avoid the entities worshiped as the sun, moon, and stars because they had been allotted to the nations *as their gods.*

Furthermore, if the entities who masqueraded as the gods of the sun, moon, and stars were imaginary, then what do we make of this prophecy from Isaiah?

> On that day the LORD will punish
> the host of heaven, in heaven,
> and the kings of the earth, on the earth.
> They will be gathered together
> as prisoners in a pit;
> they will be shut up in a prison,
> and after many days they will be punished.
> Then the moon will be confounded

and the sun ashamed,
for the LORD of hosts reigns
on Mount Zion and in Jerusalem,
and his glory will be before his elders. (Isaiah 24:21–23)

It's hard to imagine how the sun, moon, and stars could literally be "confounded," "ashamed," and held like "prisoners in a pit," much less punished. No, this prophecy is about the entities who inspired and accepted worship by presenting themselves to the ancient world as the gods of the sun, moon, and stars. Remember, in Revelation 12:4, Satan brings a third of the "stars of heaven" with him when he descends to Earth. It is generally agreed by Bible scholars that these stars are angels. If they are not the same third that is prophesied in Revelation 8:12, the verses at least support the idea that John's fourth trumpet vision was about the spirit realm and not an astronomical calamity.

The fifth trumpet (Revelation 9:1–11). This is one of the more intriguing sections of the Book of Revelation. "A star fallen from heaven" unlocks the abyss and lets out a horde of locust-like creatures who are given five months to torment those who are not sealed by God. Why five months? It's not a coincidence; it bookends the one hundred fifty days (five thirty-day months on the lunar calendar) that Noah and his family were aboard the ark before it came to rest in the mountains of Ararat.[197]

In our view, this confirms that the terrifying locust-things that swarm out of the abyss are not symbols that represent man-made objects, such as modern attack helicopters, but supernatural beings—specifically, the Watchers of Genesis 6 (i.e., the Titans of Greek myth), who were power-less to save their children, the gigantic Nephilim, as they were destroyed during the five months that the Flood covered the earth. The five months the Watchers are allotted to torment humanity during the end times is a bit of payback on the children of men—but only those without the seal of God on their foreheads.

An in-depth study of this section is beyond the scope of this chapter and this book, but it's safe to say that the star that falls from heaven, the locusts, and Abaddon/Apollyon, the king over those in the abyss, are supernatural beings.

The sixth trumpet (Revelation 9:13–21). After blowing his trumpet, the sixth angel is commanded to release the four angels bound in the Euphrates, who in turn lead an army of two hundred million that kills a third of humanity. Again, a deep study of this section is beyond the scope of this book; whether the horsemen of the prophecy are literal cavalry, John's best effort to describe modern weapons, or angelic warriors is immaterial here. The point is that this trumpet, like the previous five, summons supernatural agents to carry out God's will.

The seventh trumpet (Revelation 11:15). This triggers a series of events that culminates in the arrival of Antichrist, the Beast who emerges from the sea in Revelation 13:1. While Christian theologians have speculated on the identity of this character for nearly two thousand years, we're still searching for a consensus candidate. Many in the first-century church believed he was Nero, not just because he'd been an evil ruler who had persecuted the church, but because of a popular rumor that the emperor had not actually died in 68 AD. The Nero Redivivus legend held that the disgraced ruler had staged his death and fled east to Rome's enemy, Parthia, from which he would lead a mighty army to reclaim his throne. As strange as it sounds today, this belief persisted into the fifth century![198]

Focusing on a human candidate misses the point. John's description of a seven-headed monster emerging from the sea, which often represents the abyss and/or chaos in the Bible, is a symbol that would have been familiar to nearly any religious person in the ancient world, regardless of their belief. Stories of monsters or dragons from the sea, some with seven heads, were common in the ancient Near East, and they have been documented as far back as the middle of the third millennium BC. (And, we should note, Apophis was one of the chaos monsters of the ancient world.) A thorough study of this topic is, again, beyond the scope of this chapter and book, but it does illustrate that all seven of the trumpet judgments are connected to supernatural actors.

Discerning the future requires understanding the past. Studies of end-times prophecy often impose our modern worldview onto texts that were written between two and three thousand years ago, which yields interpretations that would have been meaningless to those who lived in the days of the prophets.

The timing of the arrival of asteroid Apophis makes it a strong candidate to fulfill the Wormwood prophecy. April 13, 2029, coincides with the date on the Hebrew calendar that marks the anniversary of the destruction of Jericho, the Israelites' first conquest as they entered the Promised Land. Three and a half years earlier, October 13, 2025, is Tishri 21, the final day of the annual Feast of Tabernacles, the celebration of God's victory over the rebellious gods of the nations. A few days earlier, 17 Tishri, is the anniversary of the fall of Babylon, which foreshadows the destruction of Mystery Babylon, the end-times church of Antichrist, during the seven-year period commonly called the Great Tribulation.

Many of the prophecies in Revelation, the seven trumpet judgments in particular, involve the active participation of supernatural beings—angels, devils, demons, and things that don't easily fit into any categories that we've been taught in church. Yet, the evidence is there, and these things were well known to the prophets and apostles. So, it is possible that the second and third trumpets—the "burning mountain" and the great star "blazing like a torch" that bring destruction to the waters of the world—are judgments carried out by powerful angels traveling with or upon calamities that are set to fall from the sky.

Are we correct that the asteroid of Revelation 8 will impact the earth in 2029? Will a pre-Tribulation Rapture occur 3.5 years earlier, during the prophetic Feast of Tabernacles? Or a few days earlier, during the prophetic

Feast of Trumpets (placing the Church at the arriage supper of the Lamb in heaven for the real Feast of Trumpets gathering around the "House" of God, as was mirrored in the Old Testament?) Time will tell. If nothing else, our appointment with Apophis is an urgent reminder that we, the Church, must get busy fulfilling our Lord's command to make disciples of all nations. Time is growing short.

8

Is Apophis Carrying an Alien Microbe That Will Initiate the Mark of the Beast?

If Apophis turns out to be biblical Wormwood, as I (Tom) believe it will, it will collide with earth in the middle of the Great Tribulation period, generally around the same moment in dispensational history as when the Mark of the Beast arrives. As I believe Apophis is carrying an "Andromeda Strain"-type alien microbe, I suggest it has a hitchhiker virus living off of it that, on impact with our terra firma, will be jettisoned into the atmosphere and rain down a global contagion that will make Covid-19 look like a day at the park.

Let me explain.

As described on Wikipedia, the *Andromeda Strain* "is a 1969 techno-thriller novel by Michael Crichton documenting the efforts of a team of scientists investigating the outbreak of a deadly extraterrestrial microorganism in Arizona."

A team from an air force base is deployed to recover a military satellite which has returned to Earth, but contact is lost abruptly. Aerial surveillance reveals that everyone in Piedmont, Arizona, the town closest to where the satellite landed, is apparently dead. The duty officer of the base tasked with retrieving the satellite suspects that it returned with an extraterrestrial contaminant and recommends activating "Wildfire," a protocol for a government-sponsored team of scientists intended to contain threats of this nature.

The Wildfire team, led by Dr. Jeremy Stone, believes the satellite—intentionally designed to capture upper-atmosphere microorganisms for bio-weapon exploitation—returned with a deadly microorganism that kills through nearly instantaneous blood clotting.[199]

Though fiction, Crichton was lauded at the time by scientists who appreciated his attention to detail about the ability of extraterrestrial microbes or extremophiles to live in harsh environments like space where temperatures range from hundreds of degrees Fahrenheit to hundreds of degrees below zero. An extremophilic alien bacteria could not only survive such an environment, but an entire field of astrobiology called "panspermia" exists to explain how earth may have been host to such intergalactic lifeforms in the distant past.

Might such an Andromeda Strain on Apophis be the "trigger" that results in a global pandemic that leads to a mandatory universal vaccine? The Mark of the Beast?

This is an important question, because some years ago my wife Nita brought up a point we had never considered before then. Her idea quickly spread online after I mentioned it on the radio during an interview with Steve Quayle (Steve still credits Nita with this theory, one which has been often repeated by other writers and commentators since, many of whom have not given her the credit she deserves). She asked if the biblical Mark of the Beast might be a conspiracy employing specific implantable health-technology only now available. Her theory was gripping: In her narrative, instead of a virus from an asteroid, she suggested an occult elite operating behind the US government might devise a virus that is a crossover between human and animal disease—let's say, an entirely new and highly contagious influenza mutation—and intentionally releases it into the public. A pandemic ensues, and the period between when a person contracts the virus and death is something like ten days. With tens of thousands dead in a few weeks and the rate of death increasing hourly around the globe, a universal cry for a cure goes out. Seemingly miraculously, the government then steps forward with a vaccine. The only catch, the government explains, is that, given the nature of the animal-human flu, the "cure" uses animal DNA and nanobots to rewrite one's genetics so that the person is no longer entirely human. The point made was that those who receive this antidote would become part "beast," and perhaps, thus, the title, "Mark of the Beast." No longer "entirely human" would also mean—according to her original outline—that the individual could no longer be "saved" or go to heaven, explaining why the book of Revelation says that "whosoever receiveth the mark" is damned forever (while also explaining why the ancient *nephilim*, whose DNA was part human and part angel and/or animal, could not be redeemed). For believers, they would know this is the mark of the Beast, as we believe the Spirit of God would confirm it in their conscious and Spirit. If they take this "cure," they will know at the moment they have willfully submitted to damnation regardless how it is justified.

Another possibility came to me one day when watching *I Am Legend* starring Will Smith. If you've seen the film, you know it starts out with a doctor on television claiming a cure to cancer via a chimeric vaccine. The world celebrates as the global inoculation does indeed cure cancer. However, because the vaccine was a blend of human and animal genetics, it ultimately leads to a human form of rabies that nearly wipes out all life on earth. One virologist (Will Smith) appears to be the only man of earth naturally immune to the disease, and he sets out to find a cure using his blood for a new vaccine.

The show *I Am Legend* made me wonder if in the future a global pandemic would ensue only to have one man step forward whose blood holds the key to a cure. It turns out, he is the Antichrist and, like a dark version of Communion, one can only be healed by receiving his flesh and blood via the 'mark' or vaccination of the beast.

In either scenario above, if one imagines the global chaos of such a pandemic, the concept of how the Antichrist "causes all," both "small and great," to receive this mark becomes clearer. When looking into the eyes of dying children, parents, or a spouse, it would be incredibly difficult to allow oneself to die or to encourage others to do the same when a "cure" was readily available. Lastly, this scenario would mean that nobody would be allowed to "buy or sell" in the marketplace without the Mark-cure due to the need to quarantine all but the inoculated (a real-world possibility we are witnessing right now during the coronavirus), thus fulfilling all aspects of the Mark of the Beast prophecy.

To find out if the science behind this abstract was as reasonable as it appeared on the surface, I contacted Sharon Gilbert, whose graduate work included molecular biology. This was her troubling response:

Tom:

What is human? Until recently, most of us would readily respond that *we* are humans. You and I, we might argue, are *Homo sapiens*: erect, bipedal hominids with twenty-three pairs of matched chromosomes and nifty little thumbs capable of apposition to the palm that enable us to grasp the fine tools that our highly developed, bi-lobed brains devise.

Humans, we might argue, sit as rulers of the Earth, gazing down from the pinnacle of a pyramid consisting of all plant and animal species. We would remind the listener that natural selection and evolution have developed mankind into superior thinkers and doers, thereby granting us royal privilege, if not infinite responsibility. The Bible would take this definition much farther, of course, adding that mankind is the only part of God's creation formed by His hands, rather than spoken into existence, and that you and I bear God's unique signature as having been created "in His image" (Genesis 1:27).

Many members of the "illuminated brotherhood of science" would likely demur to the previous statement. These have, in point of fact, redefined *human*. Like Mary Shelley's *Modern Pro-*

metheus, Victor Frankenstein, today's molecular magicians play "god" not by stitching together rotting corpses, but by reforming the very essence of our beings: our DNA.

So-called "postmodern man" began as a literary reference but has evolved into an iconic metaphor representing a collective image of perfected humanity beyond the confines of genetic constraints. Transhumanism, also known as the H+ movement envisions a higher life-form yet, surpassing *Homo sapiens* in favor of *Homo sapiens 2.0*, a bioengineered construct that fuses man's original genome with animal and/or synthetic DNA.

While such claims ring of science fiction, they are indeed science fact. For decades, laboratories have created chimeric combinations of animal, plant, and even human DNA under the guise of medical research. The stated goal is to better man's lot by curing disease, but this benign mask hides an inner, sardonic grin that follows an ancient blueprint to blend God's perfect creature with the seed of fallen angels: "You shall be as gods."

You and Nita speak to the heart of the matter when you warn of a day when true humans may receive transhuman instructions via an implant or injection. A seemingly innocuous vaccine or identification "chip" can initiate intracellular changes, not only in somatic or "body" cells, but also in germ-line cells such as ova and sperm. The former alters the recipient only; the latter alters the recipient's doomed descendants as well.

In my second novel, *The Armageddon Strain*, I present a device called the "BioStrain Chip" that employs nanotechnology to induce genetic changes inside the carrier's body. This miracle chip is advertised as a cure for the H5N1/ebola chimera that is released in the prologue to the book. Of course, if you've read the novel, then you know the BioStrain Chip does far more than "cure"—it also kills.

Though a work of fiction, *The Armageddon Strain* raises a chilling question: What limitations lie within the payload of a biochip? Can such a tiny device do more than carry digitized information? Could it actually serve as the *Mark of the Beast?*

The answer is yes.

DNA (Deoxyribonucleic acid) has become the darling of researchers who specialize in synthetic constructs. The "sticky-end" design of the DNA double-helix makes it ideal for use in computing. Though an infinite number of polyhedra are possible, the most robust and stable of these "building blocks" is called the double crossover (DX). An intriguing name, is it not? The double-cross.

Picture an injectable chip comprised of DNA-DX, containing instructions for a super-soldier. Picture, too, how this DNA framework, if transcribed, might also serve a second, *sinister*, purpose—not only to instruct, but also to *alter*.

Mankind has come perilously far in his search for perfection through chemistry. Although millennia passed with little progress beyond roots, herbs, and alchemical quests for gold from lead, the twentieth century ushered science into the rosy dawn of breathless discovery. Electricity, lighter-than-air travel, wireless communication, and computing transformed the ponderous pace of the scientific method into a light-speed race toward self-destruction.

By the mid-1950s, Watson and Crick had solved the structure of the DNA molecule and the double helix became all the rage. Early gene splicing, and thus transgenics, began in 1952 as a crude, cut-and-paste sort of science cooked up in kitchen blenders and petri dishes—as much accident as inspiration. As knowledge has increased (Daniel 12:4), genetic scientists learned to utilize microbiological "vectors" and sophisticated methods to insert animal or plant genes from one species into another. It's the ultimate "Mr. Potato Head" game, where interchangeable plastic pieces give rise to an infinite number of combinations; only, in genetic splicing, humanity is the unhappy potato.

Vectors provide the means of transport and integration for

ve new science. Think of these vectors as biological trucks
ry genetic building materials and workers into your body's
uch "trucks" could be a microsyringe, a bacterium, or a
(a virus particle). Any entity that can carry genetic information (the larger the load capacity, the better) and then surrepti-
tiously gain entry into the cell is a potential vector. Viruses, for
example, can be stripped of certain innate genes that might harm
the cell. Not only does this (supposedly) render the viral delivery
truck "harmless," it also clears out space for the cargo.

Once inside the cell, the "workers" take over. Some of these
"workers" are enzymes that cut human genes at specific sites, while
others integrate—or load—the "cargo" into appropriate reading
frames—like microscopic librarians. Once the payload is stored in
the cell's nuclear "library stacks," the new genes can be translated,
copied, and "read" to produce altered or brand-new, "alien" poly-
mers and proteins.

The resulting hybrid cell is no longer purely human. If [it is]
a hybridized skin cell, it may now glow, or perhaps form scales
rather than hair, [or] claws rather than fingernails. If [it is] a brain
cell, the new genetic instructions could produce an altered neu-
rotransmitter that reduces or even eliminates the body's need for
sleep. Muscle cells may grow larger and more efficient at using
low levels of calcium and oxygen. Retina cells may encode for
receptors that enable the "posthuman being" to perceive infrared
or ultraviolet light frequencies. The hybrid ears may now sense
a wider range of sounds, taste buds a greater range of chemicals.
Altered brains might even attune to metaphysics and "unseen"
gateways, allowing communication with supernatural realms.

Germ-line alterations, mentioned earlier, form a terrifying
picture of generational development and may very well already be
a reality. Genetic "enhancement" of sperm-producing cells would
change human sperm into tiny infiltrators, and any fertilized
ovum a living chimera. Science routinely conducts experiments

with transgenic mice, rats, chickens, pigs, cows, horses, and many other species. It is naïve to believe humans have been left out of this transgenic equation.

If so many scientists (funded by government entities) believe in the "promise" of genetic alteration and transgenic "enhancement," how then can humanity remain human? We cannot. We will not. Perhaps, *some have not*.

Spiritually, the enemy has ever sought to corrupt God's plan. Originally, fallen angels lay with human women to corrupt the original base pair arrangements. Our genome is filled with "junk DNA" that seemingly encodes for nothing. These "introns" may be the remains of the corrupted genes, and God Himself may have switched them off when fallen angels continued their program, post-Flood. If so, today's scientists might need only to "switch them back on" to resurrect old forms such as Gibborim and Nephilim.

I should point out that not all "trucks" (vectors) deliver their payload immediately. Some operate on a time delay. Cytomegalovirus (CMV) is a common infective agent resident in the cells of many humans today. It "sleeps" in our systems, waiting for a window of opportunity to strike. Recently, genetic specialists began utilizing CMV vectors in transgenic experiments. In 1997, the Fox television program *Millennium* featured an episode in the second season called "Sense and Antisense" (referring to the two sides of the DNA molecule). In this chilling story, a scientist named Lacuna reveals a genetic truth to Frank Black: "They have the map, the map, they can make us go down any street they want to. Streets that we would never even dream of going down. They flip a switch, we go east. They flip another switch, we go north. And we never know we have been flipped, let alone know how."

In the final days of this current age, humanity may indeed "flip." Paul tells us that Christians will be transformed in a moment (1 Corinthians 15:51–53). Is it possible that the enemy also plans an instantaneous "flip"? Are genetic sleeper agents (idling "trucks") already at work in humanity's DNA, waiting and ready to deploy at the appropriate moment?

Science is ready. Knowledge has been increased. The spiritual players have taken the stage.

All we need is the signal. The sign. The injection. The mark. The *trigger*.

We shall ALL be changed. Some to incorruptible bodies ready to meet the Lord. Others to corrupted genomes ready to serve the Beast.

Sharon's response to my inquiry raises some interesting questions. As noted in the news lately, scannable implants and tattoo transmitters are becoming more sophisticated, adding "prophetic" components—such as merging human biological matter with transistors to create living, implantable machines. Related science also envisions "smart" chimeric vaccines that literally rewrite DNA. Add to that the draconian commentary from America's top health advisors lately, and it is not difficult to imagine how the dreaded mark of the Beast could unfold in the very near future. Bill Gates wants a "digital certificate" to show who has recovered from Covid-19 before they can fully move around in the marketplace. Dr. Anthony Fauci has joined Gates in calling for some type digital tracking system without which people will not be able to return to work or shop at their local grocery. High tech companies like SuperCom have even produced scalable electronic monitoring and tracking platforms they say are ready now to keep an eye on all, both small and great. And some countries have already passed legislation to make the coronavirus vaccine mandatory. I personally believe the possibility that the Mark of the Beast could arrive through a version of one of these vaccine technologies is plausible, if not altogether likely.

I also believe *THE MESSENGER*, aka the Apophis-Wormwood asteroid, is carrying an alien microbe with a virus that will serve as the "trigger" that sets in motion this end-times activity.

Will you be "accounted worthy to escape all these things that shall come to pass" (Luke 21:36)?

There is only one way to know for sure. Accept Jesus Christ as your Lord and Savior and repent of your sins. If you will or have done this, He promises:

> Because thou hast kept the word of my patience, I also will keep thee from the hour of temptation, which shall come upon all the world, to try them that dwell upon the earth. (Revelation 3:10)

More Mid-Tribulation Connections to Apophis-Wormwood:
From the Mark of the Beast and "Trigger Event" Alien Viruses to the Judgment of Rome and the False Prophet

In addition to Wormwood and the Mark of the Beast playing out in the middle of the Great Tribulation period, *THE MESSENGER* also mysteriously and dynamically connects my vision of the pope in chapter 1 of this book, and the second vision of Apophis from 2019, to the judgment of Mystery Babylon, which I believe will also transpire in the midst of Daniel's seventy weeks. I explained this connection and why it is important recently in my 2020 Defender Virtual Conference presentation. From the transcript, here is what I told the audience of thousands:

Now earlier I said, if the visions I had were meant to tie what at first appear to be two unrelated things together: 1) The resignation of Pope Benedict, which paved way for the election of Pope Francis; and 2) the vision of Apophis striking earth in 2029, then we have uncovered a marvelous and very concerning revelation.

Why do I say that?

First, I have always said these moments of *ecstasis* are like pieces of a larger puzzle I do not yet understand. I was asked recently by the host of one of the largest Christian TV programs what my seeing the resignation of Pope Benedict a year in advance has to do with the 2019 vision of Apophis. Why would God show me such random, seemingly unrelated things? Until now, my response has been "I don't know." It's like I am seeing pieces of a much larger picture I do not yet comprehend.

But I will share the bottom line with you now, and why I had not seen this until very recently is a mystery to me, because now it seems so clear how these events are tied together.

BOTH WORMWOOD-APOPHIS AND THE JUDGMENT OF ROME AND ITS FALSE PROPHET OCCUR SIMULTANEOUSLY IN THE MIDDLE OF THE GREAT TRIBULATION! THE VISIONS I HAVE RECEIVED ARE NOT TWO SEPARATE THINGS, BUT A BIRD'S-EYE GLIMPSE OF TWO MAJOR PARTS OF THE END TIMES, SOON TO UNFOLD BILATERALLY, AND I PREDICT BETWEEN NOW AND 2029.

Now, let me explain a bit more about how Rome and the Pope will soon be combined with arrival of Wormwood.

Both Catholics and protestant evangelicals see the current Pope echoing a prophesied roll in pushing socialism, the system Antichrist will employ. In fact, several Catholic defenders of the faith—including the largest Catholic news agencies in the world (CAN and EWTN News), as well as Rome's leading theologians like Archbishop Carlo Viganò—have recently stated publicly that Francis is this man from the books of Revelation and Daniel, even writing letters to President Trump to warn him that Francis is leading the way for the "children of darkness" we see on the streets calling for a Marxist/Socialist uprising.

BUT FOR MYSTIC CATHOLICS…IT'S MUCH MORE THAN THAT. Many of them believe in *The Prophecy of the Popes*, which predicted nine hundred years ago that 112 pontiffs—from the day St. Malachy had his divine vision in Rome and forward—would arrive, with the last one ruling over the Vatican when the church and world enter the Great Tribulation period according to that prophecy. Francis is #112 on this list, and his namesake, Francis of Assisi, predicted this final pope would be a deceiver.

Now follow me here. In our bestselling book *Petrus Romanus*, I especially featured retired professor of the Pontifical Biblical Institute, eminent Catholic theologian, and former Jesuit priest, Malachi Martin, who had privileged information pertaining to secretive Church and world issues, including the Third Secret of Fátima, which many believe has never been released and that Martin hinted spelled out parts of a plan to formally install the dreaded False Prophet during a "Final Conclave." Martin's book, Windswept House depicted how a pope would be secretly forced from office (Benedict?) and replaced by a Jesuit-backed leader who would help establish a final New World Order (Francis?) under Antichrist.

More recently, in a shocking interview titled "**Is Francis the Last Pope?**" which you can Google and read for yourself, published by the two largest Catholic news agencies in the world, the personal secretary to Pope Benedict and the Prefect of the Papal Household for Pope Francis, Archbishop George Gänswein, was specifically asked about this "Prophesy of Malachy," better known as the Prophecy of the Popes, the retirement of Benedict, and whether Francis himself believes *he is this last pontiff.*

The interview began by making direct reference to questions that I myself had raised regarding the **dual lightning strikes** atop St. Peter's Basilica on the evening of February 11, 2013, on the same day of Benedict's public resignation announcement. I followed that with commentary about the inauguration of Francis and how, "for a few adepts of history and secret orders," this sign from heaven was deliciously staged. I had written that because the term "inaugurate" is from the Latin *inauguratio* and refers to the archaic ceremony by which the Roman augurs ("soothsayers") approved a king or ruler through lightning omens as being "sanctioned by the gods." As for Petrus Romanus, his "inauguration" was sealed by the same omen the ancient augurs used in determining the will of the gods for a king in that part of Rome—thunder and lightning as the most important auspice and sign that Jupiter—the father of Apollo—was watching.

It turns out that I was not alone in my ponderings, as the Catholic news agencies confirmed, writing: "Many observers chose to interpret this (lightning strikes) as a divine reaction to the historical announcement of Pope Benedict's resignation, made that very morning." Then the article went on to say, "As his personal secretary, Archbishop Gänswein reminisced about how both he and Benedict only found out about the lightning strike after the event and that the impression to them was "one of a sign from above, a reaction," Ganswein told Badde, who conducted the interview. When Ganswein showed Benedict images of the spectacular incident a few days later, the pope asked whether this was some kind of digital montage, Gänswein said, before adding: "However, nature had spoken,'" echoing what I had published online in 2013.

But then the astonishing report made an important disclosure, adding: "During the interview, Paul Badde referenced...the "Prophecy of the Popes"—according to which Pope Francis may be considered to be **the last pope, to which** Archbishop Gänswein admitted: "Indeed, when looking at the prophecy, and considering how there was always a sound reference to popes mentioned in its history—that gives me the shivers [and] speaking from historical experience, one has to say: Yes, this is a wake-up call."

Now think about that folks: Given that both current popes and their closest advisors at the Vatican have considered whether Pope Francis is the last pope—Petrus Romanus—and that the reality gives them "the shivers" and is perceived by them as "a wake-up call," is it any wonder that conservative scholars within the Catholic Church have taken an increasingly careful view of Pope Francis? And is the subsequent question of whether Pope Francis is the False Prophet the reason Canon Lawyers and Theologians for the Vatican hosted a conference in Paris a while back to discuss "how to depose a heretical pope"?

Keep in mind that Catholic and Protestants historically have viewed the Prophecy of the Popes as only one of many omens predicting the role that Rome would play in the end times and that ultimately the predicted destruction of the seven-hilled city of Rome—which I believe could very well happen as Apophis rains down asteroid debris in 2029—also identifies the Roman Catholic Church as "MYSTERY, BABYLON THE GREAT,

THE MOTHER OF HARLOTS AND ABOMINATIONS OF THE EARTH" (Revelation 17:5). This woman who rides the scarlet-colored beast is very clearly described by John as a city that sits on seven mountains that rules over the kings of the earth (cf. Revelation 17:9, 17:8). At the time John wrote this, there was only one city on seven hills that ruled over the kings of the earth, and that was Rome. Now, while Rome as a military and political force eventually disappeared from history, the seven-hilled city continued as a spiritual and religious force that continues to this day to host the kings of the earth, which bow to kiss the pope's ring.

If one accepts the veracity of Malachy's vision, which many Catholics do, then the Roman Catholic Church is necessarily the woman who rides the beast.

But how else might this connect to 2029, Apophis as Wormwood, and the final pope? The final lines of the Prophecy of the Popes also predict that Rome will be destroyed:

> In extreme persecution, the seat of the Holy Roman Church will be occupied by Peter the Roman, who will feed the sheep through many tribulations; when they are over, the city of seven hills will be destroyed, and the terrible and fearsome Judge will judge his people.

This seems to corresponds with:

- The book of Revelation 17–18, which speaks of her fiery destruction.
- The seven hundred-year old Zohar, which says just before Messiah arrives, the "kings of the earth" will gather in Rome and will suddenly be killed by fiery objects falling from the sky. Could that be asteroid debris from the breakup of Apophis/Wormwood?
- Allegedly, the true Third Secret of Fatima and other Catholic sources likewise describe Rome being destroyed by fiery heavenly objects.

- Even the Sibylline Oracles, Book 2, prophesied of end-times Rome and what sounds like asteroid debris: *And then shall, after these, appear of men, The tenth race, when the earth-shaking Lightener Shall break the zeal for idols and shall shake the people of seven-hilled Rome, and riches great shall perish, burned by Vulcan's fiery flame. And then shall bloody signs from heaven descend.* Of course, Vulcan, mentioned here by Apollo's seer, is the god that Manly P. Hall said empowers the Freemasons hands with "the seething energies of Lucifer," and it was Malachi Martin who said the Freemasons would be the Superforce behind bringing Rome under control of Antichrist.

By the way, it wasn't only Malachi Martin who said the Vatican under the papacy of a Jesuit would become a machine of Antichrist's final world order. Numerous other famous priests and theologians in the Catholic Church have taught and warned the same for hundreds of years.

One of the most famous was Dr. Henry Edward Cardinal Manning, the Lord Archbishop of Westminster from 1865–1892. Before conversion to Catholicism, he was an influential Anglican cleric, but lost faith in the Church of England in 1850. He became a significant presence in setting the direction of the modern Catholic Church, and achieved particular fame for his doctrine of papal infallibility (the dogma that the pope is preserved from even the possibility of error when he speaks *ex cathedra*), which became dogma during the First Vatican Council of 1870. Manning's unrelenting emphasis on the prerogatives and powers of the pope, including authority over local temporal and spiritual hierarchies such as local bishops, defined *ultramontanism* in his day—the idea that papal superiority should exist even over councils and kings.

But those facts make Manning all the more remarkable, given how, during the 1800–1900s, a series of scholarly opinions was published outlining how events in the Roman Catholic Church combined with long-time, anti-papist goals by secret Masonic infiltrators would give rise in the last days to great apostasy in Rome and the advent of Antichrist. Among the strongest proponents of this eschatology was Cardinal Manning himself, who delivered a series of lectures in 1861 under the title "The Present Crises of the Holy See Tested by Prophecy" (later incorporated into a larger study entitled "The Temporal Power of the Vicar of Jesus Christ"), in which Manning foresaw a future crisis in the Roman Catholic Church initiated by the type of ecumenism and flexible dogma that many modern conservative Catholics have loathed following the Second Vatican Council and the teachings of the current pope Francis. Manning believed this change to orthodoxy would undermine the authority of the Church and finally result in a departure from the profession of Catholic faith by the nations together with the displacement of the true pope by a False Prophet, thus ushering in the Antichrist and global apostasy. Manning also believed, like Malachi Martin later echoed, secret societies like the Freemasons were part of this conspiracy. He wrote: "The secret societies have long ago undermined and honeycombed the Christian society of Europe, and are at this moment struggling onward towards Rome, the center of all Christian order in the world."[200] But when he looked at the prophecy in Revelation 18 concerning the end-time destruction of Mystery Babylon, Manning saw it was the hand of God in judgment of worldwide apostasy emanating from Rome:

> We read in the Book Apocalypse, of the city of Rome, that she said in the pride of her heart, "I sit as a queen, and am no widow, and sorrow I shall not see. Therefore shall her plagues come in one day: death, and mourning, and famine; and she shall be burned with fire, because God is strong who shall judge her." Some of the greatest writers of the Church tell us that...the great City of Seven Hills...the city of Rome will probably become apostate... and that Rome will again be punished, for he will depart from it; and the judgment of God will fall...[201]

Thus, just as the Prophecy of the Popes and numerous Catholic visionary conveyances do, Manning foresaw the destruction of the city of Rome as a result of its partnership with Antichrist. This doctrine would have been unfamiliar to most Catholics in those days, so Manning went on to explain how Catholicism's greatest theologians agreed with this point of view. He wrote:

> The apostasy of the city of Rome…and its destruction by Antichrist may be thoughts so new to many Catholics, that I think it well to recite the text of theologians, of greatest repute. First, Malvenda, who writes expressly on the subject, states that Rome shall apostatize from the faith and return to its ancient paganism, saying: "But Rome itself in the last times of the world will return to its ancient idolatry, power, and imperial greatness. It will cast out its true Pontiff, altogether apostatize from the Christian faith, terribly persecute the Church, shed the blood of martyrs more cruelly than ever, and will recover its former state of abundant wealth, or even greater than it had under its first rulers."
>
> Then he quotes Lessius, who said: "In the time of Antichrist, Rome shall be destroyed, as we see openly from the thirteenth chapter of the Apocalypse," and again: "The woman whom thou sawest is the great city, which hath kingdom over the kings of the earth, in which is signified Rome in its impiety, such as it was in the time of St. John, and shall be again at the end of the world." And Bellarmine: "In the time of Antichrist, Rome shall be desolated and burnt, as we learn from the sixteenth verse of the seventeenth chapter of the Apocalypse." On which words the Jesuit Erbermann comments as follows: "We all confess with Bellarmine that the Roman people, a little before the end of the world, will return to paganism, and drive out the Roman Pontiff."
>
> Viegas, on the eighteenth chapter of the Apocalypse says: "Rome, in the last age of the world, after it has apostatized from the faith, will attain great power and splendor of wealth, and its sway will be widely spread throughout the world, and flourish greatly. Living in luxury and the abundance of all things, it will worship

idols, and be steeped in all kinds of superstition, and will pay honor to false gods. And because of the vast effusion of the blood of martyrs which was shed under the emperors, God will most severely and justly avenge them, and it shall be utterly destroyed, and burned by a most terrible and afflicting conflagration."[202]

Throughout history, including recent times, numerous Catholic priests have built on the foundation laid by Cardinal Manning and other early Catholic authorities, and have often been surprisingly outspoken in their agreement regarding the inevitable danger not only of apostate Rome but of the False Prophet rising from within the ranks of Catholicism itself as a result of secret satanic Illuminati-Masonic influences. According to Catholic priests in more recent times, such as Father E. Sylvester Berry, whose book *The Apocalypse of Saint John* foretold the usurpation of the papacy by a false prophet; Father Herman Bernard Kramer, whose work, *The Book of Destiny*, painted a terrifying scenario in which Satan enters the church and assassinates the true pope in order that his false pope can rise to rule the world; as well as similar beliefs by priests like Father John F. O'Connor, Father Alfred Kunz, and Father Malachi Martin, who taught this will happen because secret-society and sinister false Catholic infiltrators understand that the geopolitical influence of Rome in the world is indispensable for controlling future global elements in matters of church and state. The Roman Catholic Church represents one-sixth of the world's population and over half of all professing Christians, has its own diplomatic corps of ambassadors posted in industrialized nations globally, and more than one hundred eighty nations of the world send their ambassadors to the capital city, the Vatican.

In a two-hour presentation that last I knew was still available on YouTube, Father O'Connor gave a homily titled "The Reign of the Antichrist," in which he described how changes within society and in the institution were already at work before his death to provide for the coming of Antichrist. In this sermon and elsewhere, O'Connor outlined the catalyst for this scheme unfolding as a result of "Masonic Conspirators" within the organization whose plan, called "Alta Vendita," would essentially take control of the papacy and help the False Prophet deceive the world's faithful (including Catholics) into worshipping Antichrist.

Now...I need to hurry and bring all this to a specific conclusion.

As stated in our bestselling book, *Petrus Romanus*, the idea by some Catholics that the final pope from St. Malachy's list heralds the beginning of "great apostasy" followed by "great tribulation" and sets the stage for the imminent unfolding of apocalyptic events, this could give rise to the False Prophet, who, according to the book of Revelation, leads the world's *religious* communities into embracing a *political* leader known as Antichrist. This marriage of Church and secular government would give unprecedented global influence to the Man of Sin during this period known as the Great Tribulation.

Before you doubt that Pope Francis may be this man, consider how accusations of apostasy are stacking up against him with numerous top Catholic theologians, websites, blogs, and discussion forums deliberating how he is leading the Church toward schism, ironically a fulfillment of the pope's namesake, Francis of Assisi, who famously predicted about the final pope:

> At the time of this tribulation a man, not canonically elected, will be raised to the Pontificate, who, by his cunning, will endeavor to draw many into error and death.... Some preachers will keep silence about the truth, and others will trample it under foot and deny it...for in those days Jesus Christ will send them not a true Pastor, but a destroyer.

A respected Italian monsignor and former consultor to the Vatican's Congregation for the Doctrine of Faith—Monsignor Nicola Bux—has even gone on record saying that Pope Francis needs to stop the "confusion and apostasy" he is sowing among priests and bishops by "correcting" his "ambiguous and erroneous words and acts."

Perhaps moreso than any others, influential Catholic television network director Jose Galat publicly claimed not long ago that Pope Francis is the "false prophet" who, he says, is "paving the way for the Antichrist." Galat also argues the "real pope" is Benedict XVI, who was somehow forced to resign. Francis "was elected by a mafia of cardinals," Galat said, agreeing with other Catholics already mentioned who see a conspiracy behind this first ever Jesuit pope.

And then there is Benedict himself who recently said the Catholic Church is "on the verge of capsizing."

Pope Francis has in fact been accused of heresy by more than sixty priests, theologians, and academics who published a twenty-five-page letter in which the signatories issued a "filial correction" to the pope, a measure last employed in the fourteenth century. The document accuses Francis of propagating numerous heretical positions.

Perhaps strangest of all was an inquiry not long ago in which the Vatican launched an investigation into a Catholic group of exorcists (the Heralds) who, *after having discussions with Satan, have determined that Pope Francis "is the Devil's man."*

But... let me ask an unexpected question—what if Francis is not Petrus Romanus, the final pope of Malachy's prophecy? What if that dark Superforce (Catholic Freemasons) that Malachi Martin warned about is using Francis and his left-leaning theology to play a complex end-times game aimed at manipulating and reconfiguring Rome into a Socialist-Marxist instrument for the real Final Pope's arrival? What if the same George Soros-globalist one-worlders who have teamed up against Trump with men like Barack Obama are working with Francis to lay the groundwork for Antichrist's global order ala the book of Revelation?

Too crazy to believe?

Here is what popular Catholic website LIFE SITE recently said:

Most astonishingly, the Vatican itself seems involved as Pope Francis, the German bishops and others around him have openly developed close relationships with many leading One-Worlders, inviting them to the Vatican to give talks and advice. This has been a radical change from all past popes. Reports suggest George Soros favored Bergoglio [Pope Francis] during the Conclave that elected him pope. For the first time ever, the New World Order movement has gained powerful public backing for many of their agendas from the head of the Roman Catholic Church, who has aggressively insisted that climate change, open borders, anti-capitalism and more are now issues of moral and religious obligation for a new, worldly Catholic Church. It also appears that some in the Vatican may be laying the groundwork for a moral and religious case in favor of population control.... Many signs point to this.

And what if I told you the rabbit hole of evidence to support this global conspiracy doesn't stop there, and actually ties the resignation of Pope Benedict, the election of Pope Francis, George Soros, Barack Obama, Hillary Clinton, John Podesta, the possible arrival of the False Prophet, Antichrist, the Final Pope, discussions of a Messiah, and the election of 2016 and upcoming election of 2020 to those SHADOWLAND occultists now at work to overthrow the Trump administration's agenda?

Are you aware that a group of respected Catholic leaders sent a letter a while back to President Trump asking him to launch an official investigation into activities connected to the people I just mentioned? It appears that Team Obama was involved in a different coup similar to the one currently focused on Trump, but this time against the Vatican and which the authors of the letter believe forced the aging Pope Benedict to step down for sinister reasons.

In a top-notch piece of investigative journalism, William F. Jasper at the *New American* asks:

Did billionaire speculator George Soros, President Barack Obama, Secretary of State Hillary Clinton, Vice President Joe Biden, and Obama/Clinton adviser John Podesta conspire to overthrow the conservative Pope Benedict XVI and replace him with a radical, Pope Francis? Did they use America's intelligence agencies, and our nation's diplomatic machinery, political muscle, and financial power to coerce and blackmail "regime change" in the Roman Catholic Church?

Far from being some wild conspiracy theory, there is sound prima facie evidence to indicate that this is a serious effort to expose a political scandal of the highest order, involving flagrant, criminal abuse of power at the top levels of the U.S. government.

The letter that Jasper refers to is too long to read in this presentation, but was written and sent by Catholic leaders from *The Remnant* newspaper to President Trump and included this:

The campaign slogan "Make America Great Again" resonated with millions of common Americans and your tenacity in pushing back against many of the most harmful recent trends has been most inspiring. We all look forward to seeing a continued reversal of the collectivist trends of recent decades.

Reversing recent collectivist trends will, by necessity, require a reversal of many of the actions taken by the previous administration. Among those actions we believe that there is one that remains cloaked in secrecy. Specifically, we have reason to believe that a Vatican "regime change" was engineered by the Obama administration.

We were alarmed to discover that, during the third year of the first term of the Obama administration your previous opponent, Secretary of State Hillary Clinton, and other government officials with whom she associated proposed a Catholic "revolution" in which the final demise of what was left of the Catholic Church in America would be realized. Approximately a year after this e-mail discussion, which was never intended to be made public, we find that Pope Benedict XVI abdicated under highly unusual circumstances and was replaced by a pope whose apparent mission is to provide a spiritual component to the radical ideological agenda of the international left. The Pontificate of Pope Francis has subsequently called into question its own legitimacy on a multitude of occasions.

[They then go on to list numerous concerns over Pope Francis's hostility toward Trump and advocacy of Socialism-Marxism, then say]:

With all of this in mind, and wishing the best for our country as well as for Catholics worldwide, we believe it to be the responsibility of loyal and informed United States Catholics to petition you to authorize an investigation into the following questions:

- To what end was the National Security Agency monitoring the conclave that elected Pope Francis?
- What other covert operations were carried out by US government operatives concerning the resignation of Pope Benedict or the conclave that elected Pope Francis?
- What actions, if any, were actually taken by John Podesta, Hillary Clinton, and others tied to the Obama administration who were involved in the discussion proposing the fomenting of a "Catholic Spring"?
- What was the purpose and nature of the secret meeting between Vice President Joe Biden and Pope Benedict XVI at the Vatican on or about June 3, 2011?
- What roles were played by George Soros and other international financiers who may be currently residing in United States territory?

The letter goes on to list why these conservative Catholic leaders believe that the very existence of these unanswered questions provides sufficient evidence to warrant their request for an investigation.

At the end of the letter on the *Remnant's* official website, they provide links to documents and articles that support their charges, including some released by WikiLeaks, which caught Soros, Clinton, and Podesta conferring on how to bring the "Middle Aes dictatorship" at the Vatican to an end.

In another *New American* report from last October, the emails in question were investigated involving the Clinton campaign's secret anti-Catholic agenda. They noted:

> Podesta, a longtime Clinton adviser/confidante and hand-picked top activist for left-wing funder George Soros, revealed in a 2011 e-mail that he and other activists were working to effect a "Catholic Spring" revolution within the Catholic Church, an obvious reference to the disastrous "Arab Spring" coups organized that same year by the Obama-Clinton-Soros team that destabilized the Middle East and brought radical Islamist regimes and terrorist groups to power in the region. The Podesta e-mail is a response to another Soros-funded radical—Sandy Newman, founder of the "progressive" Voices for Progress. Newman had written to Podesta seeking advice on the best way to "plant the seeds of the revolution" in the Catholic Church, which he described as a "middle ages [sic] dictatorship."

Of special interest to me in the letter to Trump from the concerned Catholics is where they specifically note: "Approximately a year after this e-mail discussion, which was never intended to be made public, we find that Pope Benedict XVI abdicated under highly unusual circumstances and was replaced by a pope whose apparent mission is to provide a spiritual component to the radical ideological agenda of the international left" and that they "remain puzzled by the behavior of this ideologically charged Pope, whose mission seems to be one of advancing secular agendas of the left rather than guiding the Catholic Church in Her sacred mission…. It is simply not the proper role of a Pope to be involved in politics to the point that he is considered to be the leader of the international left."

It's not hard to read between the lines of their letter to find the insinu-ation that Pope Francis is—or is paving the way for—the False Prophet, which will guide the world's religious faithful into supporting the political figure called Antichrist.

With all this in mind and given my personal exhaustive investiga-tion into the Vatican, extensive research into the Prophecy of the Popes, and correct prediction regarding the resignation of Benedict before the fact, I have a bombshell announcement to make. I am reaching out to those concealed friends in Rome who assisted me in the past to confirm my belief that Pope Francis will either retire soon or be taken out of the way, and that this really is tied to something strange that unfolded in bringing him temporarily to the pontificate. I believe, as they suggested, that Francis was not "canonically elected," as his namesake originally pre-dicted. And the church members who helped me before…the ones I've already mentioned in this presentation…are only the tip of the iceberg of those who will eventually voice how "illegitimate" activity went on behind closed doors during the last papal election, and that, for reasons we do not yet understand, Francis was put in as a temporary "placeholder" until the real Pope #112 (Petrus Romanus) could be installed. The mysterious rea-sons surrounding this "placeholder" false pope may never fully be known, but was foreseen by such mystics as Father Herman Bernard Kramer in his work, *The Book of Destiny*. During an unusual interpretation he made of the twelfth chapter of the book of Revelation concerning "the great wonder" mentioned in verse 1, Father Kramer wrote:

> The "sign" in heaven is that of a woman with child crying out in her travail and anguish of delivery. In that travail, she gives birth to some definite "person" who is to RULE the Church with a rod of iron (verse 5). It then points to a conflict waged within the Church to elect one who was to "rule all nations" in the man-ner clearly stated. In accord with the text this is unmistakably a PAPAL ELECTION, for only Christ and his Vicar have the divine right to rule ALL NATIONS…. But at this time the great

powers may take a menacing attitude to hinder the election of the logical and expected candidate by threats of a general apostasy, assassination or imprisonment of this candidate if elected. (capitalized emphasis in original)

Although I disagree with Kramer's interpretation of the book of Revelation, his fear that "great powers may take a menacing attitude to hinder the election of the logical and expected candidate" echoes the sentiment of priests I mentioned earlier, who saw a crisis for the Church coming, and the False Prophet and Antichrist rising as a result.

This, too, was in the news recently when a report was published by Sébastien Maillard, a Vatican correspondent in Rome. He noted how a large array of conservative bishops fear that Francis is bypassing critical Church doctrine and fear he has already gone too far. Even those cardinals who voted for Francis now want him to step down so that the Holy See's secretary of state, Cardinal Pietro Parolin, can be elected the real pope. And these electors understand something else, too. Parolin's name means "Peter the Roman" from the final line of the *Prophecy of the Popes*.

9

Charles Manson, Chaos, and the Coming Great Reset

In my mind's eye, my thoughts light fires in your cities.
—CHARLES MANSON

Now the last age by Cumae's Sibyl sung
Has come and gone, and the majestic roll
Of circling centuries begins anew:
Justice returns, returns old Saturn's reign,
With a new breed of men sent down from heaven.
—VIRGIL, *ECLOGUE IV*

Power is inflicting pain and humiliation.
Power is in tearing human minds to pieces and putting them
together again in new shapes of your own choosing.
Power is not a means; it is an end.
—George Orwell, *Nineteen Eighty-Four*

The opening quotes to this chapter represent a strange amalgam of sources, but each reveals an aspect of our current age. Manson and Orwell tapped into streams that offer insight into a coming apocalypse where old beliefs are stripped away and replaced by new. But the ancient writer Virgil seemed also to tap into this prescient future vision in his *Eclogue* series, especially *Eclogue IV,* which haughtily trumpets a day when the old gods return:

> The iron shall cease, the golden race arise,
> Befriend him, chaste Lucina; 'tis thine own
> **Apollo reigns**. And in thy consulate,
> This glorious age, O Pollio, shall begin,
> And the months enter on their mighty march.
> Under thy guidance, whatso tracks remain
> Of our old wickedness, once done away,
> Shall free the earth from never-ceasing fear.
> He shall receive the life of gods, and see
> **Heroes with gods commingling**, and himself
> Be seen of them, and with his father's worth
> Reign o'er a world at peace.[203] (Emphasis added)

Notice the emboldened lines. The death of the age of iron and the birth of the golden refers to the ever-cycling *ouroboros,* the snake eating its tail and the cycle of the years that sees the end to the base metal years and the return of the glorious age of gold! As with the statue in Daniel's vision, this ever-decaying cycle runs from gold to silver, then bronze to iron, and finally the iron becomes clay or mixes with the race of old gods to return the world to a shimmering age of gold. We are living in such a paradigm shift, and the engine driving this entropy is chaos. The old god Set, who ushers in the age of Saturn—ruled over by Apollo.

But this new age will be anything but golden; it will be the blackest period of human history: quite literally, hell on earth.

George Orwell foresaw a glimpse of such a time. The brilliant English novelist endured the heartache, delusion, fears and cultural shocks of the pre- and post-World War II Britain, and he portrayed the ultimate end to totalitarianism and total government surveillance through his novels *Nineteen Eighty-Four* and *Animal Farm.* Finding these disquieting themes couched within the safety of fiction somehow grants them a sense of sur-realism, but it teaches a lesson to those who hope to learn from history.

Orwell died in January of 1950, long before the *actual* emergence of the very society which he so feared: a world of mechanized eyes and soft-ware slogans; a realm of memespeak, thought police, and the false percep-tion of universal exceptionalism (which by its very nature makes everyone the same—except for "protected classes"). However, this oppressive and fear-based environment is but the harbinger of darker worlds still to come.

Ordo ab chao. Order out of chaos. Apophis. Set. The return of old Saturn's reign.

The Coming "GREAT RESET"

If this phrase is new to some of you, you're not alone; but it has perco-lated through elitist brains for centuries in one form or another. In 2010, Richard Florida, a sociologist who studies economic cycles in city systems, authored a seminal book called *The Great Reset*. The primary thesis of this sleeper seed-book is that major paradigm and organizational shifts occur in economic systems when cities lose sight of diversity and creativ-ity. For Florida, it's the creative classes of individuals who stoke the engine of innovation and hence drive invention and industry. Without such big thinkers, Florida would assert, mankind's forward momentum grinds to a halt.

Of course, critics of Florida's metropolitan model disagree on the grounds that he insists this so-called creative class must be composed of a high percentage of gender-fluid individuals. Yes, you read that correctly. To achieve the "great reset" of mankind, cities must be restructured with a new elitist class that favors artists, musicians, novelists, and other creators whose ideologies skew heavily to the socialism and trans philosophies (as opposed to "cis" philosophies). As an aside, for those unfamiliar with the terms, "trans" and "cis" are mirror-image configurations of biochemical structures. God's design is trans (the dominant configuration), which means anyone opposed to God would choose the "cis" version.

Florida's logical end, therefore, is socialist Darwinism. Such a philosophy paints mankind as ever striving towards greater levels of achievement and centralized organization. First, he moves from living alone in caves to hunter-gatherer tribes, followed by agrarian communities, then to industrialized cities where farming is no longer required, to today's information-addicted, hashtag-loving big-thinkers who can't fix their own flat tires, much less grow a tomato—and finally, the cities die and the community disbands. The only way to fix this, Florida asserts, is to inject cities with artists and trans-fixed socialists, who will kick us into a new age of innovation.

And we are being forced into this very shift. Don't believe it? Just recall the social-media-driven, hashtag revolution that is currently overwhelming cities and law enforcement agencies across the globe. At present, thousands of protesters bearing slogans and signs, neatly printed with the most fashionable hashtags (#fillintheblank) have taken to the streets—with Molotov cocktails in hand—ready to defend their right to desecrate our homes and sow destruction in our towns. They seek to erase more than history, more than statues—the current age itself. And in an era where nearly all learning is digital, it's easy to imagine how history might be changed to suit a rising dictator. Like the Nazis, book-burning removes old ideas and brands them heretical or damaging, but if a child's only source of information is the Internet, then all knowledge is subject to editorial alteration and erasure.

And with the loss of printed history and commemorative structures and statues—without a hard copy of humanity's flawed past—future generations will have to rely upon the plays, poetry, and propaganda written by government-approved authors via online sources that can instantly be updated to reflect the ideology of the moment. With a single keystroke, what has been will cease to be.

It is just as George Orwell feared:

The past was alterable. The past never had been altered. Oceania was at war with Eastasia. Oceania had always been at war with Eastasia.[204]

In Orwell's *Nineteen Eighty-Four*, the ruling English government, "Ingsoc" (short for "English socialism") reigned over the new nation of Oceania. Ingsoc controlled her citizens' thoughts and activities by requiring each to communicate using only "Newspeak." The concept of free speech had vanished in Oceania in favor of ironically positive and often self-contradictory words and phrases.

Joycamps replaced labor camps, presumably making them "fun" (not).

Goodthink was any thought that supported the ruling political party.

Oldspeak was the former English language (one can see our current trends towards shorthand communication—i.e., emojis—replacing actual, cogent expression through entire sentences).

Oldthink was outdated ideas held by individuals before the rise of the current regime.

Thinkpol was the thought police, who used false-flag operations to lure unsuspecting renegades into "outing" themselves.

Teledep, was the Ministry of Truth's telecommunications department of the regime, which broadcast Big Brother's daily briefings and propaganda.

Telescreens provided two-way communication between government entities and citizens.

Orwell foresaw our current society, where social media and twenty-four-hour news cycles shape and influence public opinion—and even shame those who refuse to accept the new "truths." Think of how the hashtag generation is using peer pressure to force netizens to rethink their positions and beliefs. We are being changed, dear friends. We're slowly being moved towards the new paradigm by a maniacal minority of keyboard warriors. Power is being concentrated into the hands of fewer and fewer individuals, and soon it will reside in only one.

J. R. R. Tolkien would call it the "One Ring to Rule Them All." Today's community organizers might paraphrase it as "One Meme to Rule Them All."

But before you can restructure society—before you can design a new Tower of Babel or raise Sauron's Dark Tower or lay the foundations for

Orwell's Oceania—all the old foundations must be destroyed and forever removed from memory. That is what's happening right now—today.

This is what Florida meant by the "Great Reset."

Today's hashtag movement is intent on destroying all of humanity's past, leaving behind a void that requires filling. Think of this as societal brainwashing that leaves the formerly filled and "prejudicial" brain empty and ready for Orwell's Newspeak to take hold. But this did not originate with Richard Florida—or with Black Lives Matter—or with ISIS—or with Charles Manson.

It is an ancient idea, found in the book of Genesis.

> And the earth was **without form, and void**; and darkness was upon the face of the deep. And the Spirit of God moved upon the face of the waters. (Genesis 1:2; emphasis added)

"Without form and void"—empty. What does that mean? After the LORD created the heavens and the earth in verse 1, some catastrophic event, most likely a rebellion, occurred that left this world altered, emptied of its former glory, its identity. Like the aforementioned brain that must be emptied for retraining, our own earth had to be made void before it could be reordered. It's been hiding in plain sight: *Ordo ab chao*—order out of chaos. Quite literally, for it is a primordial entity known as Chaos that lurks beneath the global waters. The war that preceded verse 2 of Genesis 1 is called the *Chaoskampf*. It refers to a war before Adam and Eve—before the creation of the sun and moon. Before our current animal life. We don't know what that former world was like, but we know how it ended. With a deluge. The earth, covered in water, with the Holy Spirit hovering over the leader of that rebellion, Chaos. The Dragon. Tiamat. Leviathan, Apophis. It is this creature that slithers in the heart of Gaia worshipers, placing creation above the Creator. It is a topsy-turvy doctrine akin to Orwell's Newspeak.

Today, it's called "climate change."

The Great Reset's climate-change agenda not only reveres Gaia as our "mother" but even depicts an ancient Egyptian god as the good guy. The hero of the *Chaoskampf.* The one who brings order out of chaos.

SET. Yes, you read that correctly. Set, the entity now associated with death, was once revered as the heroic conqueror of Chaos.

Here's the myth, and we'll follow it with an examination of the Great Reset Initiative as it's laid out by the World Economic Forum. The various agendas within this overarching initiative are:

1. COVID-19
2. Racism and injustice
3. LGBTQ+ agenda
4. Climate change
5. Mental health
6. Trade
7. Globalization

The last two items, trade and globalization, lie neatly within the wheelhouse of an organization calling itself the "World Economic Forum" (WEF), but it's clear from the subcompartments of the Great Reset Initiative that much more is at work here. Under the globalization heading is the notion of both an "Industry 4.0"[205] and "Globalization 4.0." Florida implies that each Great Reset does so on the backbone of a societal revolution, the first using steam power, the next electric power, the third electronic and information power, and now this fourth revolution builds upon the information system to lead us into a fifth turning of sorts, where humanity has become merged with technology, i.e., we are transhuman.

Trade, according to the WEF website, requires the removal of all national identities:

> With more and more voters demanding to **"take back control" from "global forces"**, the challenge is to restore sovereignty in a world that requires cooperation. Rather than closing off economies

through protectionism and nationalist politics, we must forge a new social compact between citizens and their leaders, so that everyone feels secure enough at home to remain open to the world at large. Failing that, the ongoing disintegration of our social fabric could ultimately lead to the collapse of democracy....

The changes that are underway today are not isolated to a particular country, industry, or issue. They are universal, and thus **require a global response. Failing to adopt a new cooperative approach would be a tragedy for humankind.** To draft a blueprint for a shared global-governance architecture, we must avoid becoming mired in the current moment of crisis management.[206] (Emphasis added)

Note the author's use of "scare quotes" in the phrases "take back control" and "global forces," implying that such beliefs pose a danger to the world's survival. Schwab continues with: "Globalism is an ideology that prioritizes the neoliberal global order over national interests.[207]" This Fourth Industrial Revolution even has its own manifesto, called the 2020 Davos Manifesto,[208] which is itself a continuation and reimagining of the 1973 Davos Manifesto.[209] Both agreements center around the need for economic cooperation with an end goal of making money for investors (not surprising), but the 2020 manifesto adds the imperative that:

In creating such value, a company serves not only its shareholders, but all its stakeholders—employees, customers, suppliers, local communities and society at large. The best way to understand and harmonize the divergent interests of all stakeholders is through a shared commitment to policies and decisions that strengthen the long-term prosperity of a company.[210]

The WEF website also reveals a link to the current COVID crisis as a driving factor for this future reset.

2020

d **action** by business, **combined with global**, mul-
)peration—at exceptional scale and speed—can
te the risk and impact of this unprecedented crisis.
urgent need for global stakeholders to coop-
erate in simultaneously managing the direct consequences of
the COVID-19 crisis. **To improve the state of the world, the
World Economic Forum is starting The Great Reset initiative.**[211]
(Emphasis added)

In January of 2021, members of the World Economic Forum will
meet to plan our futures.

We only have one planet and we know that climate change could
be the next global disaster with even more dramatic consequences
for humankind. We have to decarbonize the economy in the
short window still remaining and bring our thinking and behav-
iour once more into harmony with nature," said Klaus Schwab,
Founder and Executive Chairman of the World Economic
Forum.... "**COVID-19 has accelerated our transition into the
age of the Fourth Industrial Revolution.** We have to make sure
that the new technologies in the digital, biological and physical
world remain human-centred and serve society as a whole, providing everyone with fair access."

"If there is one critical lesson to learn from this crisis, **it is
that we need to put nature at the heart of how we operate.** We
simply can't waste more time," said HRH The Prince of Wales.
(Emphasis added)

COVID-19 and climate change are used as the excuse to force the
world to accept the reset. But there's more to this than just a slew of
wealthy businessmen and royals, and it leads us far back into antiquity. As
Solomon once said:

The thing that hath been, it is that which shall be; and that which is done is that which shall be done: and there is no new thing under the sun. (Ecclesiastes 1:9, ESV)

Set, the Hero and Villain of Old

Some might remember studying Egyptian deities in a high school or college mythology class, or perhaps as part of a course on Old Testament history, but let this be stated now and without reservation: *Set actually existed.* He was not a human invention. He wasn't just a means for an unsophisticated mind to try to explain meteorological or seasonal effects. Set was a real entity—and a fallen one at that—which means his story has been twisted, first one way and then another, to fit the narrative and purpose of whatever leader was presently in power. Sometimes, he was the good guy. Sometimes, the bad. He either provided the king with protection and supernatural abilities, or else he was the enemy of the deity who offered those things to the king.

Defender author and SkyWatchTV host, Derek Gilbert, has been studying the gods of Egypt and the ancient Near East for many years now for a bestselling series of books, including: *The Great Inception, The Day the Earth Stands Still, Last Clash of the Titans, Bad Moon Rising,* and *Veneration.*

Derek provides us a brief introduction to Set, the mysterious, ever-changing god of chaos:

Most of us are familiar with the Egyptian god Set as the evil villain of the story of Osiris and Isis. Set, also called *Seth* or *Sutekh*, was the jealous brother, who killed and dismembered his sibling Osiris. With no son to avenge this heinous crime, the newly widowed Isis devised a cunning plan: She would revive her dead husband long enough to become pregnant. First, Isis collected her late husband's body parts, thirteen in all (she never recovered the fourteenth part, the phallus, which had been eaten by a fish). But clever Isis circumvented this problem by fashioning a substitute generative member from either her own thumb or from a bit of gold. Lastly, taking the form of a kite (type of bird), and with the aid of the god Thoth's magical working, Isis revived Osiris just long enough for him to beget the falcon-headed god Horus. Thus, Isis foiled Set's plans by producing an heir who would avenge his father. And Osiris, whose skin is green to represent death, now reigns as Lord of the Underworld.

However, this negative tale wasn't always the accepted version. The above account comes from the Greek historian Plutarch, compiled around AD 100. But during the Israelite sojourn in Egypt, more than *fifteen hundred years earlier*, Set was portrayed as a heroic figure; identified by Egyptians and Canaanites with the storm-god Baal. As such, Set was the rain-giver, god of storms, of the desert, and of foreigners. And it was believed that he defended the solar boat of the sun-god Re (or Ra, depending on the source) against the destructive chaos-serpent, Apophis, each night as it slipped below the horizon. Without Set, the cycle of time and the rising of the sun would cease, causing the end of all things (the Apocalypse), with the world disappearing into the belly of insatiable Apophis.

By the time the Jews returned from Babylon in the fifth century BC, roughly *a thousand years after the Exodus*, the glory days of the pharaohs were over. Egypt was overrun by armies from Ethiopia (715 BC), Assyria (671 BC), and Persia (529 BC). Therefore, the god of foreigners wasn't welcome around the pyramids anymore; and Set, once identified with the king of the pantheon, Baal (Zeus to the Greeks), became linked instead with the chaos god, Typhon.

If you've read Tom Horn's recent book, *Wormwood*, then you know the asteroid Apophis may strike the earth or graze our atmosphere on April 13, 2029. It's intriguing therefore, that the god Apophis is so inextricably linked to Set, and that the World Economic Forum proposes a Great ReSet.

By the way, Typhon, as we'll discover later in this chapter, has another connection with Apophis. Not only is this god of chaos identified with Set, but he is also the poster boy for a new occult movement called "chaos magick."

For now, if you're a movie buff, you may associate Set's personality and actions with his depiction in the recent film *Gods of Egypt*. In this updated telling of Egyptian myths, Set is very definitely the bad guy.

Here's the plot in a nutshell (note that it differs from the actual myths quite a bit): During the coronation ceremony for Prince Horus, his Uncle Set shows up and slays Osiris (Horus' father), and then steals Horus' eyes. Blinded, the heir to Osiris is exiled to a lower realm (Horus is often portrayed as an alternative god of the underworld). Grandfather Ra (who's very busy piloting the sun boat across the heavens) takes a neutral stance on his children's squabbles, but does offer his grandson a special vial of water that will weaken Set's power. Horus realizes it is up to him to avenge his father's death. The plot continues with numerous side stories (one involves a "chosen" human as helper), but the ending is a major reversal of the myth. The Egyptian story depicts Set *slaying*, not helping, the chaos dragon Apophis. According to traditional Egyptian mythology, each day, the dragon tries to devour Ra's sun barge, but Set and Re (alternately Ra) defeat him and stave off the apocalypse.

However, in the film, Set kills Ra and then frees Apophis to wreak havoc!

And here's where we get back to the coming Great Reset. As mentioned above, another name for Ra is Re. You've probably seen both names and wondered if these were two different gods. Nope. The same god, but many scholars prefer Re to Ra. So, using this terminology, let's consider the film's lesson:

If Re is killed by Set, the result is chaos (the release of Apophis). Set + Apophis = Death of Re and Reign of Chaos

However, if we prefer the old Egyptian story, Set + Ra = the defeat of Apophis (Chaos) and the restoration of order.

Set + Apophis = Chaos with Re dead.

Set + Re = Order with Apophis dead.

Now, take a look at the logo of a recent YouTube video[212] that stars Crown Prince Charles of England, promoting the Great Reset Initiative:

The profound brilliance of this design is that it combines the above two ideas. Set against Re, and Set plus Re. In essence, it distills *ordo ab chao* into a five-letter code, separated by a colon. Ironically, in mathematics, separating two numbers or unknowns (such as $x{:}y$) refers to the set of those two numbers or "the set of x and y." Also, the five letters of the logo might hold another hidden message. According to occult symbology, the number five represents divinity, grace, redemption, the "god-man," and even the incarnated conscience (being the number four, which represents the earth and/or matter PLUS the number one, which is said to represent God's in-breathed Spirit).

Though unbeknownst to most Christians, a neo-pagan practice known as "chaos magick" also reveres the idea of order out of chaos. (No, we've not misspelled "magic" by adding a *k*. That was added by the movement's founders, two British occultists: Peter J. Carroll and Ray Sherwin. Carroll and Sherwin based their new system on the ideas of turn-of-the-century artist Austin Osman Spare, author of several grimoires (i.e., textbooks for magicians). Spare had initiated the idea of connecting *sigils*—symbols based on the hidden relationship between the conscious and unconscious self—to a gnostic or altered state that empowers the sigil. In essence, these shamanistic sorcerers claim that they can create a new "god" simply by imagining and believing in one. Terrafim (pagan images of household gods) provided locality to ancient gods. A golem of mud is another example of invoking a spirit into a manmade object, but more recently, a new type of god has emerged: the one imagined through digital means. Slenderman (known as a *tulpa* or thought-form) is but one example of the power behind such mental magical workings. Slenderman's allure drew in teens and children, and in at least one case, led to a stabbing, meant to please the new "god."

But imagined entities are ephemeral and lack true power, and so (since 2010), a "post-chaos' chaos magick movement has emerged that denounces the former "imaginary gods" as useless and feeble (assuming they existed at all) and calling for the return of the old gods, worshiped by our ancestors.

Which brings us back to the ancient chaos god, Set. Whether consciously done or not, the RE:SET logo certainly holds sigilistic power, invoking both Re and Set as either allies or enemies. Both imply a return of an old, fallen realm hegemony—and both tell us that this New World Order (let's call it the "Year Zero"), will not commence without our passing through a rough transitional period: The time when chaos will reign. Think of it as being swallowed by Apophis.

Now, if you're beginning to feel like the NWO magicians are all-powerful, remember Psalm 2. This prophetic chapter begins with the picture of a coalition of fallen-realm spirit entities and humans who plot together against the Almighty:

Why do the nations rage
and the peoples plot in vain?
The kings of the earth set themselves,
and the rulers take counsel together,
against the LORD and against his Anointed, saying,
"Let us burst their bonds apart
and cast away their cords from us." (Psalm 2:1–3, ESV)

Then the psalmist continues with God's reaction to these plans:

He who sits in the heavens laughs;
the Lord holds them in derision.
Then he will speak to them in his wrath,
and terrify them in his fury, saying,
"As for me, I have set my King
on Zion, my holy hill."
I will tell of the decree:
The LORD said to me, "You are my Son;
today I have begotten you.
Ask of me, and I will make the nations your heritage,
and the ends of the earth your possession.
You shall break them with a rod of iron
and dash them in pieces like a potter's vessel."
(Psalm 2:1–9, ESV; emphasis added)

Did you catch that? Yahweh laughs at their plans! When we learn of these hideous plots and schemes, it can make us afraid—make us feel helpless. But the LORD laughs! He's known about their schemes since before the dawning of the universe, just as He knows the schemes will fail. Yet He allows them to proceed with their plots, in order to unmask their dark hearts, for He has promised to "reveal deep and hidden things; he knows what is in the darkness" (Daniel 2:22, ESV).

Here's the point: *Ordo ab chao* means that chaos (Re:Set + Apophis) must precede the establishment of a New World Order: the coming "Great Reset," as the World Economic Forum calls it. Oh, but did I mention who now serves as the public face of this *ordo ab chao* reset button? Hold onto your hats, folks, because it's evocative of Sharon Gilbert's *Redwing Saga* series, where the fallen realm and their human dupes insist that London of the nineteenth century was not only the *omphalos* of the world (i.e., the navel or connection between heaven and earth), but that the Redwing/Fallen Angel alliance would culminate in the enthronement of their spirit-inhabited ruler as king of the British Empire, and by extension, the world. And that this New Man would lead the world through a chaotic war (the planned World Wars) and into a wonderful, new *Golden Age*.

But that's just fiction, right?

No. There is a very real, planned Great RE:SET coming, which is led by none other than the Crown Prince of England: His Royal Highness, Prince Charles Philip Arthur George.

Here's what HRH Prince Charles had to say at the launch of the World Economic Forum's Great Reset, on May 27, 2020:

> There is a golden opportunity to seize something good from this crisis...global crises know no borders, and highlight how interdependent we are as one people sharing one planet.... Unless we take the action necessary, and we build again in a greener and more sustainable, more inclusive way, then we will end up having more and more pandemics and more disasters from ever-accelerating and global warming and climate change. So this is the one moment, as you've all been saying, when we have to make as much progress as we can.[213]

Charles Is the Man, Son.

We now jump from a prince called Charles to a notorious killer with the same first name. But how does Manson fit into all this? No, we didn't place his name in the title of this chapter as a tease. First off, Charles Manson and his infamous family are profoundly connected to the public psyche. Remember that conscious and unconscious formula used by chaos magick practitioners? It requires the implantation of sigils into our minds, and by repeating them, the sigils are activated. Imagining a thing creates a thing—or summons it. Charles Manson understood this concept, and his salacious crimes fractured the minds of all who lived at that time, leaving their foul impressions upon our collective consciousness.

But it goes even deeper than that, for Manson was embedded with a program that many of you have researched: MK-ULTRA.

A new book by Tom O'Neill blows the lid off preconceptions regarding the impetus behind Manson's crimes. No, it wasn't to please the Beatles or to start a race war. In his explosive exposé, *Chaos: Charles Manson, the CIA, and the Secret History of the Sixties*, O'Neill reveals his own, twenty-year trip own down the Manson rabbit hole, and uncovers the maddening truths hidden there.

For instance, most Americans know that Manson frequented the hippie locales of the Haight-Ashbury district, but few know the CIA also operated there, within the Haight-Ashbury Free Clinics (HAFCs). O'Neill connects the CIA to these clinics, but also to a secondary front of free hippie hangouts, where graduate students dispensed free LSD while pretending to be "one of the gang." While their unwitting subjects got high, the grad students asked psychologically loaded questions and employed persuasive techniques. The purpose was to learn if spy agencies could produce domestically grown "Manchurian Candidates."

According to O'Neill, Charles Manson and many of his high-profile Hollywood friends (including Dennis Wilson of the Beach Boys and record producer Terry Melcher) form a tantalizing Venn diagram with a mystery man named Reeve Whitsun, a shadowy chameleon alleged to work as a plain-clothes provocateur within the LA scene.

The operation in question commenced with a memo, explained by O'Neill:

On August 25, 1967, J. Edgar Hoover issued a memorandum to the chiefs of each of his FBI field offices in the United States, outlining the objective of COINTELPRO. (The name was an abridgment of Counter Intelligence Program.) First launched in 1956 to "increase factionalism" among Communists in the United States, COINTELPRO had been activated on and off throughout the early sixties, often to vilify civil rights leaders—Martin Luther King Jr. most prominent among them. In his '67 memo, Hoover formed a new branch of the operation, aiming to expose, disrupt, misdirect, discredit, or otherwise neutralize the activities of black nationalist, hate-type organizations.... The activities of all such groups of intelligence interest to this Bureau must be followed on a continuous basis.... Efforts of various groups to consolidate their forces or to recruit new or youthful adherents must be frustrated. **No opportunity should be missed to exploit... the organizational and personal conflicts of the leaderships of the groups...[and] to capitalize upon existing conflicts between competing black nationalist organizations.**[214]

Many of you probably already knew about this memo and the infamous program it inaugurated, but COINTELPRO's link to Black nationalism and the orders to "capitalize on existing conflicts" is incendiary. O'Neill seems to think that, either while incarcerated or through the Haight-Ashbury Free Clinic setup, Charles Manson learned to use LSD and techniques of mind-control programming (e.g., deviant sex practices, isolation, confusion, lack of sleep, etc.). After creating his own Manchurian candidates, Manson ordered them to perform ritualistic slaughter, while laying the blame on black nationalist organizations like the Black Panthers. The bloody messages left at the Tate-LaBianca sites were intended to lead to Panther members.

As he uncovered more and more of these unsettling links, O'Neill proceeded farther and farther down this labyrinthine rabbit hole:

My to-do list was now as long as it'd been in the heaviest days of my reporting. And sometimes, behind my excitement and anxiety, I could feel a lower, deeper dread…. The evidence I'd amassed against the official version of the Manson murders was so voluminous, from so many angles, that it was overdetermined. I could poke a thousand holes in the story, but I couldn't say what really happened. In fact, the major arms of my research were often in contradiction with one another. It couldn't be the case that the truth involved a drug burn gone wrong, orgies with Hollywood elite, a counterinsurgency-trained CIA infiltrator in the Family, a series of unusually lax sheriff's deputies and district attorneys and judges and parole officers, an FBI plot to smear leftists and Black Panthers, an effort to see if research on drugged mice applied to hippies, and LSD mind-control experiments tested in the field… could it?[215]

O'Neill explains his own cognitive dissonance and the moment he "woke up" in an interview with the UK online newspaper, *The Independent*:

I had never believed in conspiracies. But it is a documented fact that the CIA had a programme called Chaos, and the FBI had one called COINTELPRO. The objectives of both of those at-the-time secret operations was to destabilise the left-wing movement and make hippies appear dangerous. And if this was a government operation, then boy did they succeed. Suddenly, everybody looked at anyone with long hair and a beard as a possible Charlie Manson.[216]

Is it coincidental that one of the names for this counterintelligence operation was CHAOS? Hardly. Not if you consider the deceptive spirits that operate behind the human agencies of this world. And we see the very same *modus operandi* repeated today, via leftist community organizing"groups. Don't forget that it was the CIA, through its InQTel investment wing, that funded a nascent social-media startup called Facebook—the seminal online social media site that connected people from across the globe. Initially, the site was intended only for colleges, but it soon outgrew this design and became a network for eager netizens from all walks of life, providing microblogging and photo-sharing in a seemingly egalitarian manner—no web skills required. With the rise of smart phones and tablets, is it any wonder that social media has morphed into an intelligence-gathering monster? No longer must government agencies apply for a warrant to search your home or workplace. No! Today, we volunteer all of it through these social-media sites and our home-connected thermostats, voice-operated oracles like Alexa and Siri, and microphones and cameras.

We upload every moment of our lives without ever considering the consequences. And now, those same socially connected, sharing sites are enforcing their socialist rules upon us. Through our posts and comments, they know our likes, dislikes, religious preferences, and political beliefs. They've scraped the metadata from photos of ourselves, our family, our workplace, our cars, and our homes. They know us better than we know ourselves. You might even say social media moguls have become our masters and our teachers. They curate news to us, using it to shape our thoughts and beliefs. Just as the CIA lured hippies in with free LSD and studies them, social media has lured us in with free forums and games, and used them to study us.

It's like the opening paragraph in chapter one of H. G. Wells' prescient 1898 novel, *The War of the Worlds*:

> With infinite complacency men went to and fro over this globe about their little affairs, serene in their assurance of their empire over matter.... No one gave a thought to the older worlds of space as sources of human danger, or thought of them only to dismiss the idea of life upon them as impossible or improbable. It is curious to recall some of the mental habits of those departed days.

At most terrestrial men fancied there might be other men upon Mars, perhaps inferior to themselves and ready to welcome a missionary enterprise. Yet across the gulf of space, minds that are to our minds as ours are to those of the beasts that perish, intellects vast and cool and unsympathetic, regarded this earth with envious eyes, and slowly and surely drew their plans against us. And early in the twentieth century came the great disillusionment.[217]

Remove the instigators of this fictional war from Mars, and then replace them with human actors, intent on resetting the world according to a new paradigm, and couple these with the true enemies, those unseen, unobservable actors who pull the strings and act as *coadjutors deluxe* (that is, the spirit realm), and you have our world today. Wells used science fiction to present a coming conflict that would forever alter mankind. He lived in the lead-up to World War I, but you and I live in the lead-up to Armageddon. The final battle of a long war between light and dark, between good and evil, that will determine ownership of the earth and humanity. The fallen realm believe they can win this war.

As part of the preliminary events to Armageddon, we see the conflicts foretold by Christ begin to play out:

> And Jesus answered them, "See that no one leads you astray. For many will come in my name, saying, 'I am the Christ,' and they will lead many astray.
>
> And you will hear of wars and rumors of wars. See that you are not alarmed, for this must take place, but the end is not yet.
>
> **For nation will rise against nation, and kingdom against kingdom, and there will be famines and earthquakes in various places.** All these are but the beginning of the birth pains." (Matthew 24:4–8, ESV; emphasis added)

The Greek word translated as "nation" in verse 7 is *ethnos*. A better translation might be "tribe" or "people group," because our modern concept of nations is forever linked to countries. Jesus is telling us that we will see ever increasing periods of civil unrest. People groups would rise against other people groups, against other tribes—and kingdoms (the *basileia*) would rise up against other kingdoms. It's an unsettling picture of chaos and racial divide.

Isn't that what we're witnessing now? Racial politics has brought protests to our streets and anger to our homes. Social media is used to direct our opinions through persuasive and sometimes amusing meme posters (this is the tempting carrot) and then shadow banning or removing accounts they deem divisive (the stick). Peer pressure is a powerful weapon in these online gathering places, and those who refuse to obey are deemed irrelevant or dangerous.

As we write this book, our nation has just celebrated Independence Day. Yet, anti-patriot rhetoric is so strong now that one wonders if we'll manage to reach another such anniversary without fracturing completely. It's exactly the kind of minefield that Christ warned us about; it's a time when tribe would rise up against tribe. While there's no doubt that our country has failed many who live within its borders, the global picture presented online uses disturbing (and sometimes staged) graphic images and forceful memes as peer pressure, and it is a rabidly leftist agenda. Statues of civil war generals and even President Lincoln have found themselves victimized and torn from their footings. But how did Christopher Columbus, in 1492, promote slavery in a country not yet born? And what about missionaries like St. Junipera Serra? Three statues of the Catholic friar have been defaced and/or pulled down in California amidst chants of "Rise up, my people, rise up!"[218] Tribe (*ethnos*) will rise against nation.

Remember, also, that *"Rise"* is one of the words scrawled in the victims' blood at both the Tate and LaBianca murder scenes. Project CHAOS and its sister programs like MK-Ultra and COINTELPRO have left their marks on our society, haven't they?

And before we leave behind those programs from the 1960s, let's look at just one more: Project Camelot. It's a code name rich with meaning. Established in 1964, just one year after the assassination of President John

F. Kennedy, Camelot has become synonymous with Kennedy's presidency. As with the mythical King Arthur, who reigned at the original Camelot, John Fitzgerald Kennedy was viewed as a political knight errant, whose youth and energies could have united our nation and led it into a progressive new era.

However, Kennedy's early death ended all that—or did it? The day that forever changed the world (and damaged our psyches) is often linked with a national psychology that needed to believe in a fallen hero—that somehow, Kennedy would one day return, igniting rumors that endured for years that the president had merely been wounded and would one day return to claim his office. I remember those rumors that Kennedy was alive somewhere, recuperating—rather like Arthur on the Isle of Avalon.

We believed that Camelot would, someday, rise again.

But it's all too disquieting in light of spiritual matters. At the time, many can remember hearing pastors asking in hushed whispers if Kennedy might be the Antichrist. This champion of peace and human dignity certainly had the charisma to fulfill prophecy—and he'd been wounded in the head. But in the wake of Kennedy's death, the world he'd hoped to forge, built on racial equality and democratic principles, boiled up into a seething stew of hatred. Black Panthers, Weathermen, and many other insurgent groups worried Washington, precipitating the need for a means to redirect such divergent energies.

Enter Project Camelot.

Think of it as a military-funded social experiment. The basic mandate was to:

> …determine the feasibility of developing a general social systems model which would make it possible to **predict and influence politically significant aspects of social change** in the developing nations in the world. Somewhat more specifically, its objectives are:
>
> *First*, to devise procedures for assessing the potential for internal war within national societies;

Second, to identify with increased degrees of confidence those actions which a government might take to relieve conditions which are assessed as giving rise to a potential for internal war; and

Finally, to assess the feasibility of prescribing the characteristics of a system for obtaining and using the essential information for doing the above two things.[219] (Emphasis added)

The leaders of Project Camelot sought to develop social engineering methods and psychological profiling to get into the heads of individuals in other countries (but also our own)—and then use these methods whenever our country wanted to change the aforementioned country's regime. In other words, it was a playbook for enacting a *coup d'état.* Isn't it ironic that a project with the intent to undermine foreign politics used the name associated with a fallen president that some believe was slain by a murderous *coup d'état?*

Ordo ab chao.

Yes, order from chaos is our topic, and it certainly seems that we have been studied and categorized for decades or longer—in the same way the Martians studied earth in Wells' novel—and the final invasion is nearing. Only this invasion won't come from another planet. It will originate from an unseen dimension, from a place in the heavenlies where spirit entities live and fight against one another—and have been for eons.

The apostle Paul put it this way:

For we do not wrestle against flesh and blood, but against the rulers, against the authorities, against the cosmic powers over this present darkness, against the spiritual forces of evil in the heavenly places. (Ephesians 6:12, ESV)

We live in turbulent times, when tribe is rising up against tribe and kingdom against kingdom, but our true battle is against an unseen enemy. Spirits in high places—like the ancient god Chaos. The old dragon of Revelation, personified to the Egyptians either as Set or as Apophis—or a combination of the two. Set was once revered as the good guy, who aided the sun god Re against the sea dragon Apophis. And with an asteroid on the way bearing that very name, how are we to react?

The world now sits upon the uncomfortable edge of a sharp knife, both politically and economically, but also psychologically. The COVID-19 outbreak has forced many companies and individuals into bankruptcy, and it has caused millions to lose their jobs. People are frightened and angry. And now, rising up along with this chaotic pandemic, have come racial divisions and protests. Some mornings, it seems like our entire history is being erased. Based upon programs used by intelligence organizations in the 1960s, we're seeing a replay of the protests of those years and social engineering on a broad scale, thanks to social media.

Amongst all this, the World Economic Forum plans to reset the world through an endeavor called the Great Reset. It's a plan to construct a new world on the ash heap of the old. The devouring of the old to give birth to the new. Is Set about to slay the old dragon Apophis, or will he join forces with it? But even more ironic is this: The Great Reset is being promoted by a man who might one day take the name of a mythical hero, King Arthur. Yes, Prince Charles's full name includes Arthur, as does his son's, Prince William.

Friends, our world is about to undergo a major upheaval. And if you thought the sixties were chaotic, you ain't seen nothin' yet. This will be a thorough shakeup of all that we now know as "civilization," and many will gladly accept its bondage. Those who find this idea unpalatable will be forced to swallow it—and smile while they do it. We've been rushing towards an indigestible future since the sixties; perhaps even before. In fact, did you know that many of us have been singing about it in our churches? I only recently learned this, in a conversation with Defender author and SkyWatchTV host, Sharon Gilbert.

Ludwig van Beethoven's famous choral piece "Ode to Joy" (*An die Freude* in German) depicts the return of this sort of "golden age," and it's the basis for our popular Christian hymn, "Joyful Joyful, We Adore Thee." Henry van Dyke loved the melody of fourth movement of Beethoven's

Ninth Symphony. So in 1907, he wrote a poem that was set to Beethoven's choral melody. Many of us have sung this hymn many times. However, the lyrics to Beethoven's choral work are anything but Christian. Beethoven's master work is based on a poem by Friederich Schiller, and the English translation of the German is quite a shock! Honestly, it might easily be sung by today's chaotic protesters who demand that Christians disavow Jesus and dance to their discordant music, their new anthem, sung as they embrace the "golden dawn" ushered in by this Great Reset.

Sharon Gilbert—who, in addition to her degree in biology, holds a second major in English literature—has studied and even sung the music during her career in opera, so she provides us a translation and commentary:

> I remember singing Beethoven's Ninth for a concert at the University of Nebraska many years ago. We performed it in German, of course, but as I'd studied that language for several years, I was able to translate most of it myself, using my dictionary. Later, though, I learned that Schiller had changed some of the lines prior to publication, and the original is even more intriguing! By the way, did you know the poem was first published in 1786 in Schiller's magazine? The music periodical was called *Thalia*, named for the German goddess of comedy and poetry.
>
> Once I learned about the earlier version of the poem, I searched the Internet (yes, the Lord allows the World Wide Web to be used for His purposes, too!) and found the original words to the poem, along with a faithful translation. Emphasis is my own, and I've put my commentary in brackets.
>
> > *An die Freude* (Ode to Joy)
> > Joy, beautiful **spark of the gods**,
> > Daughter of Elysium, [Elysium is a realm within Hades, reserved only for fallen heroes and gods]
> > We enter, **drunk with fire**,

Heavenly one, thy sanctuary!

Thy magic binds again

What custom strictly divided; [A line to one of Shelley's *Adonais* states, "No more let life divide what death can bring together," implying that true lives begin at death]

All people become brothers, [This is the false promise of egalitarianism that lures in youth today]

Where thy gentle wing abides. [The image of being beneath a god's wing is a direct imitation of God's promise to protect us beneath His wing.]

Whoever has succeeded in the great attempt,

To **be a friend's friend,**

Whoever **has won a lovely woman,**

Add his to the jubilation!

Yes, and also **whoever has just one soul**

To call his own in this world!

And he who never managed it should slink

Weeping from this union! [The language of this verse uses "union" in a way that might easily compare to obtaining a physical union with the gods—evoking Genesis 6 and the original sin, a paradigm that is eagerly sought by the occult.]

All creatures **drink of joy** [as though 'joy' is a nourishing substance]

At nature's breasts. [This spiritual nourishment is provided by Gaia or "Mother Earth," whose worship is central to the occult chaos movement, currently disguised as "climate change."]

All the Just, all the Evil ["All the Just" is equated with "All the Evil"? Okay, is this saying the "just" and the "evil" become buddies or that they are equivalent? Perish that thought! This requires a deadly syncretism that reduces everything to a heretical oneism.]

Follow her trail of roses.

Kisses she gave us and grapevines,

A friend, proven in death. [Another mention of death—again, note the comment regarding Shelley's poem *Adonais* and the desire that true life follows death.]

Salaciousness was given to **the worm** [*Salacious* refers to sexual impropriety.]

And **the cherub** stands before God. [The covering cherub, Lucifer? Remember, "the worm" is another name for the dragon.]

Gladly, as his suns fly

through the heavens' grand plan [Yes, the original here is *seine Sonnen*, which is plural and implies multiple suns; one wonders if another might be the theoretical Nemesis, or the "black sun" of the Nazis.]

Go on, brothers, your way,

Joyful, like a hero to victory. [If these "suns" are brothers, then their image of being heroes to victory must mean these are god-like beings.]

Be embraced, Millions!

This kiss to all the world!

Brothers, **above the starry canopy**

There must dwell a loving Father. [One might assume Schiller meant the Creator, Yahweh, but it's unlikely, based on earlier lines of the poem.]

Do you kneel down, millions?

Do you sense the creator, world?

Seek him above the starry canopy!

Above stars must He dwell.

All right, let's examine the overall message of the poem. Schiller is supposed to have been inspired to write *An die Freude* by his friend and patron Christian Gottfried Körner, who also happened to be

a German Freemason. In fact, the poem includes many Freema-
sonic ideals, as well as echoing the current sentiments of French
revolutionaries (remember, this was written in 1785, just four
years before insurgents stormed the Bastille). And a few years later,
Ludwig van Beethoven, who was studying with Christian Got-
tlieb Neefe, another Freemason, set about putting the poem to
music—thus, the fourth movement of Symphony No. Nine was
conceived. Though other Freemasons set *An die Freude* to music,
it is Beethoven's that the world sings and loves—most without any
idea of the lyrics' true meaning.

Honestly, friends, if the idea of "brotherhood" entering some sort of
mystical (or even physical) union with the ancient gods doesn't shake you
up, then what does? Chaos is the ultimate end of the planned Great Reset.
Or rather, the Great Re:Set. Re and Set, either working as buddies, or
working as enemies. Either way, it looks as though Set intends to come
out on top, but he's just the warm-up act. The real star of this, according to Virgil's poem, is Saturn—who will emerge as the animating power
behind Apollo. With Gaia as the female component of this unholy trio,
we get the false Father, Son, and Spirit (Gnostics often refer to the Spirit
as a form of Sophia, their goddess of knowledge).

Really, if the arrival of the asteroid Apophis (which may be both an
astronomical body and an angel) is the coming of Chaos/Set, then the
fulfillment of the Great Re:Set is coming in just a few years.

Perhaps, in April of 2029.

OTHER IMPORTANT WORKS FROM
DR. THOMAS R. HORN

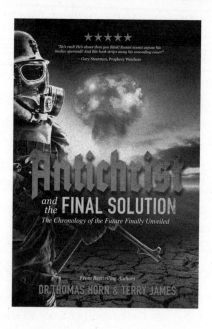

It's been assumed for centuries that a prerequisite for the coming of Antichrist would be a "revived" world order—an umbrella under which national boundaries dissolve and ethnic groups, ideologies, religions, and economics from around the world orchestrate a single and dominant sovereignty. At the head of the utopian administration, a single personality will surface. He will appear to be a man of distinguished character, but will ultimately become "a king of fierce countenance" (Daniel 8:23). With imperious decree, he will facilitate a one-world government, universal religion, and global socialism. Those who refuse his New World Order will inevitably be imprisoned or destroyed until at last he exalts himself "above all that is called God, or that is worshiped, so that he, as God, sitteth in the temple of God, showing himself that he is God" (2 Thessalonians 2:4).

Bible prophecy depicts this coming tyrant as the deadliest in human history. He will try to carry out a satanic "Final Solution" to inflict genocide far beyond that done through Adolf Hitler's plan by the same name. And this soon-to-come era is closer than many can imagine, yet most don't comprehend the events that lie just ahead.

In *Antichrist and the Final Solution*, you will learn…

- How a "man of sin" will soon appear on the world stage
- The truth about the False Prophet who will assist him
- What happens when Israel signs the upcoming "peace treaty"
- Why a third temple will be built and sacrifices resume
- How "life" will be given to an "image of the Beast"
- What happens when the "seals," "trumpets," and "bowls" described in Revelation unfold
- Why 144 Jews will be mysteriously "sealed"
- Why and how Nephilim giants will return as agents of God's judgment
- Who or what "Mystery Babylon" is
- The truth about the battle of Armageddon, the Second Coming of Jesus, the millennial reign, the Great White Throne judgment, heaven, hell, and YOUR DESTINY!

Available at: https://www.skywatchtvstore.com/

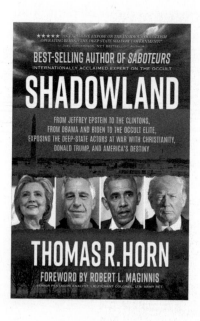

Shadowland soberly and frighteningly exposes occult influences hidden especially within Washington's Deep State and modern culture. From Jeffrey Epstein to the Clintons—from Obama and Biden to the Occult Elite—Dr. Thomas Horn uncovers terrifying realities animating from today's polarized culture and the energies operating behind the contest for dominance over values, beliefs, and religious practices.

Now, for the first time ever, readers will discover:

- Occult practices and enthroned "egregores" over a mysterious, DC-based shadow empire
- Diabolical "body count" lists and "sacrificed" whistleblowers
- Jeffrey Epstein and Shadowland's deals with the devil
- Hillary Clinton and the bizarre effort to summon Antichrist
- Whether some in "Christianity" have joined luciferian objectives
- What really was behind the Russia Hoax and Trump impeachment effort
- Shocking facts about Obama and his so-called birth certificate
- Contrasting visions for America—Progressives vs. Conservatives
- If another Great Awakening is possible
- And much more!

Available at: https://www.skywatchtvstore.com/

- Why a Bible is BOUND in a magic square INSIDE the testes of the Washington Monument…
- Where and why a buried ANCIENT MAGICAL OBELISK AWAITS UNDERGROUND nearby…
- Where the ENTRANCE to a secret crypt exists connected to American LUCIFER WORSHIP from within the Deep State…
- And, for the first time EVER, the US government-owned location where the Antichrist will be resurrected on American soil!

Available at: https://www.skywatchtvstore.com/

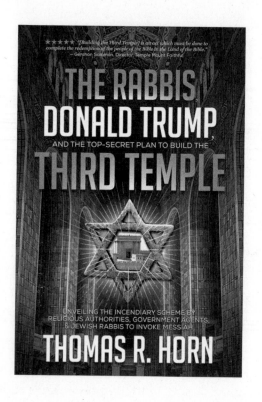

For thousands of years, the world has heard warning that there is a coming a day when the man of sin, the Antichrist, will arise to pilot the greatest deception in human history. Whereas almost anyone alive today can discuss the dictatorial global economics, societal horrors, and eventual apocalypse that follows his arrival, few appear to comprehend that there are negotiations in the workings at this precise moment to build the very location where the abomination of desolation will stand in the holy place. This, as the book of Daniel prophesied, will be the catalyst event to usher in the end of days.

Available at: https://www.skywatchtvstore.com/

Saboteurs is the most critical and groundbreaking work to date by prolific investigative author Thomas Horn. From his earliest opus on secret societies and the occult to this new unnerving chronicle, Dr. Horn returns to Washington, DC, to expose a harrowing plot by Deep-State Alister Crowley and Masonic devotees that hold an almost unbelievable secret they do not want you to understand: American society is being manipulated through a Washington-based shadow government in quest of that final world order prophesied in the books of Daniel, Revelation, and on the Great Seal of the United States! *Saboteurs* goes beyond the superficial chaos currently playing out in the public square and in media against the Trump administration to unveil a far more sinister resistance made up of sorcerous elites, their secret societies, and world power brokers who plot the insidious rise of a messianic strongman figure they call the Grey Champion.

Available at: https://www.skywatchtvstore.com/

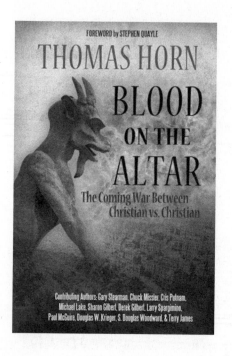

As the world races toward its momentous end-times encounter between good and evil (known in the Bible as Armageddon), a deepening antagonism is developing worldwide against conservative Christians. According to a 2014 Pew Research Center report, this hostility now includes the United States, which elevated from the lowest category of government restrictions on Christian expressions as of mid-2009 to an advanced category in only the last three years. This trend may point to one of the most overlooked aspects of Bible prophecy a war that ultimately pits born-again believers against religious Christians.

Available at: https://www.skywatchtvstore.com/

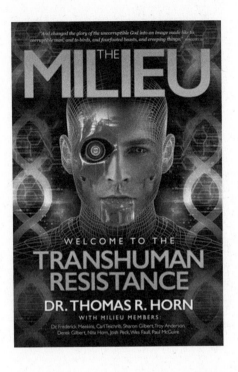

Utopia or dystopia? Shangri-La or purgatory? Paradise or perdition? What future truly awaits mankind on the other side of widespread human enhancement? With breakthrough advances in transhumanistic science and technology at an all-time high, it appears that people of all ages, backgrounds, and world cultures are lining up to embrace the alteration and augmentation of the human race. Remaining as the mere *Homo sapiens* God designed is no longer satisfactory as we rush toward the human-animal chimeric and human-machine hybrid era a point of no return.

Available at: https://www.skywatchtvstore.com/

Notes

1. https://www.biblestudytools.com/lexicons/greek/nas/ekstasis.html.
2. http://www.nytimes.com/2013/02/13/world/europe/pope-benedict-xvi-resignation.html?_r=0.
3. https://www.sciencedirect.com/science/article/pii/S00191035516307643.
4. Lear, Harry. "Open Letter to President Trump." They Fly Blog. January 29, 2018. Accessed May 29, 2019. https://theyflyblog.com/2018/02/15/open-letter-to-president-trump/.
5. https://www.youtube.com/watch?v=WFYo7X2hO_M&t=4s.
6. https://www.archives.gov/education/lessons/us-israel.
7. Meyers, C., in D. N. Freedman (Ed.), *The Anchor Yale Bible Dictionary: Vol. 6* (New York, NY: Doubleday, 1992), 544.
8. Rusten, Sharon, with E. Michael, *The Complete Book of When & Where in the Bible and Throughout History* (Wheaton, IL: Tyndale House Publishers, Inc., 2005), 8; "Timeline" tool, found by searching "Passover," Logos Bible Software, accessed from personal commercial database on April 10, 2020.
9. Ibid.
10. Booker, Dr. Richard, *Celebrating Jesus in the Biblical Feasts* (Shippensburg, PA: Destiny Image Publishers Inc.; Expanded edition 2016), 36.

11. Trumball, Henry Clay, *The Threshold Covenant or The Beginning of Religious Rites* (New York, NY: Charles Scribner's Sons, 1896), iii.

12. Ibid., 3.

13. Ibid., 3–4.

14. Ibid., 203–204.

15. Jeremias, Joachim, *Jerusalem in the Time of Jesus* (Philadelphia: Fortress Press, 1969), 84.

16. Edward M. Reingold, *Calendrical Calculations* (Cambridge: Cambridge University Press, 2008; 3rd ed.), in the *Calendar Book, Papers, and Code* series.

17. Morgenstern, Julian, "The Calendar of the Book of Jubilees, Its Origin and Its Character," January, 1955, *Vetus Testamentum*, Volume 5, 64–65.

18. Hoehner, Harold W., *Chronological Aspects of the Life of Christ* (Grand Rapids, MI: Zondervan Academic, 1977), 87.

19. Pesachim 108b–109a, *The William Davidson Talmud*, last accessed May 13, 2020 from *The Sefaria Library*, https://www.sefaria.org/Pesachim.108b.8?lang=bi&with=all&lang2=en.

20. Eisler, Robert, "Das Letzte Abendmahl," *Zeitschrift für die neutestamentliche Wissenschaft* (Vol. 24; 1925), 161–192.

21. Shurpin, Yehuda, "Why Do We Hide the Afikoman," *Chabad*, last accessed May 20, 2020, https://www.chabad.org/holidays/passover/pesach_cdo/aid/2910434/jewish/Why-Do-We-Hide-the-Afikoman.htm.

22. "Modern Jewish History: The Tribes Today—Kohens, Levis, & Yisraels," *Jewish Virtual Library*, last accessed May 13, 2020, https://www.jewishvirtuallibrary.org/the-tribes-today-kohens-levis-and-yisraels.

23. Ibid.

24. Nadler, Sam, *Messiah in the Feasts of Israel* (Word of Messiah Ministries, Kindle ed., 2011), 87.

25. Eisenberg, Dr. R. L., *The JPS Guide to Jewish Traditions* (Philadelphia: Jewish Publication Society; 1st ed., 2004), 288.

26. Strack, H. and P. Billerbeck, *Kommentar zum Neuen Testament aus Talmud und Midrasch* (IV.1; Munich: Beck, 1928), 73; as quoted in Evans, C. A., & Porter, S. E. *New Testament Backgrounds* (Sheffield, England: Sheffield Academic Press, 1997; Vol. 43), 96.

27. Evans, C. A., & Porter, S. E. *New Testament Backgrounds* (Sheffield, England: Sheffield Academic Press, 1997; Vol. 43), 96, 102.

28. Ibid., 96.

29. Evans, C. A., & Porter, S. E. *New Testament Backgrounds*, 96–97.

30. This moniker was coined on an episode of SkyWatch Television early in the year 2016. The rest of the episode can be viewed here: "Donna Howell & John McTernan—God's Mercy and Redemption," YouTube video, 16:39–16:43, uploaded by SkyWatch TV on February 8, 2016, last accessed April 22, 2020, https://www.youtube.com/watch?v=9ookNb5am1M.

31. This was shared on an episode of SkyWatch Television late in the year 2015. It can be viewed in its entirety here: "Donna Howell & John McTernan Discuss Redemption, When Jesus Sets You Free," YouTube video, 2:19–5:02; 9:23–9:50, uploaded by SkyWatch TV on December 23, 2015, last accessed April 22, 2020, https://www.youtube.com/watch?v=EIC7rKgDBrY.

32. Nadler, *Messiah in the Feasts of Israel*, 63.

33. Booker, *Celebrating Jesus in the Biblical Feasts*, 81.

34. "Romans 11:16," *Barnes' Notes on the Bible, Biblehub*, last accessed June 5, 2020, https://biblehub.com/commentaries/romans/11-16.htm.

35. "The Epistle of Ignatius to the Trallians," as cited by *Bible Study Tools Online*: Ante-Nicene Fathers, Vol. 1, Ignatius—Epistle to the Trallians, Chap. IX, last accessed June 5, 2020, https://www.biblestudytools.com/history/early-church-fathers/ante-nicene/vol-1-apostolic-with-justin-martyr-irenaeus/ignatius/epistle-of-ignatius-trallians.html.

36. "Fragments from the Lost Writings of Irenaeus," as cited by *Bible Study Tools Online*: Ante-Nicene Fathers, Vol. 1, Fragments from

the Lost Writings of Irenaeus XXVIII, last accessed June 5, 2020, https://www.biblestudytools.com/history/early-church-fathers/ ante-nicene/vol-1-apostolic-with-justin-martyr-irenaeus/irenaeus/ fragments-from-lost-writings-of-irenaeus.html.

37. Ante-Nicene Fathers, Vol. II, Clement—Stromata, Book 6, Chap. VI., 1869.

38. Brown, F., Driver, S. R., & Briggs, C. A., *Enhanced Brown-Driver-Briggs Hebrew and English Lexicon* (Oxford: Clarendon Press; 1977), v.

39. "chodesh," Heinrich Friedrich Wilhelm Gesenius, *Gesenius' Hebrew-Chaldee Lexicon*, accessed online through *Blue Letter Bible Online* on June 16, 2020, https://www.blueletterbible.org/lang/ lexicon/lexicon.cfm?Strongs=H2320&t=KJV.

40. "yowm," Heinrich Friedrich Wilhelm Gesenius, *Gesenius' Hebrew-Chaldee Lexicon*, accessed online through *Blue Letter Bible Online* on June 16, 2020, https://www.blueletterbible.org/lang/lexicon/ lexicon.cfm?Strongs=H3117&t=KJV.

41. Ibid.

42. "Biblical World Atlas" tool, "Route of the Exodus" map, found by searching "Rephidim," Logos Bible Software, accessed from personal commercial database on June 17, 2020.

43. "Exodus 19:1," *Jamieson-Fausset-Brown Bible Commentary*, Biblehub, last accessed July 8, 2020, https://biblehub.com/ commentaries/exodus/19-1.htm.

44. "hamam," Heinrich Friedrich Wilhelm Gesenius, *Gesenius' Hebrew-Chaldee Lexicon*, accessed online through *Blue Letter Bible Online* on July 14, 2020, https://www.blueletterbible.org/lang/lexicon/ lexicon.cfm?Strongs=H2000&t=KJV.

45. Dr. Juergen Buehler, "Tongues of Fire: The Festival of Shavuot," *International Christian Embassy Jerusalem (ICEJ)*, last accessed July 16, 2020, https://int.icej.org/news/commentary/tongues-fire.

46. Shemot Rabbah 5:9, *Midrash, Sefaria Community Translation*, last accessed July 15, 2020 from *The Sefaria Library*, https://www.

sefaria.org/Shemot_Rabbah.5.9?ven=Sefaria_Community_Translat
ion&lang=bi&with=all&lang2=en.

47. Ibid.

48. "Topic Guide" tool, found by searching "Blasting," Logos Bible
Software, accessed from personal commercial database on July 16,
2020.

49. Dioscorides, Pedanius, *de Materia Medica*, 5.17; As noted in:
Liddell, H. G., Scott, R., Jones, H. S., & McKenzie, R. *A Greek-
English Lexicon* (Oxford; Clarendon Press: 1996), 780.

50. As in, "When he uttereth his voice," from LXX Jeremiah 28:16
(which would be Jeremiah 51:16 in modern Bibles). As noted in:
Liddell, H. G., Scott, R., Jones, H. S., & McKenzie, R. *A Greek-
English Lexicon* (Oxford; Clarendon Press: 1996), 780.

51. "Bible Word Study" tool, found by searching "φέρω," Logos Bible
Software, accessed from personal commercial database on July 16,
2020. Please note that this source listed countless lexicons, Bible
dictionaries, and other word-study sources that confirmed this
most basic meaning.

52. Swanson, J. (1997). *Dictionary of Biblical Languages with Semantic
Domains: Greek (New Testament)* (Oak Harbor; Electronic Ed.:
Logos Research Systems, Inc.: 1997), entry "1042 βίαιος."

53. "ὥσπερ," *Thayer's Greek Lexicon*, accessed online through *Blue Letter
Bible Online* on July 16, 2020, https://www.blueletterbible.org/
lang/lexicon/lexicon.cfm?Strongs=G5618&t=KJV.

54. Marshall, Ian Howard, *Acts: An Introduction and Commentary* (Vol.
5; Downers Grove, IL: InterVarsity Press, 1980), 73.

55. Barrett, C. K., *A Critical and Exegetical Commentary on the Acts of
the Apostles* (Edinburgh: T&T Clark; 2004), 113; emphasis added.

56. Ibid., 114.

57. "Acts 2 Benson Commentary," *BibleHub*, last accessed July 22,
2020, https://biblehub.com/commentaries/benson/acts/2.htm.

58. "Acts 2:1," *Barnes' Notes on the Bible*, Biblehub, last accessed July 22,
2020, https://biblehub.com/commentaries/acts/2-1.htm.

59. Barrett, C. K., *Critical and Exegetical Commentary*, 113.
60. Marshall, Ian Howard, *Acts*, 73.
61. Booker, Dr. Richard, *Celebrating Jesus in the Biblical Feasts*, 94–95.
62. Nadler, Sam, *Messiah in the Feasts of Israel*, 83–84.
63. "Exodus 19:1," *Benson Commentary*, Biblehub, last accessed July 27, 2020, https://biblehub.com/commentaries/exodus/19-1.htm.
64. "προσήλυτος," *Thayer's Greek Lexicon*, accessed online through *Blue Letter Bible Online* on July 23, 2020, https://www.blueletterbible.org/lang/lexicon/lexicon.cfm?Strongs=G4339&t=KJV. Note that the original προσήλυτος did not refer to a Christian because, earlier than the first Messianic Jews, there was no such thing as Christianity. However, because the earliest "Christians" involved a vast number of believing Jews—and therefore the traditions, customs, and doctrines were rooted in orthodox Judaism, eventually becoming the hybrid "Christianity"—the word προσήλυτος evolved from only representing a Gentile who converted to Judaism, to representing a Gentile who converted straight into the hybrid Judaism, also known as "Christianity."
65. Booker, *Celebrating Jesus in the Biblical Feasts*, 96.
66. Westlake, George & Duncan, David, *aniel and Revelation: An Independent-Study Textbook* (Fourth Ed.; Springfield, MO; Global University: 2013), 79.
67. Ibid.
68. Ibid.
69. Ibid., 80.
70. Ibid.
71. Strong's G1722, *Blue Letter Bible Online*, last accessed July 22, 2020, https://www.blueletterbible.org/lang/lexicon/lexicon.cfm?Strongs=G1722&t=KJV.
72. Strong's G5034, *Blue Letter Bible Online*, last accessed July 22, 2020, https://www.blueletterbible.org/lang/lexicon/lexicon.cfm?Strongs=G5034&t=KJV.
73. Westlake & Duncan, , *Daniel and Revelation*, 90.

74. Strong's G3759, *Blue Letter Bible Online*, last accessed July 22, 2020, https://www.blueletterbible.org/lang/lexicon/lexicon. cfm?Strongs=G3759&t=KJV.

75. Ibid.

76. Westlake & Duncan, *Daniel and Revelation,* 139.

77. Ibid., 141.

78. Ibid..

79. Ibid.

80. Ibid.

81. Johnson, Ken, *The End-Times by the Ancient Church Fathers.* Biblefacts Ministries, 2016, 25.

82. Lane, Tony, *A Concise History of Christian Thought* (Grand Rapids, MI: Baker Academic Group, 2006) 12.

83. Kerr, Hugh. *Readings in Christian Thought* (Nashville, TN: Abington Press, 1966) 29.

84. Henning, Heath. "The Rapture as Taught by the Early Church." *Truth Watchers Online.* June 6, 2016. Accessed July 22, 2020. http://truthwatchers.com/rapture-taught-early-church/.

85. Kremer, Don. *The Chronological Order of Revelation* (Maitland, FL: Xulon, 2007) 189.

86. Ibid.

87. Dave MacPherson, *The Incredible Cover-Up: The True Story of the Pre-Trib Rapture* (Plainfield, NJ: Logos International, 1975) 93.

88. Anderburg, Roy. *Post Tribulation Rapture: A Biblical Study of the Return of Christ.* (Tuscon, AZ: Wheatburg, 2008) 38–39.

89. Ibid.

90. "Bible and Prophetic Movement." Eds. Reed, Daniel & Linder, Robert, et al, *Concise Dictionary of Christianity in America* (Eugene, OR: Wipf and Stock, 1995) 41.

91. Anderburg, Roy. *Post Tribulation Rapture,* 39..

92. Booker, *Celebrating Jesus in the Biblical Feasts,* 115.

93. Fairchild, Mary. "Why Is Rosh Hashanah Called the Feast of Trumpets in the Bible?" *Learn Religions.* July 8, 2020.

Accessed July 22, 2020. https://www.learnreligions.com/feast-of-trumpets-700184.

94. "Feast of Trumpets: The Beginning of the Civil New Year," *Feast & Holidays of the Bible* (Carson, CA: Rose, 2004).

95. Fairchild, "Why Is Rosh Hashanah…?". https://www.learnreligions.com/feast-of-trumpets-700184.

96. Booker, *Celebrating Jesus in the Biblical Feasts,* 116.

97. Booker, *Celebrating Jesus in the Biblical Feasts*, 115.

98. "Feast of Trumpets: The Beginning of the Civil New Year/Yeshua: Jesus." *Feast & Holidays of the Bible*. (Carson, CA: Rose, 2004).

99. Booker, *Celebrating Jesus in the Biblical Feasts*, 126.

100. Ibid.

101. Ibid., 126–127.

102. "Book of Life," *Ask the Rabbi:Aish Online*. Accessed July 22, 2020. https://www.aish.com/atr/Book_of_Life.html.

103. Ibid.

104. Cohen, Peter. "Messianic Good News: Boldly Proclaiming that Jesus is the Messiah." *Messianic Good News Online*. October 4, 2012. Accessed July 22, 2020. https://www.messianicgoodnews.org/may-your-name-be-inscribed-in-the-book-of-life/.

105. "Day of Atonement: The Day the High Priest Makes Atonement for Sin." *Feast & Holidays of the Bible* (Carson, CA: Rose, 2004).

106. Booker, Celebrating Jesus in the Biblical Feasts, 128.

107. Beale, G. K. & Campbell, David. *Revelation: A Shorter Commentary* (Grand Rapids, MI: Eerdman's, 2015) 133.

108. Ibid.

109. Bolinger, Hope. "What Was the Year of Jubilee?" *Christianity Online,* 2020. Accessed July 22, 2020. https://www.christianity.com/wiki/bible/what-was-the-year-of-jubilee.html.

110. "Feast of Tabernacles: Commemorates the Forty-Year Wilderness Journey," *Feast & Holidays of the Bible* (Carson, CA: Rose, 2004).

111. Booker, *Celebrating Jesus in the Biblical Feasts*, 146.

112. Gibbs, Carl, *Principles of Biblical Interpretation: An Independent-Study Textbook,* Fourth Ed. (Springfield, MO: Global University, 2016), 270.

113. Johnson, Ken, *The End-Times by The Ancient Church Fathers* (Biblefacts Ministries, 2016) 13.

114. Parker, Andrew. *Revelation: Revealing Ancient Understandings* (Bloomington, IN: WestBow, 2017) 299–300.

115. Ibid., 121.

116. "Fathers of the Third Century: Hippolytus, Cyprian, Ca." *CCEL.* 2020. Accessed July 22, 2020. https://www.ccel.org/ccel/schaff/anf05.iii.iv.i.x.ii.html.

117. Johnson, Ken, *The End-Times by The Ancient Church Fathers,* 14.

118. Ibid.

119. Davidson, Baruch, "What Is the Significance of the Year 6000 in the Jewish Calendar?" *Chabad.* 2020. Accessed July 22, 2020. https://www.chabad.org/library/article_cdo/aid/607585/jewish/Significance-of-the-year-6000.htm.

120. Ibid.

121. Silberberg, Naftali, "More on Plag Haminchah." *Chabad.* 2020. Accessed July 22, 2020. https://www.chabad.org/library/article_cdo/aid/144443/jewish/Plag-Hamincha.htm.

122. Ibid.

123. "Scientists Planning Now for Asteroid Flyby a Decade Away," *News,* April 29, 2019. https://www.jpl.nasa.gov/news/news.php?feature=7390, retrieved 6/16/20.

124. Horn, Thomas, *The Wormwood Prophecy* (Lake Mary, FL: Charisma House, 2019), 27.

125. Exodus 34:22–23.

126. Cohen, Mark E., *The Cultic Calendars of the Ancient Near East* (Bethesda, MD: CDL, 1993) 401.

127. Ibid.

128. Ibid., 403.

129. Black, Jeremy & Green, Anthony, *Gods, Demons and Symbols of Ancient Mesopotamia: An Illustrated Dictionary* (London: British Museum Press, 1992) 136.

130. Numbers 28:16–25.

131. Numbers 28:16–27.

132. 1 Kings 8:2, 65; 2 Chronicles 5:3; Ezekiel 45:25.

133. Amar Annus, "Are There Greek Rephaim? On the Etymology of Greek *Meropes* and *Titanes*." *Ugarit-Forschungen* 31 (1999) 13–30.

134. Sharon K. Gilbert and Derek P. Gilbert, *Veneration* (Crane, MO: Defender, 2019) 85–94.

135. Annus, op.cit., 20.

136. The last aurochs died in Poland in 1627, but a breeding program to recreate the aurochs by crossing larger breeds of domestic cattle hopes to release a close match to the aurochs into the wild across Europe by 2025.

137. Wyatt, Nicolas, "A la recherche des Rephaïm perdus," in J. M. Michaud (ed.) *Le royaume d'Ougarit de la Crète à l'Euphrate: Nouveaux axes de recherche* (Proche-Orient et Littérature Ougaritique II, Sherbrooke, QC: Éditions GGC, 2007) 597–598.

138. Wyatt, Nicolas, "Calf." In K. van der Toorn, B. Becking, & P. W. van der Horst (Eds.), *Dictionary of Deities and Demons in the Bible 2nd extensively rev. ed.* (Leiden; Boston; Köln; Grand Rapids, MI; Cambridge: Brill; Eerdmans, 1999) 181.

139. Ibid.

140. Wyatt, Simon and Wyatt, Nicolas, "The longue durée in the Beef Business." In: O. Loretz, S. Ribichini, W. G. E. Watson, & J. Zamora (Eds.), *Ritual, Religion and Reason* (Münster: Ugarit-Verlag, 2013) 346.

141. Lipi ski, Edward, "El's Abode: Mythological Traditions Related to Mount Hermon and to the Mountains of Armenia." *Orientalia Lovaniensa Periodica* II (1971) 13–69.

142. Ugaritic text *KTU* 1.4 vi:46.

143. Ayali-Darshan, Noga, "The Seventy Bulls Sacrificed at Sukkot (Num 29:12–34) in Light of a Ritual Text from Emar (Emar 6, 373)." *Vetus Testamentum* 65:1 (2015) 7–8.

144. Ibid.

145. Judges 9:5–6.

146. 2 Kings 10:6–7.

147. Genesis 11:9.

148. Deuteronomy 32:8, New Living Translation.

149. Deuteronomy 32:8, Good News Translation.

150. Gilbert, Derek P., *The Great Inception* (Crane, MO: Defender, 2017). See chapter 3.

151. Darshan, "Seventy Bulls Sacrificed at Sukkot, 9–19.

152. Gilbert, Derek P., *Last Clash of the Titans* (Crane, MO: Defender, 2018) 29–43. Also, Derek P. Gilbert, *Bad Moon Rising* (Crane, MO: Defender, 2019) 81–93.

153. His last dated prophecy is in Ezekiel 29:17, "the twenty-seventh year, in the first month, on the first day of the month," which was April 26, 571 BC.

154. Garrison, Mark B., "Antiquarianism, Copying, Collecting," in *A Companion to Archaeology in the Ancient Near East*, D. T. Potts, ed. (Chichester, West Sussex: Wiley-Blackwell, 2012) 44–46.

155. Also called "Tema" or "Teman" in the Bible.

156. Genesis 25:15.

157. Humphreys, op. cit., 300.

158. Hausleiter, Arnulf, "North Arabian Kingdoms." *A Companion to Archaeology in the Ancient Near East*, D. T. Potts, ed. (Chichester, West Sussex: Wiley-Blackwell, 2012) 828.

159. Kim, Jin Yang, "F. M. Cross' Reconstruction of 4Q242." *Old Testament Story* (https://otstory.wordpress.com/2008/02/22/f-m-cross-reconstruction-of-4q242/), retrieved 11/8/18.

160. Humphreys, op. cit., 300.

161. Judges 8:21, 26.

162. Genesis 15:16.

163. Gilbert, op.cit., 84–89.

164. Lipiński, op.cit.

165. Gilbert and Gilbert, op.cit., 251–253; also, Derek P. Gilbert, *Last Clash of the Titans*, 122–125.

166. Genesis 15:16.

167. Beaulieu, Paul-Alain, *The Reign of Nabonidus, King of Babylon, 556–539 B.C.* (New Haven: Yale University Press, 1989) 150.

168. Houtman, C., "Queen of Heaven." In K. van der Toorn, B. Becking, & P. W. van der Horst (Eds.), *Dictionary of Deities and Demons in the Bible 2nd extensively rev. ed.* (Leiden; Boston; Köln; Grand Rapids, MI; Cambridge: Brill; Eerdmans, 1999) 679.

169. Cohen, op. cit., 401.

170. Black, J. A. , "The New Year Ceremonies in Ancient Babylon: 'Taking Bel by the Hand' and a Cultic Picnic," *Religion*, 11:1 (1981) 40.

171. Hall, Mark G., *A Study of the Sumerian Moon-God, Nanna/Suen* (Ann Arbor, MI: University Microfilms International, 1985) 336.

172. Ibid.

173. Cohen, op. cit., 402.

174. Wolters, Al, "Belshazzar's Feast and the Cult of the Moon God Sîn," *Bulletin for Biblical Research* 5 (1995) 201–202.

175. Horn, op. cit.

176. Ornan, Tallay, "The Bull and Its Two Masters: Moon and Storm Deities in Relation to the Bull in Ancient Near Eastern Art," *Israel Exploration Journal*, Vol. 51, No. 1 (2001) 3.

177. Peterson, Jeremiah, "Nanna/Suen Convenes in the Divine Assembly as King," *Aula Orientalis* 29 (2011) 279.

178. Ibid., 284–285.

179. Jacobs, Joseph; Seligsohn, M.; Bacher, Wilhelm, "Sinai, Mount." *The Jewish Encyclopedia* (New York; London: Funk & Wagnalls, 1901), http://www.jewishencyclopedia.com/articles/13766-sinai-mount, retrieved 7/6/20.

180. Joshua 6:1.

181. "Calendar for April 2029 (Israel)." *TimeAndDate.com* (https://www.timeanddate.com/calendar/monthly.html?year=2029&month=4&country=34), retrieved 7/6/20.

182. Revelation 8:10–11.

183. Stone, Adam, "Enlil/Ellil (god)." *Ancient Mesopotamian Gods and Goddesses* (ORACC and the UK Higher Education Academy, 2016), http://oracc.museum.upenn.edu/amgg/listofdeities/enlil/, retrieved 7/6/20.

184. Brian B. Schmidt, *Israel's Beneficent Dead: Ancestor Cult and Necromancy in Ancient Israelite Religion and Tradition* (Winona Lake, IN: Eisenbrauns, 1996) 36.

185. 2 Peter 2:4.

186. Homer, *The Iliad with an English Translation by A. T. Murray, Ph.D. in two volumes* (Cambridge, MA: Harvard University Press; London: William Heinemann, Ltd., 1924). http://data.perseus.org/citations/urn:cts:greekLit:tlg0012.tlg001.perseus-eng1:8.1-8.40, retrieved 7/8/20.

187. Gilbert, *Last Clash of the Titans*, 84–91 and 118–120.

188. George W. E. Nickelsburg, *1 Enoch: The Hermeneia Translation* (Minneapolis: Fortress, 2012) 39.

189. 1 Enoch 21:1–5, in Nickelsburg, op.cit., 41.

190. Strong's Hebrew Concordance H8313, https://www.blueletterbible.org/lang/lexicon/lexicon.cfm?strongs=H8313&t=KJV, retrieved 7/7/20.

191. Ezekiel 1:7, 13.

192. Xella, Paolo, "Barad." In K. van der Toorn, B. Becking, & P. W. van der Horst (Eds.), *Dictionary of Deities and Demons in the Bible 2nd extensively rev. ed.* (Leiden; Boston; Köln; Grand Rapids, MI; Cambridge: Brill; Eerdmans, 1999) 160.

193. Xella, Paolo, "Resheph." In K. van der Toorn, B. Becking, & P. W. van der Horst (Eds.), *Dictionary of deities and demons in the Bible*

2nd extensively rev. ed. (Leiden; Boston; Köln; Grand Rapids, MI; Cambridge: Brill; Eerdmans, 1999) 701.

194. Ibid.

195. Zechariah 1:1 dates the vision to "the eighth month, in the second year of Darius," who ruled Persia 522–486 BC.

196. 2 Peter 2:4; Jude 6.

197. Genesis 8:4.

198. Augustine of Hippo, *City of God* XX.19.3, https://www.ccel.org/ccel/schaff/npnf102.iv.XX.19.html#iv.XX.19-p6, retrieved 7/9/20.

199. https://en.wikipedia.org/wiki/The_Andromeda_Strain

200. Cardinal Manning, *The Present Crises of the Holy See Tested by Prophecy*, reprinted in 2007 under the title,"*The Pope & the Antichris*" (Tradibooks, Dainte-Croix du Mont, France, 75.

201. Ibid., 79–80.

202. Ibid., 81–82.

203. Virgil, *Eclogue IV*, lines 11-22, found online via http://classics.mit.edu/Virgil/eclogue.4.iv.html.

204. Orwell, G. *Nineteen Eighty-Four* (United Kingdom: Penguin Modern Classics, 2003) 318.

205. For information on Industry 4.0, see: Marr, Bernard, "What Is Industry 4.0', September 2, 2028, Forbes Magazine online, https://www.forbes.com/sites/bernardmarr/2018/09/02/what-is-industry-4-0-heres-a-super-easy-explanation-for-anyone/#612814869788 (accessed July 13, 2020).

206. Schwab, Klaus, "Globalization 4.0, What Does It Mean?", November 5, 2018, World Economic Forum Website, https://www.weforum.org/agenda/2018/11/globalization-4-what-does-it-mean-how-it-will-benefit-everyone/ (accessed July 13, 2020).

207. Ibid.

208. 2020 Davos Manifesto can be read here: https://www.weforum.org/agenda/2019/12/davos-manifesto-2020-the-universal-purpose-of-a-company-in-the-fourth-industrial-revolution/ (accessed July 13, 2020).

209. 1973 Davos Manifesto can be read here: https://www.weforum. org/agenda/2019/12/davos-manifesto-1973-a-code-of-ethics-for-business-leaders/ (accessed July 13, 2020).

210. See note vi.

211. World Economic Forum website: https://www.weforum.org/great-reset/ (accessed July 13, 2020)

212. YouTube Video, "Prince Charles Says Pandemic a Chance to 'Think Big and Act Now'" The Royal Family Channel, found via https://www.youtube.com/watch?v=BucTwPegW5k (accessed June 27, 2020).

213. Ibid.

214. O'Neill, Tom, with Piepenbring, Dan, *Chaos: Charles Manson, the CIA, and the Secret History of the Sixties*, (New York: Little, Brown & Co., (June 25, 2019) 212.

215. Ibid., 394–395.

216. Williams, Alex, "New Charles Manson Book Blows Holes in the Race-War Theory," August 8, 2019, *The Independent*, found online via https://www.independent.co.uk/arts-entertainment/manson-family-new-book-a9039666.html (accessed July 6, 2020).

217. Wells, H. G., *The War of the Worlds* (William Henemann: UK; Harper & Brothers: US, 1897..

218. Catholic News Agency Staff, "St. Junipero Serra Statue Destroyed at California Capitol," published July 5, 2020 by Catholic News Agency, accessed online July 6, 2020, via https://www. catholicnewsagency.com/news/saint-junpero-serra-statue-toppled-at-california-state-capitol-in-sacramento-74631.

219. Hunt, Ryan, *Project Camelot and Military Sponsorship* (2007), p. 26. (Doctoral dissertation from Duquesne University); Pdf available online via https://dsc.duq.edu/cgi/viewcontent. cgi?article=1688&context=etd. (accessed July 6, 2020).